Effective

pastoring

ALSO BY BILL LAWRENCE

Beyond the Bottom Line (coauthor)

EffECTIVE
pastoring

Giving Vision,
Direction, and Care
to Your Church

BILL LAWRENCE

CHARLES R. SWINDOLL, *General Editor*
ROY B. ZUCK, *Managing Editor*

THOMAS NELSON PUBLISHERS
Nashville

EFFECTIVE PASTORING
Swindoll Leadership Library

Published in association with Dallas Theological Seminary (DTS):
General Editor: Charles R. Swindoll
Managing Editor: Roy B. Zuck
The theological opinions expressed by the author are not necessarily the official
position of Dallas Theological Seminary.

Library of Congress Cataloging in Publication Data:

Lawrence, William D.
Effective pastoring / William D. Lawrence
p.   cm.—(Swindoll Leadership Library)

ISBN 0-8499-1353-5
1. Clergy—Office. 2. Pastoral Theology. I. Title. II. Series

BV660.2.L39   1999   99-41679
253–dc21   CIP

Printed in the United States of America
00 01 02 03 04 05 06 BVG 9 8 7 6 5 4 3 2

DEDICATION

To Howard G. Hendricks,
"Prof" as they call you.
All I owe you is my marriage,
my family, and my ministry—
How can I ever repay you?

Contents

FOREWORD

EVERY PASTOR MUST BE, at heart, a shepherd. Without a shepherd's heart, he's probably not an effective pastor. A pastor who watches over God's flock without a shepherd's heart, serving with wrong or insincere motives, is as Jesus said, merely a "hired hand" (John 12:12).

A hired hand takes on the same task as a true shepherd, but for vastly different reasons. Whether because of pride, the pursuit of riches, or even some secret desire for power or authority, a hireling leads from selfish motives. Will a hireling move to a new church assignment? That depends on the salary being offered. Will he accept an invitation to speak at a day-long spiritual retreat or an evening celebration banquet? That depends on the number of people attending or the size of the honorarium being offered. Sad, isn't it?

By contrast, a true shepherd serves God's people out of a debt of gratitude for all the Father has done and is doing in his life. The upright pastor desires above all else to use his gifts and talents as a "spiritual service of worship" (Rom. 1:21, NASB).

Both pastors, the selfish hireling and the sincere shepherd, may seem to be undertaking God's word in God's way. However, over time the flock begins to sense the difference between the two. The congregation of the hireling begins to feel used and manipulated. Hurts and needs either go unattended or are met in a reluctant, superficial manner. Preaching becomes harsh and accusatory. Joy is missing from the congregation. Love and grace are nowhere to be found.

What a contrast to those cared for by a loving, faithful pastor. The shepherd who tends his flock year after year, feeding them a steady diet of God's truth, finds over time he has nurtured a healthy band of maturing believers, people who are willing to step out in faith and trust God to dream great dreams. In the fulfilled flock, friendships flourish, a caring community is encouraged, laughter abounds, emotional wounds are treated, and peace prevails. The pastor's preaching is marked by positive words of exhortation as well as loving warnings of dangers in the road ahead. Compassion flows freely. Enthusiasm is contagious.

My friend and colleague, William Lawrence, has a genuine pastor's heart, as you will observe when you read this book. Bill has spent his entire adult life serving in the church and training pastors in the class-room. He is one of those gifted individuals who could be called a "pastor to pastors." As executive director of the Center for Christian Leadership and professor of pastoral ministries at Dallas Seminary he has trained hundreds of young pastors who have moved into full-time vocational ministry.

Effective Pastoring is the result of Bill Lawrence's passionate pursuit of training leaders to serve in the body of Christ. Here, no punches are pulled. Bill does not give seven easy steps or ten top secrets of effective shepherding. The material in this book is "straight talk" about life lived in the fishbowl called "full-time pastor." By the time you finish reading these pages, the differences between a hired hand and a true shepherd will stand out in stark contrast.

So, grab your shepherd's staff, take this book, and head off to a quiet place. It's not only the sheep who need rest and refreshment; effective shepherds do too. Much encouragement awaits you!

—CHARLES R. SWINDOLL
General Editor

PREFACE

In the Democratic Senate primary in 1974 Howard Metzenbaum challenged John Glenn by saying, "How can you run for the Senate when you've never held a job?" Glenn had pursued a military career, but he had never worked in the corporate world. Metzenbaum's question reminds me of the question pastors sometimes hear following a sermon. "So what do you do with the rest of your time? I wish I had to work only thirty minutes a week."

Glenn responded by describing the wars he had fought, the friends he had lost, and the risks he had taken—all part of the price he had paid. He'd certainly had a job. And pastors do too. Although pastors do not face the physical dangers a military officer does, they bear the scars of spiritual warfare, personal struggle, and emotional stress. With Paul, we know something of the cares of the churches (2 Cor. 11:28).

Peter Drucker has said that leading the church is the most difficult job in the world. Pastors have little ultimate authority and work with volunteers whose fears and desires frequently have to be considered, if not fulfilled, and who ultimately decide the pastor's fate. It is very difficult to fire a volunteer—and rather easy to fire a pastor.

On the other hand, most of us who have pastored know it is one of the greatest privileges of life. To be there when someone is born into God's family, to stand by the bedside of a dying saint and pray with that person, to preach a life-changing sermon by God's grace—what could be more challenging?

Because of both the discouragement and the delights of pastoring, I am pleased to write a book designed to help pastors be more effective. In this volume I look at the kind of person a pastor must be, at the pastor's purpose, and at several vital practices a pastor must implement. Because so much is written in the areas of counseling and preaching, I have chosen not to write about these tasks. Instead I have written on areas frequently not dealt with in seminary courses, issues that are becoming increasingly significant in the pastorate today.

As a pastor you have one of the most demanding jobs in all the world. I hope this book will encourage you to delight increasingly in the Lord, who has made pastoring the desire of your heart.

Acknowledgments

Every author feels profound relief and immense gratitude when he finishes a book. I am grateful to my mentors, Howard Hendricks and Ray Stedman, who have had untold influence on me. To the elders and people of South Hills Community Church, San Jose, California, where I first pastored, I say thank you for your patience, long-suffering, and faithful support. No church ever stood by its pastor more steadfastly. I also wish to say thanks to Roy B. Zuck, who has been a most encouraging editor.

Every author also thanks his wife, of course, but none more than I. Lynna has been my first editor. She has pointed out how to make the confusing clear and the dull interesting, as well as how to transform clutter into focus. What could assist a writer more? If this book helps anyone, it will be due in large part to her hard work.

PART ONE

THE PASTOR'S PERSON

CHAPTER ONE

———

TO KNOW HIM

THE RETURN ADDRESS told me the letter was from my mentor, Ray Stedman. With anticipation I opened the envelope and read the words "an invitation to teach a nation." I was invited to be part of a team Stedman was putting together to teach the principles of Ephesians 4:7–16 in a number of cities in the Philippines. What a challenge—an opportunity to touch an entire nation for Christ under the leadership of my model for pastoral ministry. Little did I know this invitation would end in the blackness of burnout and my first taste of brokenness. Nor did I know it would take years for me to understand what God was doing in my life.

Ray Stedman, pastor of Peninsula Bible Church in Palo Alto, California, had recently written the book *Body Life*, a seminal work redefining how pastors should understand their role. No longer could we minister only by ourselves; we had to equip the saints to do the work of the ministry, as Paul directed so long ago. Pastors and pew-sitters are to serve together in order to bring the gifts and energies of all the body of Christ into ministry and so multiply the impact of God's Spirit throughout the world.

As common as that thought is today, it was revolutionary when Stedman first wrote it. Because of this book, he had been asked to teach these principles to churches in the Philippines. In a span of five weeks we would speak throughout the country, each of us spending three weeks ministering individually in different parts of the islands. We would speak in a total of eighteen conferences, blanketing the nation with the principles he had applied so effectively in his ministry for nearly twenty years.

This was heady stuff for me, a recent seminary graduate. I visited a former classmate in Tokyo and another in Manila. In Indonesia I visited a couple who were launching their missionary career and had interned in our church. Despite the excitement of all this, something happened in the Philippines I never anticipated: I failed. My "invitation to teach" a nation turned out to be an invitation to failure.

Looking back now, I'm not sure I was qualified to do what I did. Was my teaching lacking? I don't know. It seemed to be well received, but I couldn't accept the affirmation offered me. My feelings of failure were based on one thing: my conclusion that I wasn't the best preacher on the team. I was consumed with the need to be the best, something I had never consciously struggled with before. I had no idea such terrible drivenness lay within me, and I didn't know how to cope with it. It was this drivenness that turned the challenge of the invitation into the darkness of burnout. I came home angry—angry at the American church's lack of concern for lost people (a valid but misplaced indignation), but mostly angry at my failure.

Why did I think I had failed? The six of us on the team were never together, and I never heard anyone else preach. How did I know I wasn't the best? More importantly, what difference did it make how I compared with the others? Why did that matter? Who cared besides me? Why did I care? The answer is obvious to me now: My whole identity depended on my being the best. If I weren't the best, in my way of thinking, I felt my life wasn't worth living.

If you were counseling me thirty years ago, what would you have said to me? That I was seeking significance in the wrong place and in the wrong way? Undoubtedly. That I was success-driven? Absolutely. That I was achievement-dependent? Obviously. That I was proud? What an understatement! That I was a deficit thinker? Totally. For seven long months I struggled, going deeper and deeper into burnout without understanding what was happening to me. I had no idea God was bringing me to the point of brokenness or that He had the grace I needed to find my way out of my confusion. I failed to understand what it meant to know Christ, but more than that, I did not fully understand God's grace.

4

Toward the end of that seven months I read *Mere Christianity*, by C. S. Lewis. Then I began to understand my situation. Reading this book was like reading my autobiography; it was as if he knew my thinking and feelings intimately. *Mere Christianity* helped me discover the root of my problem: I was comparing myself to others and defining my identity on the basis of how good I thought I was in comparison to them. I was using a performance standard as the basis of my existence as a person. If I decided I was better than those I compared myself to, I felt I was somebody—I had a sense of significance based on my superiority over them. If I decided I wasn't as good as those to whom I compared myself, I felt I was nobody. I had a sense of insignificance, even nonexistence, based on my inferiority to them. My standard was subjective, consisting of my feelings, plus others' comments, plus my own imaginations. If I felt I was the best, I was emotionally up; if I felt I was less than the best, I was emotionally down. I was competing, and it was all or nothing, win or lose—and I was losing.

Lewis's book showed me that my comparison was competition and competition means pride. He wrote:

Pride is *essentially* competitive—is competitive by its very nature—while the other vices are competitive only, so to speak, by accident. Pride gets no pleasure out of having something, only out of having more of it than the next man. We say that people are proud of being rich, or clever, or good-looking, but they are not. They are proud of being richer, or cleverer, or better-looking than others. If every one else became equally rich or clever or good-looking there would be nothing to be proud about. It is the comparison that makes you proud: the pleasure of being above the rest. Once the element of competition has gone, pride has gone.[1]

Worse than this, I felt God would never let me minister cross-culturally again. Despite my struggles I discovered a facility for expressing myself in cross-cultural settings, but I concluded that my failure meant God would never again give me such an opportunity. This was because I had not focused on knowing Christ. Despite eight years of seminary training and a lifetime of growing up in a Christian family and attending church, I did not really comprehend what it meant to know Christ.

"To know Him." I knew those words, but I did not understand what they meant when I began pastoring. Part of my blindness had to do with the way I grew up in the faith. All I knew about Christianity was behavioral, not relational. I had been taught to obey God, and I was committed to utter, radical obedience. In my understanding of God's Word I thought I was righteous because I was obedient, and I *could* be righteous because I *could* obey. I simply had to do whatever the Bible said. The problem was that I had never heard that I could be obedient to God only as I was dependent on Christ. My legalism blinded me to my need to know Him in a deep, growing way. Besides, knowing Christ seemed abstract to me. What does a person do to know Him? I couldn't comprehend what that meant or how I could do it. I thought I was called to serve Christ and I didn't realize I needed to know Him to do that.

Preaching, on the other hand, was something I could grasp. To me, preaching was real, concrete, definite, utterly tangible, and I could get hold of that. Each sermon has a beginning, a body, and a conclusion. When I preached, I knew I fulfilled my purpose. After all, the Bible says, "Preach the word" (2 Tim. 4:2). That's what I was taught and that's what I did. "If you preach the Word, people will come to your church," I was told. Tell people what they need to know, and they'll be what they ought to be. Coming out of seminary, I failed to understand how to connect preaching with knowing Him. I'm sure I exercised selective hearing and heard what I chose because I wanted to succeed as a preacher.

Don't get me wrong. I knew that to preach effectively I needed to depend on Christ. I knew I couldn't do it on my own. As I studied and prepared to preach, I prayed. I sought the Holy Spirit's insight into the biblical text and I prayed for spiritual strength from the risen Lord. There never was a Sunday when I consciously entered the pulpit depending on myself. God did use me and worked through His Word, mostly in spite of me, of course. But I failed to see how mixed my motives were, and I didn't realize how this was affecting my ministry.

I also didn't understand that I was driven to define my identity through my preaching. I thought preaching was what made me somebody. Through preaching I mattered and gained the lasting significance I craved. Success as a preacher would make me somebody others would admire. Until I consciously sought to know Him, I attempted to define myself by what I did, specifically what I did as a preacher. However, we can never fully define ourselves by what we do. All identity—all of who we are—grows out of relationships, not accomplishments, specifically our relationship with Christ and then with His church. I was attempting to make myself significant in the wrong way, because significance comes only through knowing Christ. Little wonder rough times lay ahead for me. I did not know God was finally getting me in the place where He could use me.

After reading *Mere Christianity*, I said to God, "All right, Lord, I'm a proud man, but You have given me gifts." That was the bottom point of my life, and the beginning of my way up to a new awareness of God and His grace. For the first time I could acknowledge what was obvious to so many for so long: I was a proud man. Yet, also for the first time in my memory, I could think well of myself. I had never been able to think good thoughts about myself and be comfortable inside. Clearly I was what I call a deficit thinker.

DEFICIT THINKING

A deficit thinker is someone who thinks he is a nobody who must make himself into a somebody by what he does.

I thought that as a nobody I could make myself into a somebody by being the best preacher there was. As a deficit thinker I was marked by emptiness where there should have been an identity. I had an inner vacuum that I needed to fill; otherwise I had no sense of existence and value.

The deficit thinker believes achievements make him somebody, and this is how he gains an identity for himself; what he does is what truly matters.

However, it's not possible for anyone to fill an identity void through achievements. We become ourselves only through relationships, first through knowing Christ and then through knowing those in and out of His family. As a result, the deficit thinker gets the exact opposite of what he is striving for, because he ends up with more emptiness than he had in the first place.

The deficit thinking person is a *driven* person, that is, all his energy is focused on himself, on seeking to buy an identity through his accomplishments. *Drivenness is the desperate effort of a deficit thinker to define his identity, all done in God's name, but apart from God's resources.* Because he is desperate—after all, he senses he has no life if he has no identity—he may sacrifice even those who are most precious to him: his wife, his children, his friends, even his Lord, to gain the sense of identity he so greatly needs. He is like a starving man scrounging in the garbage for food.

Even though I was a deficit thinker, I was totally committed to Christ.

I truly wanted to serve and glorify Him. I had turned away from everything to follow Christ and I fully intended to pursue Him wherever He led. Nevertheless, even as a dedicated follower of Christ, I ended up burned out and broken. Deficit thinkers are confused. Here are six ways they think about themselves and life.

Deficit Thinking	
Resource-limited:	There's only so much to go around.
Time-bound:	You only go around once.
Death-defined:	I am what I am when I die.
Competitively driven:	Win-lose.
Independently motivated:	I can make it on my own.
Fear-based:	It's do or die.

Resource-Limited: There's Only So Much to Go Around

The deficit thinker sees all resources as limited. Whether it's power, influence, position, possessions, or glory, there is only so much to go around, and he must get as much as he can or he loses. Frequently this drivenness is masked by "God language." Phrases like "for God's glory" or "being jealous for God" frequently fall from his lips, but we see his real heart through the strife and division he causes when he seeks to glorify God by getting all the glory he can for himself. A deficit thinker says things like, "If only I can get Billy Graham to endorse my book, I can make a *great* impact for Christ." But this is not the way to buy an identity. For such a person power is the key resource and control is the primary prize.

Time-Bound: You Only Go Around Once

A deficit thinker measures himself by thinking of where he should be at a certain age. "I'm forty years old and I should be pastoring a church of a thousand by now. I feel like a failure because I'm not where I thought I would be at forty." He feels bound and measured by time, as if his arbitrary and false standards actually define who he is. A deficit thinker always measures his personal value by his achievements rather than by his character and growth. Rarely do we hear someone say, "I'm far more loving at forty than I expected to be." That's because, for many of us, the number of people in our churches is more important to us than the amount of love in our hearts. This is a sure sign of deficit thinking.

Death-Defined: I Am What I Am When I Die

A deficit thinker feels he doesn't have an identity, and that there is nothing worse than being nobody. A person without an identity is one who doesn't matter, who knows only a living death, who is void and without significance. A deficit thinker seeks to define who he is and to prove that he matters. He concentrates on his achievements. He thinks that what he does makes him somebody and gives him significance. So if we are deficit thinkers, we try to prove we are valuable by doing something we think others will admire. Then we die, and all our efforts become futile. We do everything we can to prove we matter, and we still end up dead. This is why our efforts to find fullness only produce more emptiness.

Competitively Driven: Win-Lose

For the deficit thinker life is a zero-based game. He starts every day at zero and must show an identity profit for the day or he thinks he is a failure. Each day he fails makes him more driven than the day before. Since failure and nonidentity are never more than one day away, he can never stop driving lest he fail utterly and lose all hope of ever achieving success. He wins or loses on a daily basis, and the winner takes all, so if he doesn't win, there isn't anything left for him to take. The fact that his sermon last Sunday was good doesn't mean a thing after a few minutes of satisfaction on Monday. The message he hears from others is, "Don't tell me what you did for me last Sunday; tell me what you're going to do for me next Sunday."

The chips in the zero-based approach to life are typically money, sex, power, and fame. Most pastors have rejected money and sex as life chips, but many have yet to settle the issues of power and fame. This explains why the struggle for control dominates so many in the ministry. Control is the way pastors become powerful and famous, and power and fame are the way pastors keep score, just as money is the way entrepreneurs keep score. So there is tension, competition, anger, and bitterness on church staffs and boards since so many leaders are deficit thinkers with a win-lose mentality.

Relationships always break down among zero-based players because they believe that relationships mean weakness, since you have to be vulnerable to connect with others, and deficit thinkers can't be vulnerable. This is why many driven pastors take advantage of their wives, ignore their children, and disregard their staffs. They don't have time for relationships because they must make an identity profit before the day ends. Deficit thinkers always focus on what they don't have and desperately need. For them the glass isn't half full or half empty—it's always empty because they are always looking at the wrong glass.

Independently Motivated: I Can Make It on My Own

Deficit thinkers rarely admit they need others to succeed in life because they can't afford to trust. If they do, they'll have to admit they can't make it on their own, and that's like saying they can never be themselves. They may say they need others and claim they're dependent on Christ, but they don't truly understand what this means or they would make knowing Him their number-one priority. Frequently they resist accountability, reject authority, and trust very few people. For them control is the primary issue, and they mean *their* control even though they have made a sincere commitment to Christ's lordship. They trust almost no one because they can get where they want to go only through *their* controlling others. Words like "team" and "family" roll off their tongues and land with a deadening thud since all who hear them know they are utterly incapable of such commitments. No matter what they say, they will almost never truly acknowledge a need for others.

Fear-Based: It's Do or Die

Fear reigns supreme in the deficit thinker's heart. Fear of failure; fear of success; fear of being discovered as a nobody; fear of being known as empty and futile; fear of being found out for what they truly are. Fear is lord of all in their lives. Even as I felt God would never give me another cross-cultural opportunity, so all deficit thinkers have a distorted view of God and how He responds to their failures. But if they truly understood God, they wouldn't be so afraid.

AN ORIGINAL DEFICIT THINKER

Before his conversion Paul was a deficit thinker of the highest order (Phil. 3:3–6). We know this because he did what all deficit thinkers do: He put his confidence in the flesh to be all he thought God wanted him to be (3:3–4). We, too, put confidence in the flesh when we strive to define our identities by relying on ourselves. Then we are drawing on human resources, not God's, and we measure our identity by what we think makes us superior. For deficit thinkers to feel fulfilled, they have to see themselves as better than others. For Paul those ways, before his conversion, came from his religious roots, family heritage, and personal accomplishments, and especially his self-righteousness (3:5–6). His supreme confidence that he was blameless before the Law gave him his ultimate identity as a man who satisfied God in every way.

I, too, was a deficit thinker. I was totally committed to Christ and made a sincere effort to serve and please Him. However, as long as I drew my identity from trying to be the best preacher rather than knowing Christ, I could do nothing more than run a deficit in life. With Paul, I had to learn that everything I counted on for gain was futile and empty; in fact, it was all a loss (3:7–8). Paul used accounting language when he said all he had counted on for identity was loss apart from knowing Christ. Like the company owner who carefully reviews his business's profit-and-loss statement, so Paul was concerned about the profit-and-loss statement of his life. And he discovered he was taking a loss on his life investments; he was going in the hole.

Despite all his efforts and investments—his religious roots, his family heritage, his personal accomplishments, his self-righteousness—his deficit was increasing. The emptiness in his soul was getting bigger; he was not fulfilled, no matter how hard he worked or how many more life resources he poured into his efforts. He did not have any more capital to invest. He was broke, with nothing to show for all his hard work. In fact, he was worse than broke, if that were possible. He used the Greek word *skybala* ("refuse to be flushed away") in describing what he got in return for his life resources. It wasn't just a dry hole or a bad investment; it was a shameful, ugly, rotten life, full of trash that brought dishonor, grief, and pain to his soul. Paul, the deficit thinker, was driven, in the *skybala* of the flesh to find his identity.

ABUNDANCE THINKING

Abundance thinkers see life in a radically different way from deficit thinkers. The difference between them is not in what they do, but in how they think. Abundance thinkers rely on the Holy Spirit, while deficit thinkers are bound by their sinful perspective. *Abundance thinkers understand that they don't define their identity through their accomplishments; instead they discover and develop their identity through knowing Christ.* The abundance thinker does exactly the same things the deficit thinker does: He prays, he prepares, he preaches, he pastors. However, he is at rest. He is approachable, peaceable, willing to listen, full of drive, but not driven.

Driven people act out of emptiness and focus their energy on making themselves somebody by pursuing the achievements they have decided bring them identity. Those who find their identity in knowing Christ have an abundance of drive, but not self-centered drivenness. They are fueled by the fullness of knowing who God made them, and they grow each day in the exciting discoveries such assurance brings. Achievements take on new meaning for them as they invest their drive in service and find significance in giving themselves to others rather than seeking to get recognition and affirmation from others. Unlike the spiritually starving driven man scrounging in the *skybala* of the flesh to find his sustenance, the abundance thinker directs his energies to serve others and to help them find themselves in the fullness of knowing Christ.

Now they are truly free—free from comparison and competition, from envy and jealousy, from fear and anger, from covetousness and self-protection. They are able to encourage and support others when they once would have competed. This is true even when the others are more talented than they are and may replace them at some point in the future. Because they have learned that their unique, special identity is a free gift of grace, their praying, preparing, preaching, and pastoring become their ways of serving as they grow from somebody to somebody, from fullness to greater fullness, from glory to glory (2 Cor. 3:18). All of their actions grow from the security of their identity. They are no longer trying to buy an identity through what they do.

Abundance thinkers have a totally different mind-set because they see themselves from God's perspective. The only limits they have are the limits the sovereign God places on them to help them grow in faith and glorify Him. The following paragraphs outline six ways abundance thinkers think of themselves and life.

Resource-Unlimited: God Has Every Resource I Need.

In contrast to the deficit thinker, those who experience God's abundance know that all His resources are infinite. There is no limit to His glory. There is no limit to the power He can exercise through us or to the positions He may have for us. Everything God has for us is ours. All we need to do is trust Him for it. None of us has to end life bitter and broken, full of regret. If we trust God, we will see His greatness through us in ways we never dreamed possible.

Abundance Thinking	
Resource-unlimited:	God has every resource I need.
Time-aware:	I am accountable for my time.
Resurrection-defined:	What we do matters, but life *fully* begins when we die.
Community-driven:	Serving is the point, not winning.
Dependently motivated:	I can't make it on my own.
Security-based:	The abundant life is in Christ.

Time-Aware: I Am Accountable for My Time

We are not time-bound, but we are time-accountable. We must buy up every moment God gives us in light of our evil days (Eph. 5:15–16). Time is more important than the name we make for ourselves. The most precious resource we get in life is time. So we must use every moment God gives us to glorify Him and reveal who He is, and not waste it by trying to show others who we are.

Deficit thinkers treat time in crass and plastic ways. Instead of investing it, they spend their time seeking success. But sooner or later, deficit thinkers run out of time and they must leave behind all they gained. They throw it away on cheap, fruitless efforts to exalt themselves. Abundance thinkers, on the other hand, invest time as they bring God's fullness into human emptiness. When they run out of time, they have a heritage to leave behind and a treasure that has already been sent on ahead. There is no greater stewardship of the years our Father gives us than to invest them for eternal values.

Resurrection-Defined: What We Do Matters, but Life Fully *Begins When We Die*

What we do today matters, but it is preparation for our eternal tomorrow. Our Lord's parables were filled with the truth that God is preparing us for an eternal trust, the privilege of serving Him forever. We will face the judgment seat of Christ, and we must prepare for that scrutiny now through what we do with the gifts and opportunities God gives us. All of us long to hear our Lord say, "Well done, good and faithful servant," but even that is not the end of opportunity for us.

Death does not end our service nor define us in a final way. Only in heaven will we become our true selves fully and totally. We will enter into our greatest opportunities to serve when we enter God's presence free from sin, the flesh, and all physical limitations. Although we are preparing for our Lord's evaluation and must make every effort to send gold, silver, and precious stones on ahead, we must remember that death is the doorway to resurrection and the richest service we will ever know. Death is not the end; it is the beginning of what we were truly created to be, and we must live our lives in that light.

Community-Driven: Serving Is the Point, Not Winning

Abundance thinkers give themselves to others, because they realize they become what God created them to be only through serving Him and other people. The only ones who can enter into this kind of fellowship are those who no longer have anything to hide, who taste in some small way the freedom the Trinity has in its relationships. There you see Father, Son, and Holy Spirit, each of whom both leads and subordinates Himself to the other without fear of control or competition, with no concern for who wins or loses, with concern only for love and accomplishing their agreed-on purpose. Deficit thinkers can never enter into such a relationship. They aren't even remotely capable of doing so. Abundance thinkers, however, find their greatest joy in serving, not in winning.

Dependently Motivated: I Can't Make It on My Own

Just as abundance thinkers need community, they need Christ even more. Increasingly they grasp the meaning of our Lord's words, "Without Me you can do nothing" (John 15:5). What was once abstract and incomprehensible gradually becomes the single greatest reality of their lives: Knowing Him is the greatest gain there is in life (Phil. 3:7–8).

Security-Based: The Abundant Life Is in Christ

Deficit thinkers are fear-based, driven by the terror that they are nobodies and that they might never become more than that. But abundance thinkers have found the abundant life that is in Christ—the true abundance of being themselves and all that means through God's grace—and they are confident He will give them more than they could ever ask or think (Eph. 3:20). They do not fear what life brings so long as Christ is there with them and they get to know Him better. *Entering into this relationship ourselves and then helping others enter into it with us is what pastoring is all about.* Nothing is greater than this—no position, or power, or pulpit, nothing!

AN ORIGINAL ABUNDANCE THINKER

Just as Paul is a model of deficit thinking, so he is a model of abundance thinking (Phil. 3:7–14). Once he turned from the loss of *skybala* to the gain of knowing Christ, he became a radically different person. Thirteen years elapsed between his first efforts in Jerusalem (Acts 9:30) and Barnabas's invitation for Paul to go from Tarsus to Antioch (11:25–26). During this "wilderness" time Paul became the kind of individual God could thrust into prominence as the apostle to the Gentiles.

Now Paul, the accountant viewing the profit-and-loss statement on his life investments, became an athlete running a race with every ounce of energy in his being. His eyes were on the finish line, he ran toward the tape, seeking only to hear the Judge declare him a prize winner (Phil. 3:10–14). That prize, the prize for which he was created, filled his thoughts. His goal was to fulfill the call of God on his life. He knew he was still on the track, and, although he was not certain how many more laps he had to go, he was faithful to give his best and go his hardest until he entered the last lap and saw the finishing tape in front of him. He was driven, not by a vision of himself but by a vision of his Lord. He knew he was just another runner on life's track, and that was good enough for him because he also knew that was what he was created to be. Nothing could fulfill him more than knowing Christ. Once he gained Christ he had everything; before he had nothing. Now he had true abundance.

For such a pastor the size of his church is only as important to him as it is to Christ. To him fame means nothing except as it exalts Christ. In his mind preaching is not an issue of his identity; it is an expression of Christ's glory. He is at rest, striding confidently and steadily in Christ, no matter what turmoil he faces. He is delivered from the death of deficit thinking through the abundance he finds in knowing Jesus Christ his Lord.

An abundance thinker is ready to face himself, including his fears and his flaws. He learns to know Christ better when he confronts his sin in deeper ways. He does not need to reduce God's Word to the banal relevance of the words "That'll preach." He understands preaching must come from the depths of his walk with Christ, not from a shallow immersion in the culture around him. He knows the real purpose of preaching is to change lives, not merely to "preach." And he knows that true power in preaching comes first from an intimate relationship with Christ and second from an insightful understanding of his times.

An abundance thinker also comprehends the connection between leadership competence and the leader's character. Each time he comes to the question of competence versus character, he realizes he can't grow in skill without facing flaws in his being. He will never come to know Christ fully until he chooses the pain of character growth in the process of skill development. Here is one of the most vital principles a spiritual leader must grasp: *The higher up a leader goes in competence demand, the deeper down that leader must go in character discipline.* We can be certain of this: *For every new level of opportunity God gives us, He will demand a new depth of growth from us.*

If we resist facing our flaws, we will soon find ourselves functioning without any inner strength, and our ministries will collapse under us. This is why men with such great gifts, knowledge, and charisma have such great falls: They learned to manipulate, but not to minister. They acted as if they knew Christ, but they never entered into the suffering that sin demands—the pain of facing our own shame, the grief of having to acknowledge to others what they already knew about us, the humility of knowing we're just as ordinary as everyone else. They thought being good at what they did—rather than who they were—was the way to buy success and become somebody.

New opportunities demand new competencies, but every new skill we develop brings us face to face with new character flaws we must confront, no matter how great the pain. If we refuse to face these flaws, we can do only one thing: cover up our sin with our achievements. But all cover-ups lead to the same end, namely, ministry collapse. One of the most significant ways we come to know Christ is through confronting and confessing our sin. In those moments He draws near to us to cleanse, comfort, and commission us to the new tasks for which we are now ready. Moses (Exod. 3:1–4:14), Isaiah (Isa. 6:1–9), and Paul (Acts 9:1–14) all learned that *the closer we get to the holy God, the clearer our life call becomes.* God appeared to each of them in His holiness, not to condemn them, but to commission them once they had confessed their sin. Like Moses, Isaiah, and Paul, all pastors come frequently to the intersection of competence and character, and like them, we must be ready to face our sin, not cover it up. Then we will know Christ and grasp what Paul learned: Our ultimate aim, as runners in life's marathon, is to pursue the purpose for which Christ pursued us.

This is what I discovered when I confessed my pride to God. Amazingly, eight months after my failure in the Philippines God led me back to Southeast Asia. Failure was not the end for me. Instead it brought the beginning of true life and opportunity. Although it has taken years for me to grasp the significance of God's grace in my life, He has continued to use me and teach me through the opportunities He gives. I have found God doesn't reject us when we fail. Rather, He redeems and restores us and then pours out on us greater blessings than we could ever imagine.

Christ is the true Source of all identity, and the better we know Him the better we know ourselves. All identity, influence, ministry, and impact come from knowing Him. In fact, everything that matters comes from knowing Him. The greatest source of ministry competence lies in knowing Christ. Here is where we find vision; here is where we find courage; here is where we find our gifts; here is where we find spiritual power. Without Him all we do is nothing.

I wish I could tell you my recovery from burnout delivered me from pride and instantly freed me from deficit thinking, but I can't. The process is long and slow, and I have discovered times of brokenness continue throughout life. I have learned about knowing Christ through private prayer and public worship. I have learned my own attitude is my greatest barrier to being a servant leader. No matter what others do to hinder me or even oppose me, I am always free to be the person Christ made me to be if I choose to trust Him.

I have discovered the joy of serving Jesus just for the delight of it. I have learned that preaching without fear comes when I am preaching without concern for myself, but this takes consistent prayer, confession, and cleansing, all of which come only through God's grace. I have also discovered one of the most important ways to know Him is to stand at the intersection of competence and character and say yes to Christ when I'd rather say no. At times that has meant staying where He wanted me to stay when I wanted to go elsewhere. What is it He wants me to face? I discovered it a few years ago when I was studying the Gospel of Mark; it was my hardened heart.

THE EFFECTIVE PASTOR

In this book on effective pastoring, I want you to know what I mean by "effective." Certainly it includes powerful preaching, visionary leadership, new plans for the twenty-first century, productive boards, strong teams— all the things that make pastoring the joy God intends it to be. But no pastor can be effective unless his number-one commitment is to know Christ. Unless we are willing to pay any price to know Christ, our ministry will collapse. Our own sermons will mock us and convict us of our unholy lives; our own vision will reveal that we are powerless and ineffective; our own plans for the twenty-first century will show that we are nothing more than empty talkers; our board and staff will reject us and judge us for the hypocrites we are. The very Lord who died for us and called us into ministry will set us aside, take our lampstand from us, and give it to another who will make knowing Him more important than anything else in life. Let's know Him and serve Him. This is what pastoring is all about.

CHAPTER TWO

———⌄———

THE DREADED LEADER'S DISEASE

Hardened hearts. These are two ominous words we associate with the arrogant, proud pharaoh of the Exodus; the idolatrous tribes of Canaan; the stiff-necked, rebellious Israelites; and the willfully self-righteous Sadducees and Pharisees, but not with Christ's disciples. Yet this is exactly how Jesus described His men (Mark 6:52; 8:17). What led Jesus to accuse His own followers of having hardened hearts? In response to His call they had given up everything to follow Him—financial security, family normalcy, their occupations. Still He said they had hardened hearts.

Were Christ's disciples like the Pharisees and Sadducees, who demanded that Jesus be what they wanted Him to be? In some measure, yes. They resisted Him because He did not live according to their terms. Their hearts were hardened because they didn't trust Him and His sufficiency. Each of the twelve disciples struggled with this flaw. They made the right decisions, said the right things, confessed the right theology, did the right miracles, and yet the terrible shackles of this debilitating struggle held them prisoners. Because of it, they brought frustration to their Lord and shame to themselves, even as many of us do as pastors. What can this mean for us? Are we possibly doing the same in our pastoral ministry?

Could our hearts be hardened? Like the disciples, we have turned away from all other pursuits to follow Christ, but we can also mix our commitment with expectations that keep us from seeing Him for who He truly is and what He intends to do through us. We fill our minds with our puny plans and miss His powerful purpose for us, even as the disciples did. We have "Leader's Disease," that is, hardened hearts.

Leader's Disease is epidemic among pastors. Nothing holds us back more. Nothing infects our souls, stains our spirits, or paralyzes our hands so completely as this issue of the heart. When we are in the grip of Leader's Disease, we are unable to respond to our Lord's plans for us; we cannot learn from Him or see His greatness through us. The disciples revealed this through their response to two miracles that became models of ministry for them—and us.

A SUPERNATURAL ASSIGNMENT

Jesus commissioned the Twelve to preach, drive out demons, and anoint many sick people with oil (Mark 6:7–13). They obeyed and had a powerful ministry. Who wouldn't long for such accomplishments? Any modern minister would regard their impact as an unparalleled success and would declare the pastor who did these things a spiritual giant. Yet the disciples had hardened hearts. They had given up finances and family to follow Christ, and they had cast out demons and prayed with power for physical healings. Why would their hearts be hardened?

At the end of a long, demanding day Jesus sent His men across the Sea of Galilee while He went up on a mountain to pray (Matt. 14:23). Well into the night, in the midst of wild winds and churning waves, He walked on the water to meet them (Mark 6:48). When they saw Him, they thought He was a water spirit and they cried out with terror. Then He spoke to them, and they knew it was Jesus. With that He got into the boat and the wind died down (6:51). His disciples were amazed, but they shouldn't have been. They should have expected Jesus to deliver them, and to do it in an amazing way.

Why should they have expected Him to rescue them? Because He had already stilled one storm and also demonstrated His power over nature, sickness, demons, and death. Furthermore earlier that same day they saw Him feed five thousand people with a little boy's lunch. What more could the Son of God do to earn their trust? Yet they were terrorized and amazed. Why? Because their hearts were hardened (6:52).[1] This is stunning! How could the disciples be spiritually imperceptive? How could they have the same problem as the Pharisees (3:5)?

Their condition expressed itself in their astonishment when Jesus walked on water and stilled the storm. Why had they learned nothing from the incident of the loaves? Because their hearts were hardened.

MODEL MIRACLES

Jesus designed these miracles to be a model of the ministry demands that both the disciples then and pastors today must meet to be effective. The feeding of the five thousand is the class and walking on water is the lab, and together they become a model of ministry for all who desire to know and serve Christ.

Involved Disciples

The feeding of the five thousand is one of the few events in Christ's life recorded in all four Gospels. It marks the first time Jesus involved His disciples in doing a miracle with Him. Up until now they had been passive observers, spectators watching what He did, but they themselves were not engaged. Now they came to Him with a problem—too many people and not enough food—but they didn't think of a miracle. All they wanted was to get rid of the crowd (Mark 6:35–36). Like so many of us, they wanted the Lord to remove their overwhelming problem, but He didn't do that. Instead He said a very startling thing: "You [emphatic][2] give them something to eat" (6:37).

John explained that Jesus planned this miracle as a test for the disciples. When He asked Philip, "'Where shall we buy bread for these people to eat?'" (John. 6:5), He already knew "what He was going to do" (6:6). Jesus wanted them to think of a solution, but the problem was too big for them. Philip showed their frustration by telling Jesus something He already knew. "Eight months' wages would not buy enough bread for each one to have a bite" (6:7). Jesus wanted them to feed the crowd, but even if they had eight months' worth of a working man's wages, no one would get more than a single bite. What kind of a solution is that? They were incredulous, utterly unprepared for Jesus to tell them to give the five thousand something to eat.[3]

William Lane makes these interesting comments: "Jesus, in contrast to the circumstances depicted in all of the other miracles, appears deliberately to create the situation in which the people must be fed. His instructions to the disciples to feed the people and to count their reserves of bread signify unambiguously that the food had to be provided through the disciples, not from the multitude. Jesus knows from the beginning what He will do and the exchange with the Twelve moves toward a well-defined end. The Twelve, however, display an increasing lack of understanding; their attitude of disrespect and incredulity declares that the conduct of Jesus is beyond their comprehension."[4]

Jesus wanted to engage the disciples in the process. "In contrast to their usually passive stance Jesus actively involved them in the total proceeding. His extended discussion with them prior to the event baffled them, while His wordless disclosure of His divine power through the event exceeded all understanding."[5]

What was the purpose of this test? To raise their trust in Him to a new level by showing them what He could do *through* them, not just *for* them or for others. He also acted to show them how they could depend on Him even as He depended on the Father. Thus He acted to teach them a new approach to ministry. Not only would they preach, cast out demons, and heal the sick, but they could also meet the deepest inner spiritual hunger of others through trusting in Him. They had passed the first part of the course; now it was time to move on to the next level and learn about the true nature of ministry. He wanted to teach them they were inadequate for ministry, that all ministry is beyond ordinary human resources.

Ministry Realities

Ministry is life permanently lived in the deep end of the pool with no time-outs. The odds will always be five thousand to seven, that is, there will always be five thousand hungry men (plus women and children), and all we'll ever have in ourselves to give them is five loaves and two fish. The pastorate will always be beyond us—beyond our gifts, our training, our experience, beyond everything except radical trust in Christ. If we are seeking to become adequate as pastors, we are seeking something that will never happen. The best and brightest among us will never have more than a little boy's lunch. Ministry is permanently beyond our adequacy.

Jesus gave His apostles and us a model of ministry that demonstrates our need for Him in all we do. He will never give us something we can do apart from Him, whether it is preaching, counseling, visiting the sick, leading a staff, or developing elders or deacons. Whatever it is, we can't do it without Him. We must bring our little boy's lunch, place it in His hands, wait for Him to bless it, and then see Him distribute its life-giving nutrition and energy through us. All we can ever do is carry bits and pieces of loaves and fish from Jesus to the hungry multitude. One thing is certain: On that day no disciple forgot that only Jesus had the food. To prevent the hungry multitude from becoming an angry mob, they needed to stay dependent on Him. Jesus alone is adequate for the task we face, and only as we trust Him and His resources will we be able to feed the hungry multitude. Relying on our own resources reveals a hardened heart.

Jesus' Adequacy for Our Inadequacy

Jesus was telling His men, in essence, "I will replace your inadequacy with My adequacy." The message Jesus communicated to His disciples through this miracle was this: *To minister for Me you will have to do what you can't do with what you don't have.* Nothing has changed since then. This is as true for us today as it was on the day the disciples faced the five thousand. However, Jesus communicated more than this to His men and to us in that moment. His actions were a promise: *I will do what I can do with what I have.* We are never adequate, but He is always adequate through us. For this reason we must expect Him to intervene when we face storms, and only our hardened hearts cause us to be amazed when He walks on water to deliver us from the storms we face in life.

Because only Christ can meet the overwhelming needs of others through us, none of the means we normally use to build and accomplish ministry ever work. Means such as the following are inadequate for ministering for Christ:

- our thinking
- our knowledge
- our planning
- our energy
- our influence
- our power
- our preaching
- our control
- our personality.

All the ways we seek to succeed in ministry fail us when we face five thousand hungry men plus women and children, because none of them has any power to change lives. Jesus does use our thinking, planning, energy, influence, power, and personalities when He feeds the five thousand through us. Surely each disciple had his own individual way of putting bread and fish in the people's hands on that amazing day, yet the power to make the difference came not from the disciples but from the Discipler. So it is with us. The power to make a difference comes from Christ, not us.

This is the essence of ministry: *Jesus fills our hands with His adequacy so we can go from Him to the hungry multitude.* Jesus taught this to His disciples when He fed the five thousand. He expected them to remember this when He walked on water, but they didn't remember. Why? Because their hearts were hardened; they were relying on themselves.

Hardened Heart, Sinking Feet

Hardness of heart was the reason Jesus spoke so strongly to Peter following his failed effort to walk on water. Some may not think Peter's effort was heroic, but I believe it was amazingly so. I have always been stunned at our Lord's words to him. I would have expected Him to congratulate Peter as the only man with enough courage to get out of the boat and do what Jesus was doing. Remember the situation before you judge Peter. It's easy for us to stand in a pulpit and make great sermon grist by criticizing Peter for being afraid when he lost sight of Jesus because of the pounding waves. We proclaim from our landlocked pulpits on Sunday mornings,

"Never let the waves of life overcome your faith in Jesus." This is good advice, even good preaching, although many of us who preach it so blithely might well have been throwing up over the side of the boat instead of walking on water. Our good preaching, however, misses the point of Peter's failure in faith. Peter's problem wasn't that his eyes were overcome by the waves, but that his heart wasn't up to the task.

Jesus' rebuke to Peter seems harsh. "You of little faith, why did you doubt?" (Matt. 14:31). Peter had done what no other disciple would do; he went over the side of the boat and onto the water. So why did Jesus speak so strongly to him? What did Jesus want? There is only one answer: Jesus *expected* Peter to walk on water. Our Lord's point is this: "You have just failed at what I *expect* you to do for the rest of your life. You will face storms that will demand all the energy you have, but they will be supernatural storms brought on by supernatural forces which demand faith in My supernatural resources. Learn this point now, because this is what your ministry will be about. I expect you to do the supernatural through My supernatural resources. Anything less is doubt and failure and reveals a hardened heart."

This is what our Lord expected His men to learn from the lecture and to apply in the laboratory of life. We are to take our Lord's words and works seriously. He is God, and He plans to speak the Word of God and do the works of God through us. What could be more challenging? How can we be satisfied with ordinary—even less than ordinary—ministries when the Lord of the universe wants to act through us? Only He is adequate for ministry. Our hardness of heart keeps us from grasping this truth and trusting Him for what He can do through us. For this reason, Jesus never ceases to put us in circumstances designed to deliver us from hardened hearts, circumstances that give Him every opportunity to demonstrate His glory through our frailties.

FOUR MIRACLES, FOUR MESSAGES, THE SAME POINT

The disciples' hardness of heart became our Lord's greatest obstacle in developing His leaders. Mark focused on this struggle through a series of four "message miracles" in Mark 7–8. Each miracle had a message designed to demonstrate a different way hardness of heart impacts us.

Darkened Understanding (Mark 7:24–30)

On learning where Jesus was, a Syrian Phoenician woman, a Gentile, went to see Him about her little daughter who had a demon. He represented her only hope. Despite His efforts to rebuff her, she persisted, and Jesus did something He did only one other time: He healed her daughter without going to her, touching her, or saying a word about her.[6] This woman's heart was tender toward the Lord despite her lack of understanding, and she trusted Him to meet her need.

In contrast to the Syrian Phoenician woman, consider the disciples, who had had a lifetime of instruction from the Old Testament concerning the Messiah. Further, John the Baptist had identified Jesus as the Messiah, and they had heard His words and seen His works. Yet because their hearts were hardened, their minds were darkened. So they couldn't grasp the true significance of who He was.

What's the point of this miracle? This woman had a faith far beyond her knowledge, but the disciples, by contrast, had a faith far short of their knowledge.[7] The woman who knew almost nothing of Christ had great faith, while the disciples, who knew much more about Him, had little faith. The disciples' knowledge blinded their understanding so they could not trust Him for supernatural actions. In contrast, the woman's faith enlightened her understanding so she could trust Him to meet her needs. Her heart was soft, but the disciples' hearts were hardened.

The message of this miracle is that hardened hearts darken our understanding so that we don't trust Christ for what He can do through us. We don't sense our inadequacy or His adequacy for us. We may say the words and sound as if we get the point, but our behavior belies our claim, just as it did in the disciples. What the head knows, the hand cannot do until the heart is broken, and the disciples were a long way from this.

Deafened Ears, Crippled Tongues (Mark 7:31–37)

The next message-miracle follows immediately. In this event, recorded only by Mark and designed to prefigure the opening of the disciples' ears,[8] Jesus healed a deaf man who could not talk clearly. Could there be a clearer message to His disciples? Hardened hearts deafen the ears and cripple the tongue. The disciples heard the truth, but only partially; they spoke the truth, but not clearly. They would never hear or speak properly until full faith finally opened their ears.

A Rerun Miracle (Mark 8:1–10)

In the next miracle Jesus fed four thousand, a "rerun" miracle echoing the feeding of the five thousand. Some critics regard this as a mistaken record of the feeding of the five thousand, but the differences are specific and clearly described, and Jesus referred to both miracles in this same chapter (8:19–20). Our Lord was an excellent teacher, and, as any excellent teacher knows, repetition is an effective weapon in an instructor's arsenal. This time the demand was different, a little easier perhaps, since there were only four thousand to feed, and the disciples had seven loaves and a few small fish. However, whether the odds are five thousand to seven or four thousand to seven and more, they are still overwhelming.

What message was Jesus sending through this rerun miracle? He was telling His disciples and us, "I mean it, men. I'm not playing with you. Do you want to become fishers of men? Do you want to make a difference for Me? Then understand My message. You will never be adequate for ministry without relying on Me. You are utterly inadequate apart from Me and you always will be. I will replace your inadequacy with my adequacy, and this is the only way you can serve Me." Yet hardness of heart—depending on our own resources—keeps us from grasping His point.

The Point: Hardened Hearts (Mark 8:11–21)

Immediately after this, some Pharisees came and asked Jesus for a sign, but He rejected their demand because their intent was to judge Him, not trust Him (8:11–12).[9] Then Jesus and His disciples got into a boat and headed across Galilee (8:13). While in the boat Jesus issued a stern warning that His disciples misunderstood. Jesus gave them orders telling them to watch out for the yeast of the Pharisees and the Herodians (8:15). By yeast Jesus referred to their evil intention to test Him, not trust Him. The disciples missed Jesus' point entirely and became confused because they had only one loaf of bread in the boat. They thought He was rebuking them for not having enough bread to eat, a ridiculous thought in light of His having fed the five thousand and the four thousand. When our Lord heard them discussing this, He rebuked them and raised several penetrating questions, thus bringing the message of His miracles together for His disciples.

Twice He asked them if they still did not understand (8:17, 21) despite His words and works. This was in contrast to the Syrian Phoenician woman who saw and heard so little but understood so much. He also asked them if they had ears but failed to hear (8:18), just like the deaf man He healed in Decapolis. Didn't they remember, He inquired, how many basketfuls were left over after the feeding of the five thousand and how many large basketfuls (8:20) were left over after the feeding of the four thousand? They did remember, of course, but though they had the facts they missed the point. He made His point clear by asking, "Are your hearts hardened?" (8:17). A darkened understanding, deaf ears, and crippled tongues could mean only one thing: Their hearts were hardened; they failed to rely on Him.

Blinded Eyes (Mark 8:22–26)

Now that Jesus had made His point, He did one more miracle to confirm and emphasize His message to the disciples. They entered Bethsaida, and some people brought a blind man to Him for healing. Jesus took the man outside the village and touched His eyes, but when He asked if he could see anything, the man replied, "I see people; they look like trees walking around" (8:24). So Jesus touched his eyes again, and the man saw clearly.

This two-stage miracle was the only one of its kind in Jesus' ministry. With all His other miracles, healing occurred when He spoke or touched, but this miracle was unique because it took two touches.[10] Why? Surely not because Jesus was unable to do it with one touch. Could it be a message to the disciples that they had eyes to see but could not see? They grasped enough of Jesus' message to know He was God,[11] but their hearts were hardened. Their eyes were blinded just as their understanding was darkened, their ears deafened, and their tongues crippled. For this reason, like the blind man who confused men with trees, the disciples mistook Messiah for a forest of their own making.

WHO AM I? (MARK 8:27–33)

When Jesus and His disciples arrived at a remote area near Caesarea Philippi in the far north of Israel, He asked them, "Who do people say I am?" (8:27, NIV). Of course they gave Him all the popular answers. Then He made His question more specific by asking, "But what about you? . . . Who do you say I am?" (8:29). Peter responded, "You are the Christ, the Son of the living God" (Matt. 16:16). Peter and the rest of the disciples knew He was God. They had gotten the message, but missed its meaning. Yet Jesus approved Peter's response and blessed him with a special commendation. "Blessed are you, Simon son of Jonah, for this was not revealed to you by man, but by my Father in heaven" (16:17). Peter was personally tutored in Christology by God Himself. Surely his theology was accurate.

Next Jesus did an amazing and baffling thing; He began to speak plainly about the Cross (Mark 8:31). He had never mentioned the Cross before, and the disciples were even more unprepared for this message than they were for His message-miracles. Peter reacted by taking Him aside and rebuking Him (8:32). Peter may have said something like this: "What are you doing? Messiahs aren't crucified. You're not making any sense. You will kill Rome; Rome will not kill you! You're scaring us." By speaking to Jesus privately, Peter was trying to respond politely, but Jesus had no concern then for politeness; truth was more important to Him. As Jesus turned to look at Peter, He saw the other disciples (8:33) and rebuked Peter with some of the most amazing words in the Bible. "Get behind me, Satan!" How can a man who was privately tutored by God in Christology be called Satan? What does this mean?

This is the dreaded Leader's Disease and shows that it takes more than an accurate theology to have an accurate faith. Our Lord identified Peter's core problem: He was pursuing man's interests rather than God's (8:33). Peter's expectations conflicted with God's purposes. He was looking for position and power, while God was looking for sacrifice and humility. He was afflicted with the dreaded Leader's Disease.

Jesus' words show us that *Leader's Disease is a chronic condition of the heart that is contaminated by expectations of self-reliance, position, power, recognition, and control.* It pursues man's interests rather than God's, while serving Christ. This faith must be purified, and until this happens, those with Leader's Disease will turn from the Cross with the same motives, fears, and pride Satan has.

All this comes because of hardened hearts. We can think of hardened hearts as Mark's image for the flesh. The disciples were not like others with hardened hearts in the Bible such as Pharaoh, the Canaanites, or Israel's religious leaders. Their hearts were not hardened in the same way as those rebellious people any more than believers who walk according to the flesh are the same as unbelievers who are totally controlled by the flesh. But like unbelievers, we can and do walk according to the flesh and fulfill its desires. So sometimes it's difficult to tell believers and unbelievers apart.

CONCLUSION

The dreaded Leader's Disease is a chronic condition in which hardness of heart blinds us to the real meaning of the truth we hold. The problem does not lie in our heads; it lies in our hearts, and this affects our hands, making us powerless and ineffective. What does this Leader's Disease look like and how can we gain deliverance from it? This is what we see in our next chapter.

CHAPTER THREE

DELIVERANCE FROM
THE DREADED LEADER'S DISEASE

Is IT POSSIBLE for people who are completely committed to Christ to have Leader's Disease? How can people who have given up financial security and family living have this malady? How would Peter, who had power to cast out demons and who knew who Jesus is, suffer from the blindness caused by a hardened heart? How could Peter be called Satan?

If anything ever showed the folly of judging a man's spirituality by his ministry success, this does. How could a man do what Peter did and not be spiritual? The answer becomes increasingly obvious as we consider what happened to Christ's men, starting in Mark 6. From the moment Jesus introduced them to their supernatural responsibilities through the feeding of the five thousand until His Resurrection, all twelve men were on a downward spiral. They reached the point where they could not deliver a demonized boy (Mark 9:14–32). They had fallen from great success to great failure, and Jesus was frustrated with their fall. "O unbelieving generation . . . how long shall I stay with you? How long shall I put up with you?" (9:19). These men had great success until they met the supernatural demands of ministry. Then they fell apart and grew increasingly ineffective.

HANDS, HEAD, HEART

The disciples had two of the three elements they needed for lasting impact. Peter represents them well. We know that Peter was a man of action, a man of the hands, a doer, always ready to take on a task. Like Peter, we must be doers, men of action. Things will not get done if we just stand around and talk about them. We need to act, to lead the church forward, to present and develop new ideas that will move our ministries into new directions. But Peter was more than a man of the hands; he was also a man of the head. Although we might not expect this of him, Peter turned out to be a thoughtful man, a theological thinker, who understood who Jesus is on the basis of his knowledge of Scripture and his observation of Jesus' words and works. Peter identified Jesus as the Christ. The others must have thought it, but it was Peter who spoke and declared that Jesus is the Son of the living God. Peter, like the rest of the apostles, was a man of the hands and a man of the head. But what about the heart?

Here is the root of the disciples' problem, and of ours as well. At times they came to right conclusions and did right actions, but they could not accomplish the supernatural things that serving Jesus demands. Why was this? Because their hearts were hardened. It is not enough to hold accurate theology and do what is right. Unless the heart is softened and sensitive to depend on Christ, truth of doctrine and rightness of action will make little difference. The hands do and the head knows, but the heart is hardened because it is focused on its own interests rather than God's. We may have the right theology, but our ministry will be powerless if we are self-focused. How many ministries do we see like this—hands full of programs and heads full of knowledge, but hearts full of self?

The dreaded Leader's Disease takes root in our hearts when we pursue our own interests in God's name. We proclaim ourselves to be Christ's servants, but in reality we are self-serving. Each Sunday as we pray from the pulpit or preach from the Word we claim to be serving the sheep for the Savior's interests, yet when our hearts are hardened, we use the sheep to serve ourselves.

We can tell our hearts are hardened if we resent the refusal of the sheep to make us successful, as if their responsibility before God is to enhance our careers and promote our causes. When we become angry and seek to desert one fold for another because the sheep don't appreciate us or help us gain the fame we deserve, we have hardened hearts. Who among us has not struggled with such thoughts? Blackaby puts it well when he says, "The people are not there to help you be a successful pastor. You are there by divine assignment to work with God to bring His people to their fullest potential in knowing and doing the will of God for His glory."[1] We "are the steward and God is the owner! [We] are called by God to join Him in what He has been doing, and now wants to do through you for them."[2]

FOUR SYMPTOMS OF LEADER'S DISEASE

What does this dreaded Leader's Disease look like? It can be recognized by four symptoms.

Symptom 1: Careerism Marked by Selfish Ambition and Shameful Competition

We find the first symptom of Leader's Disease in Mark 9:30–34. For the second time Jesus told His disciples He would be betrayed, killed, and would rise after three days (9:31; compare 8:31). They were mystified by what He was saying, but they were too scared to ask Him any questions, perhaps because if He made it any clearer they would have to accept His words. His message as Messiah and their expectations of the Messiah conflicted, but by ignoring what He said they continued to hold their false concept of the kingdom. Their expectations kept them going, and, if they were not true, the apostles' motivation to follow Christ was shattered.

> The disciples consider that if Jesus is the anointed one they can only benefit from their association with Him. The disciples expect ... eventual prosperity (to gain the world), importance, and positions of power.... What they had previously experienced of Jesus in the story until now reinforced these expectations: the healings, exorcisms, works of power over nature, and the huge crowds.... this conflict between Jesus and the disciples on the way to Jerusalem exemplifies the clash between the values of the disciples and those of Jesus. The disciples share the values of the authorities. The disciples hope to

prosper, to be important and powerful. . . . But Jesus defines their values as "thinking the things of men" and turns those values upside down.[3]

Many pastors have the same expectations as the disciples, expectations of position, power, fame, triumph over our enemies, and vindication as true men of God. It is both difficult and confusing to turn from these desires for ourselves and trust Christ for what He has for us. Like these apostles, many of us have given up certain comforts with the expectation that we would get even more back. For many pastors money may not be a concern, but position, power, recognition, and fame are. Size and influence turn out to mean far more to us than we ever dreamed.

What the disciples did not know, but what we can and must know, is the total emptiness of power and position, the futile desires of our sinful natures. We can leave a lasting heritage only if we don't care about such fleshly goals and if, instead, we take up our crosses daily. This is how we become difference-makers as pastors. But the apostles did not understand this and were afraid to ask. Tragically, they didn't understand what He said about His dying and being raised again.

One day Jesus and His men returned to Capernaum and, after entering a house, He asked them, "What were you arguing about on the road?" (9:33). The disciples kept silent because they were driven by the same motives as those who rejected Jesus: They wanted a Messiah who would meet their terms and fulfill their expectations. Just like those around them, they were full of selfish ambition and shameful competition.[4] While Jesus spoke of the greatest self-sacrifice in divine and human history, the apostles argued among themselves as to who was the greatest. Their total focus was on their status in the future kingdom, and so they neither understood nor accepted the Cross.[5] Don't we do the same?

Think of the conversations we have at pastors' conferences when we talk about baptisms, buildings, budgets, books, and broadcasts. Aren't we attempting to determine who is the greatest among us? Don't selfish ambition and shameful competition darken our dreams and foul our language? Are we not forced to be silent before our Lord's searching questions? We have nothing to say when we stand before the Cross. All we can do is fall on our faces and confess our sin, and, until we are ready to do this, we must keep silent. Peter had nothing to say because there was nothing he could say. The Cross strips us of all pretense and leaves us only two choices: silence or confession.

Like the apostles we are too taken up with careerism, with success as our culture defines it. Eugene Peterson describes it well when he tells us why we have such difficulty being pastors. It is

because we are awash in idolatry. The idolatry to which pastors are conspicuously liable is not personal but vocational, the idolatry of a religious career that we can take charge of and manage. . . . But it is both possible and common to develop deep personal pieties that coexist alongside vocational idolatries without anyone noticing anything amiss. If the pastor is devout, it is assumed that the work is devout. The assumption is unwarranted.

Pastors commonly give lip service to the vocabulary of a holy vocation, but in our working lives we more commonly pursue careers. Our actual work takes shape under the pressure of the marketplace, not the truth of theology or the wisdom of spirituality. I would like to see as much attention given to the holiness of our vocations as to the piety of our lives. . . . The so-called spirituality that was handed to me by those who put me to the task of pastoral work was not adequate. I do not find the emaciated, exhausted spirituality of institutional careerism adequate. I do not find the veneered, cosmetic spirituality of personal charisma adequate. I require something *biblically* spiritual—rooted and cultivated in creation and covenant, leisurely in Christ, soaked in Spirit.[6]

The apostles were committed to careerism; their concept of the kingdom was defined by their own interests. They were committed to expectations of position and power while Christ was committed to service and sacrifice. Though the disciples and the Messiah spoke the same language, the chasm between the apostles' idea of the kingdom and Christ's cross could never be bridged. The apostles had to turn from their selfishly ambitious and competitive silence to Christ's love and humility before they could have anything to say. They had to turn from their careerism to the Cross, and we must do the same. The only way we can do this is if the

Cross penetrates our blinded minds and humbles our hardened hearts. Then we will experience a growing freedom from our selfish ambition and shameful competition.

Symptom 2: Shameless Use of Power

As Jesus and His followers continued on their way to Jerusalem, He took the Twelve aside privately and spoke to them of the Cross a third time (Mark 10:32–34). At this point He gave them the longest and most complete statement about the Cross in any of His communications. It was stark, specific, comprehensive. He would be betrayed—what an ugly word. How could He be betrayed except by a friend? What friend would do that? Weren't virtually all His friends with Him? This made no sense to the Twelve. He would be condemned, handed over to the Gentiles, mocked, spit on, flogged, killed. What message could be more unwelcome and more confusing?

Christ's promise that three days later He would rise from the dead was lost in the disciples' denial of the Cross. How else can we explain what happened next? "Then James and John, the sons of Zebedee [also known as the sons of thunder] came to Him" (10:35). "Then" is an amazing word. No "then" could be more misplaced; no "then" could convey greater irony; no "then" could reveal a greater grab for power. This shows us "the degree to which selfish ambition and rivalry were the raw material from which Jesus had to fashion the leadership for the incipient Church."[7] James and John came with an incredible demand: "Teacher, we want you to do for us whatever we ask." How could they have such audacity to ask Jesus to do whatever they wanted?

Matthew 20:20 records that they brought their mother, Salome, apparently Mary's sister,[8] and came kneeling before Jesus. (They looked so humble, but they were so proud.) If the disciples were to argue over who was the greatest, James and John—and their mother—would settle the issue through a direct appeal to family connections. For them blood really was thicker than water. We wonder why Jesus chose to entrust His mission and message to such men. Couldn't He have selected better candidates? The answer isn't difficult to discern: He had no choice because they were the only kind of men available to Him. This is why we must not judge the disciples too severely. We are exactly the same type of men, the only kind Jesus can choose.

Our Lord's response was as stunning as the disciples' request. He actually asked them what they wanted. He was patient with these shamelessly proud men; He listened to them, asked them a guiding question designed to help them realize why they were wrong, and explained to them why He couldn't give them what they wanted. Then He taught them that true greatness is giving your life on behalf of others, even when they betray you, condemn you, mock you, spit on you, flog you, and kill you. From this we realize that shameless use of power never gets us what we want.

Of course, we also have these drives. Don't you see those who want to sit on the right and the left at denominational conventions and organizational meetings? Can't you see them striving to be noticed? Seeking to be heard? Calling for attention? Using their networks to exalt themselves? Do you see yourself in James and John? We would be angry, just as the other disciples were, not just because James and John were so shameless in their use of power, but because they got to Jesus first. And their timing was ironic. They made their power grab just days before the Crucifixion; they were standing in the very shadow of the impending cross and didn't even know it.[9]

Do you see the pattern that is developing in the symptoms of Leader's Disease? Every time the Cross came up, competition came out. Every time Jesus mentioned the Cross, the disciples competed with each other to deny His message and assert their ambition. The disciples met Christ's first mention of the Cross with a rebuke, the second with silence, and the third with a shameless grab for power. There is not one tear, not one statement of shock, amazement, thanksgiving, or stunned disbelief. Their only concern was for themselves and their advancement.

They had their minds on *their* concerns, not God's. God's mind is concerned about sin and evil, grace and love for all; their minds were concerned about position, power, and success for themselves. They had futile expectations—personal, selfish, shameless seeking for power. Their expectations were based on a selfish view of life—and ours may be too. The Cross reveals these expectations in both the disciples and us.

Symptom 3: Insensitive Arrogance

The third symptom of Leader's Disease is the insensitive arrogance that blinded His disciples to our Lord's vulnerable longing for fellowship and love from them (Luke 22:14–24). No one could be as vulnerable as our Lord was with His disciples the night He was arrested. Gathered in the Upper Room with those He loved most on earth, He alone knew what a profound moment it was. As He spoke to them, He revealed His heart for them, a heart as full of eagerness to be with them as it was heavy to think of the Cross. "I have eagerly desired to eat this Passover with you before I suffer" (22:15). There's the Cross again. How would the disciples respond?

Throughout His life, Jesus must have experienced the Passover festival as a very sacred and significant celebration. When He was growing up as a child in Galilee, He learned of God's deliverance of Israel from Egypt through the Passover. He knew He was the very fulfillment of this special meal. What a mix of memories and thoughts He must have had in the Upper Room. He must have thought back to His family, to Mary and Joseph and His brothers and sisters, and the days when they celebrated the Passover together. That night, however, He concentrated on His new family, on the men who were called His disciples, the men He had been preparing to take His place, not just in Israel, but all over the earth. These men were destined for special honor far greater than they could have ever imagined. He said they would sit in seats of honor when Jesus establishes His kingdom; they would be guests of honor the next time Jesus celebrated this Passover event. Jesus knew their expectations would come true, though not in the way they thought. In anticipation of that wonderful event, Jesus gave His disciples a meal to celebrate during the period of His absence, the simple but powerful Lord's Supper.

Yet there was something else on our Lord's mind, something sinister, evil, unbelievable, that weighed Him down as nothing else could. One of those at that table was a betrayer. The disciples couldn't believe it. "Could I be the betrayer?" they all wondered. They questioned each other as to who this could be, perhaps even accusing each other. Their questioning degenerated into their typical dispute of who was the greatest among them (22:24). Once again, this is shocking, stunning, beyond comprehension.

On that night Jesus stripped Himself to the waist, took a basin, and washed their feet, thus demonstrating His total love for them. Yet they were so concerned for themselves that they were unable to share His joy, see His grief, or feel His vulnerability. All they could do was fight among themselves about who was the greatest.

How would we have reacted that night? I'd like to think I would have been radically different from those disciples, but I fear I would not have been. Have we not come to the Lord's Supper with the same concerns and expectations as the disciples? Have we not been concerned about being the best preacher or leading the best worship, even in those most sacred moments? How have we responded when others have betrayed us by leaving our churches or rejecting our love? Have we been concerned with our own greatness, acting with the insensitive arrogance of those who seek to be the greatest?

Symptom 4: Blind Self-Confidence

Another symptom of Leader's Disease is blind self-confidence (Mark 14:27–31). Jesus told His men that they would all fall away because He, their Shepherd, would be struck that night, and the sheep would scatter. When He spoke of striking the shepherd, He spoke of the Cross, as He made clear by saying, "'But after I have risen, I will go ahead of you into Galilee'" (14:28). Immediately Peter protested, which showed he still suffered from Leader's Disease. Again he confused God's truth with his own expectations. His heart was hardened. Thus he asserted, "Even if all fall away, I will not" (14:29).

What misguided self-confidence! When Peter said, "Even if all fall away," he was speaking of his fellow disciples. Thus in blind self-confidence he asserted his superiority over them. Viewing himself superior to the others, he thought he would stand when everyone else would fall. Peter spoke with great strength. "But not I," he said, using a strong contrast and strongly emphasizing the word "I" (14:29).[10] In essence, he said, *I* will *never* fall away because I am not like these others.

Peter's claim was the ultimate in foolishness, the product of a baseless self-confidence so blinded by his hardened heart that he was helplessly

· unable to see reality. Because of this, Jesus responded just as emphatically as Peter. He spoke solemnly and firmly in an effort to get Peter's attention. When He said, "Truly [literally, 'amen']¹¹ I say to you" (14:30, NASB), He was introducing an absolute assertion that is without doubt or question. "Tonight—this very night—you will do more than fall away, you will do more than run away like the rest; you will deny Me. You will deny you ever knew Me. You are no better than the rest; you are just more foolhardy." Jesus didn't merely say "you" to Peter. He spoke with the same emphasis Peter used; He said "you yourself": "Before the rooster crows twice you yourself will disown me three times." Jesus strongly confronted Peter, just as He rebuked him once before (8:33) and resisted Him another time (John 13:7–10). Yet Peter's self-confidence kept him from perceiving the truth.

Despite Jesus' warning, Peter replied with even greater vehemence, insisting again and again with one of the strongest denials possible that he would *never* deny Jesus. In fact, he said that if necessary he would die with Jesus rather than deny Him. "Ironically, a few hours later the disciples had fled (14:50) and Peter summoned the same vehemence to support his oath that he did not know the Nazarene (14:72)."¹²

Here we have the ultimate in Leader's Disease. Peter had left his business and family, and had identified Jesus as the Son of God. Undoubtedly he was a rallying point for the disciples, a man of infectious influence who through his very presence challenged the rest to be as dedicated as he was. He saw Jesus deliver his mother-in-law from a fever, and he opened his home to Jesus at the beginning of His ministry (1:29–34). After he had fished all night and caught nothing, he did what Jesus told him to do and cast his net on the other side of the boat. It was the wrong time of day to catch fish from either side of the boat, but Peter did as he was told and made one of the greatest catches of his life.

No man was more committed to Jesus than Peter, yet no man had a worse case of Leader's Disease. Peter showed every symptom of a hardened heart. How can a man as committed as Peter have a heart as hardened as his? While on the one hand Peter was dedicated to Christ, on the other he was determined to pursue his interests, rather than God's. This is why he ended up in conflict with Christ and later denied he even knew Him.

This is why he was so blinded by his own self-confidence that he could not hear the truth from the Son of God Himself, the very one Peter had earlier identified as the Christ. What could Peter do to recover from this disease? The answer lies in Christ's empty grave.

DELIVERANCE FROM LEADER'S DISEASE

To gain deliverance from the dreaded Leader's Disease, we need to understand why Mark wrote his Gospel. No writer, especially under the inspiration of the Holy Spirit, just sat down to write without a reason. In Mark's case, the reason was a critical one, in fact, a life-and-death reason.

When Mark wrote his Gospel, he was a protégé of the apostle Peter and was living in Rome. In fact, many believe Mark's Gospel is Peter's memoirs as recorded by his younger associate. Mark wrote during the time of Nero's first persecution of the church, which was primarily centered in Rome. Nero was arresting Roman believers, accusing them of atheism (because they didn't believe in the many gods of the Roman pantheon) as a pretext to cover up his burning of Rome,[13] and putting them to death in the most cruel ways possible. Naturally the believers in Rome had serious questions about what was going on. Who was this Jesus who was costing them their lives? They had to be certain He was the Son of the living God and that there was a resurrection for them. "The Gospel of Mark is a pastoral response to this critical demand."[14]

To answer this question, Mark led the Roman believers through the same discovery process the disciples experienced as they came to Christ and followed Him. Through this process they discerned for themselves that Jesus is the Son of the living God as He made it clear that what He demanded was "a radical abandonment of life"[15] in response to a call to the Cross. Here, however, there was a contrast between Jesus' mission and message and the disciples' expectations, a conflict between Christ's cross and the disciples' hardened hearts.

Like the disciples, the Roman believers had expectations of the Son of God. They knew He died, but they did not know they also would die. They expected to live, even to see His return, since this was a constant expectation in the ancient church. But instead of seeing His return, they were seeing their departure, and this was unexpected. The Romans found themselves severely tempted to deny Christ and to swear that they never knew Him, just as Peter had done.

Although our circumstances differ from those of the first disciples and the early believers in Rome, we, too, have expectations and face difficult questions. For many of us, ministry is a steppingstone to success, but we have encountered roadblocks to the accomplishments we anticipated. Elders stand in our way, and critics pick us apart for the smallest flaws, while the lost continue on their darkened way. Like the apostles and the early Christians, we are confused and unprepared for what the Cross means in our lives. We don't understand the flesh because our hearts are hardened and we don't even know it. We seek to be in control so we can become the greatest. We are tempted to deny Christ and trade in the Cross for the banality of a career. We are forced to choose between the expectations of careerism and the call of the Cross.

So all three of us—disciples, Roman Christians, and pastors—come to the same place, the tomb, and the choice between following Jesus as He truly is or trying to force Him to become what we want Him to be. For the disciples the choice was their kingdom or His Cross. For the Roman believers it was their security or His Cross. For us it is our careers or His Cross. No matter what it is, Mark's Gospel brings us all to the same place: the garden tomb. Consider what Mark wrote: "Trembling and bewildered, the women went out and fled from the tomb. They said nothing to anyone, because they were afraid" (16:8). Left to themselves these words hardly stand out, but when we think of how Mark intended them to impact his first readers, we understand how critical they are.

The abruptness of these words demands a response. Will we run from the tomb or face up to the symptoms of Leader's Disease in our lives? We are called to give up our personal dreams and ambitions, to put to death our drives for selfish success and the expectations that dominate us. Mark brought his readers to the empty tomb and to the decision it demands. All of us, disciples, Romans, and pastors, stand on the edge of death and must make the choice Mark led us to make if we are to know life.

Jesus' identity as the Son of the living God demands a response, and the response can only be to follow Him to the cross and death. This was the very call Jesus made. "If anyone would come after me, he must deny himself and take up his cross and follow me" (8:34). As He took up His Cross, so we must take up our cross and follow Him. Follow Him where? Into the grave. What does this mean? For disciples, Romans, and pastors the Cross means the same thing: death to our expectations and resurrection to a radical trust in Christ.

With the disciples and the Romans, we stand across from the garden tomb, looking into the yawning mouth of death. Will we follow Christ into His grave? Will we count on Him for His resurrection? Will we give up our expectations and stop pursuing our own interests? Will we let His Cross enlighten our understanding, unstop our ears, release our tongues, open our eyes? Will we truly trust Him for resurrection, so truly that we will turn away from everything else but trust in Him? Will we renew this commitment every day? We must consider our own hearts and make certain we are not governed more by our expectations of success and impact than by God's Spirit. It took the Cross and the Resurrection before the disciples were delivered from the pride caused by hearts hardened to anything but their expectations. The same is true for us. The only way we gain deliverance each day from the dreaded Leader's Disease is through the Cross and radical trust in Christ's resurrection power to overcome our hardened hearts.[16] This alone is what it means to pastor.

What if we choose to put our expectations to death and turn from seeking our interests to pursuing God's? What will our resurrected expectations look like? What hope do we have if we put our desires in Christ's grave? What will deliverance from Leader's Disease be for us? Note what happened to Peter. Fifty days after Jesus' resurrection "Peter stood up with the Eleven, raised his voice and addressed the crowd" (Acts 2:14).

Because of the Resurrection, Peter—a victim of Leader's Disease, confused by careerism, deafened by expectations of power, blinded by insensitive arrogance, misguided by misplaced self-confidence—was delivered from Leader's Disease and was released to be the man Jesus said he would be (John 1:42) when He first called him. If we have Leader's Disease we, like Peter, can find release in Christ.

Of course, we will not all become Peters, reaching three thousand people for Christ in one day. But we will all be like Peter in that we will become the leaders God created us to be: free to be ourselves, free from man's selfish interests, from fear, from pride, from the *skybala* of the flesh. God will be able to do through us far more than we ever expected, far more than our wildest dreams could imagine. Make the decision now to do as Peter did, and become the man God made you to be. Take up your cross daily, follow Jesus to the grave, and discover deliverance from the dreaded Leader's Disease through His resurrection resources.

PART TWO

THE PASTOR'S PURPOSE

Chapter Four

⌒

Disciple-Making Churches

To hear pastors talk, you'd think *they* own the church. All of us—pastor and other people alike—say things like, "*My* church this," "*My* church that," or "*My* church the other thing."

When pastors get together, they talk about "the vision *I* have for *my* church" or "the building *I* want to build for *my* church" or "the difficulty *I* have getting *my* elders (or *my* deacons) to do what *I* want for *my* church."

Many church members regard the church they attend as *their* church as well. It's the church *they* started, the church *they* built, the church *they* paid for, the church *they* own. This can get us into trouble, and we end up fighting over *our* church. We've forgotten the most important fact in this fight: We don't own the church. It's *not* ours.

Of course, in one sense the church *is* ours. How else do we describe where we go to church and where we serve the Lord and His sheep? Language gives us few options at this point. But it is wrong for us to think our church *belongs* to us. Church wars and divisions that so dishonor the Lord are not a matter of language, but a matter of possession. Often we really do think the church is ours, and so we fight with the intensity of people who are being mugged for the family jewels.

Too often pastor and other members are engaged in a tug of war for control of the church and its purpose. Some see it as a hospital to heal the hurting or as a counseling center to fix the broken. Young parents want it to be a nursery to raise their children, while the parents of teenagers want it to be a safe place free from bad influences. Others see it as the place to preserve the family or where singles come to meet friends and find mates. Senior citizens may see it as a center where they can gather to remember bygone days and boast about their grandchildren. Is the church a collection of unintegrated ministries intended to help us through the stages of life from birth to death? As pastors, our answer is no! We are not running a "hatch, match, and dispatch agency." The church is not to be controlled by self-centered people who are concerned for only their own interests.

Yes, the church *is* to meet the needs of families, youth, young couples, singles, and senior citizens. Meeting people's needs *is* the loving thing to do, and the church is all about love. But meeting needs is not an end in itself. What, then, is the purpose of the church? The way we answer this question tells us why we exist as pastors. We must be sure we and the members see the church's purpose in the same way, because the way we think about the church's purpose defines the expectations we have of each other.

The question we need to ask is this: What does Jesus Christ, the Owner, say the church's purpose is? He is the only one with the authority to answer this question. Since it's His church, He's the only one whose opinion matters. Remember, He said, "I will build *My* church" (Matt. 16:18, italics added). It's not *pastors* or people who build the church—it is Christ. He shed His blood for His church. So when He speaks, we must listen.

CUL-DE-SAC CHRISTIANITY

Unfortunately in our efforts to control what doesn't belong to us, many of us pursue cul-de-sac (dead-end) Christianity. For eleven years our family lived on a cul-de-sac made up of six houses with six families and a total of eighteen children. It was a nice, safe place to live. At one time the children ranged from infants to teens. The older children looked out for the younger ones, and we were virtually one big happy family.

Every day when I came home from work, I entered our cul-de-sac very slowly—hardly over five miles an hour—because I never knew what I would find. There might be a football game or a soccer game going on in the street; a mother might be scooping up a tarantula in a Mason jar; a couple of dads might be talking sports at the end of my driveway. Our cul-de-sac was a wonderful place to raise children and nurture families, but we couldn't stay there all the time. Each day we had to shop, go to work, and pursue a variety of life's activities. If we insisted on staying in our cul-de-sac all the time, we'd soon be unable to pay our mortgages, we might starve to death, or we might die of some sickness. We had to go out into the world in order to be sure our cul-de-sac continued to be a great place to live.

The church is like that. It's a wonderful, safe place for families, singles, the widowed, business people—all the kinds of people who make up our world. But it must be more than a cul-de-sac, a dead end, to which we all come after a hard week to be together and enjoy one another. When we think this way, we are confusing earth with eternity and trying to get to heaven too soon. In heaven we will be with only "our kind of people," but on earth Jesus has called us to go forth from our nice, safe churches into the real world of sin to accomplish His purpose of making disciples.

The Jerusalem Church Syndrome

When we insist on having only "our kind of people" in the church, we turn it away from its true purpose to the purposes we have for it, and we make it the Jerusalem church of our time. The Jerusalem church became self-centered, designed to meet the desires of its members with little or no thought for those who did not know Christ.

But it wasn't always like that. After its great start at Pentecost with the conversion of three thousand people from many parts of the ancient world, it continued to touch thousands more lives. Gradually, however, it became consumed with its own interests and began to give little or no thought to the needs of those around it, whether near or far away. They had little concern for sharing the gospel with Gentiles until the Lord scattered the believers through persecution.

Many American churches have gone the same way, the way of consumerism and "me first." Many churches are centered on themselves, on meeting their own needs, and they seem to be unconcerned when no one comes to Christ through their ministries. Many churches refuse to change because they like themselves just as they are. They have no vision for unbelievers, and they reject anyone who calls them to such a vision. They want to be left alone to enjoy each other, run their religious social club, and live off a heritage of past greatness and influence. Like an athlete who draws his self-image from his past trophies, even though he has grown soft and flabby, these churches draw their identities from their past and deny their present spiritual impotence.

Such churches don't want vision; they want stability. They offer all kinds of reasons why they can't reach out to others. They can't grow because they don't know the people who already come. They can't evangelize because they don't know enough of the Word yet. They can't bring others into their fellowship because they haven't solved their own problems yet. Many pastors have told me of the hurt they experienced when they called their churches to vision and were rejected because the people wanted stability rather than obedience.

Dead-End Living

Cul-de-sac Christianity is a dead-end kind of living in which the focus is entirely inward. When the Jerusalem church became a cul-de-sac, God scattered it through persecution and forced it to pursue others against its will (Acts 8:1). Because of this, a collection of nameless people in Antioch accidentally began to accomplish the Great Commission through conversations with Gentiles in the marketplace and thus they started one of the most purpose-driven churches in history (11:19–21). God does not want churches to be safe havens for insecure saints, but lighthouses for those whose minds have been blinded by the god of this world (2 Cor. 4:4). God calls us to be Great Commission pastors.

THE CHURCH'S PURPOSE

Jesus Christ has told us what the church's purpose is to be. The church, He said, is *to glorify God by pursuing the Great Commission, that is, by making disciples, through Christ's authority and presence* (Matt. 28:18–20). God calls the church to accomplish the Great Commission and thereby to glorify God. This is central to all Christ wants His church to do.

How does the church glorify God? By making disciples. Making disciples includes worship, instruction, love and care for one another, and providing for the physical needs of believers and unbelievers alike (Acts 2:42–47). It is not a narrow activity of the church; it is the all-encompassing way the church glorifies God and fulfills His aim for it. Making disciples is the way the church both worships God and adds worshipers to its number.

Out There or Around Here?

Many associate the Great Commission with "out there," with foreign missions in faraway places, but the Great Commission is an "around here" reality as well. It requires us to care about distant places such as "the uttermost parts of the earth," but Acts 1:8 is the lens that gives focus to the Great Commission. It calls us to penetrate our "Jerusalem," as well as our "Judea," "Samaria," and *then* the uttermost parts of the earth. This means we are to seek our next-door neighbors, the despised minorities among us, the masses who make up our nation, and those as far away as Nepal. No church is fully obedient to Christ if it seeks to reach only those who are far from it, any more than one that seeks to touch only those who are near it. No pastor is fully obedient to Christ if he does not lead his church to pursue the Great Commission by making disciples both locally and around the world.

Evangelism or Edification?

Another mistake many Christians make is to think of the Great Commission as only evangelism. Apparently they believe a Great Commission church is one that presents the gospel and does little to edify people. As a result, they resist or even reject the idea that a biblically purpose-driven church centers itself on accomplishing the Great Commission. But a careful study of Matthew 28:18–20 shows that it is the most comprehensive statement of the church's purpose found anywhere in Scripture. Such a church is a place where new believers are born; it is also a place where believers are raised to reproduce after their own kind. Edification is a primary focus of a Great Commission church.

In this kind of church, believers are brought to a high level of spiritual

53

health so they can reproduce as God enables them. Just as we must be physically healthy to reproduce, and emotionally and spiritually healthy to raise healthy children, so a church must be healthy to raise mature and attractive believers who can touch the souls of others through the Holy Spirit.

A GREAT COMMISSION CHURCH

The main command in Matthew 28:19–20 is "make disciples." This command is the heart of the Great Commission as Jesus gave it, the essence of the purpose He gave to His apostles and through them to us. The other three key terms, "go," "baptize," and "teach," describe the process through which we make disciples.

"Make disciples" is an imperative, a firm and definite command that says, "Do it, and do it now!" When our Lord gave this command, He gave it with a sense of urgency in His voice, so the apostles got the feeling, "This must be done at once."[1] There is no option in any command. As with all other commands Jesus gave, either we do it or if we don't we are disobeying Him. We who are pastors are disobedient to the Lord if we don't seek to lead our churches to pursue the Great Commission with a sense of urgency.

The word "Go" in Matthew 28:19 is closely associated with the main command. The word shows us there can be no making of disciples without people who purpose to do so. Believers are to have a *going* attitude, a spirit of active pursuit that always looks for opportunities. We must seek to develop a church full of people who deliberately seek to make disciples. Like the word "go," the other two terms, "baptizing" and "teaching" are participles; all three are closely related. Baptizing is part of teaching in that we instruct disciples before we baptize them, and then we teach them more for the rest of their lives. In fact, baptism is one of the best teaching tools we have, because it shows what Christ has done for us on the cross as well as God's gracious act of identifying us with Him in His death, burial, and resurrection. No picture communicates the full reality of the Christian life more effectively than water baptism.

What, then, does it mean to pastor a Great Commission, disciple-making church?

A GREAT COMMISSION CHURCH ACTS IN
CHRIST'S AUTHORITY TO ACCOMPLISH HIS PURPOSE

A Great Commission church knows it has a purpose, and it knows what that purpose is. It does not allow itself to become bogged down in the private, selfish agendas of the Jerusalem church or the soft cultural values of the modern American church. It is sharply focused, with eyes trained on the Great Commission and what that means for the church. A disciple-making pastor knows he can't accomplish his purpose without the Lord's authority, so he turns everyone to the Lord and His commands. Then he learns he can do nothing apart from Christ because he needs His authority to obey His will.

The fact that we can't accomplish Christ's purpose for us apart from His authority through us makes our purpose unique, special, totally different from any other on earth. No other entity needs Christ's authority to accomplish its purpose—neither government, education, business, nor charity. This makes our purpose the most strategic on earth, the one purpose God cares about more than any other. If we don't accomplish His purpose, humanity is left without light, life, or hope. We must pursue this purpose no matter what anyone says to the contrary. No one should be allowed to keep us from obeying our Lord and doing what His authority alone can accomplish through us.

All Authority over Spiritual Forces

Christ has all authority in heaven and on earth (Matt. 28:19), and the church that obeys Him needs that authority. Obedient churches challenge the forces of darkness, not arrogantly, but simply by what they are and do. They have the conscious aim of transforming citizens of the kingdom of darkness into citizens of the kingdom of light. They deliberately develop men and women who by their very presence as well as through their words and deeds go against evil spiritual forces and challenge their right to influence or control those whom God is calling to Himself. Disciple-makers make a difference in the world around them through the way they live.

One way to test whether you pastor a Great Commission church is to ask, What am I doing for which I need Christ's authority over evil forces?

Could your church continue to exist if Christ withdrew His authority from you? Are you seeing lives being changed by God's power? Are people being set free from evil's dark grip through those whom you are developing in your church? Are the sales of drugs being reduced in your community because of the influence of people in your church? What about alcohol sales? Or the divorce rate? Or the abortion rate? Or child abuse? Or teenage pregnancies? These are evidences of evil forces in our society today, issues we must face if we are to obey our Lord in these times. Not every individual in our churches will be involved in such front-line attacks, but gifted, burdened individuals must be developed to fight these wars in Christ's authority.

All Authority over Earthly Forces

Jesus said He has all authority on earth as well. This means He has authority over governments and educational systems and various forms of culture and the media. This authority was demonstrated, for example, when the blood of early Christians, martyred by the Romans, became the seed of the church, causing it to grow throughout the Roman Empire.

What are you doing in your community that demands His authority over earthly forces? Are individuals from your church serving winsomely as Christian leaders in local government and educational positions? What about media leaders? Have we given up on such people, thinking they are so liberal or so cynical they can't be reached? When we do, we deny Christ's claim that He has *all* authority in heaven and on earth.

The essential question is this: In all areas of our ministry as pastors, what are we doing that only Christ can do through us? *In obedience to Christ a Great Commission church does things that can be done only through Christ's authority.*

A GREAT COMMISSION CHURCH MAKES DISCIPLES

What It Means to Make Disciples

What did Jesus mean when He told us to make disciples? There are many ways to answer this question. Some say it means to transform unbelievers into committed followers of Christ. I think of it as *building people to disciple the nations,* with the understanding that "nations" refers to distinct peoples marked by cultural uniqueness whether close to us or far away. However we communicate it, making disciples means basically *to reproduce reproducers.* A disciple is a learner who can help others learn, someone who can reproduce in others what Christ is doing in him or her through the Holy Spirit's power. Our target is to help lead a person toward spiritual maturity in a steady progression according to that person's rate of growth, a rate we may have to challenge when sin gets in the way.

Think of a first-time visitor, a non-Christian, who pulls into your parking lot. What relationships, ministries, and practices must you have in place to lead that person to Christ and to bring him or her to maturity to influence others for Christ? Whatever they are, this is how you go about making disciples. The process will vary from church to church, but every ministry will have common elements.

What It Takes to Make Disciples

Making disciples calls for three steps.

Intention. A church will be a disciple-making church only when it chooses to be one. Disciple making is not accidental; it must be intentional. We must intentionally go into our community and our world in order to turn lost people into committed believers. This means everyone in the church must engage in building relationships with unbelievers and must be trained in the skills needed to relate to those who have different values and perspectives from themselves. Many of us have lost touch with our unbelieving neighbors and don't know how to talk with them or be comfortable with them. As pastors, we must gain these skills and help our people to do the same.

Do our people know what the gospel is? Can they present it clearly? Are they able to tell others what Jesus means in their lives by using language unbelievers understand? Do they know how to be winsomely righteous rather than judgmentally "holier than thou"? Do they understand how simple acts of care can open the door to reach the hurting? Will they trust Christ's authority to overcome their fears and use them to bring others to Christ? *A Great Commission church equips all its members to lead others to Christ because it is intentional about making disciples.*

Identification. The second step in the process of disciple-making is to bring new believers into identification with Christ and His church. Just as we wouldn't come home and leave our newborn baby in the hospital, so we shouldn't leave newborn believers on the spiritual streets. We bring them home to the family. This is what baptism is about.

Earlier I said that baptism and teaching are closely related. This is because no one should be baptized who hasn't been taught its meaning and because every baptism is an opportunity to teach the essence of our faith. I call this step of baptism "identification," because this is the core meaning of the word when it is used figuratively. According to Romans 6:1–14 our spiritual baptism (being placed into the body of Christ at the moment of salvation, which is pictured by water baptism) means we are identified with Christ on the cross, in the grave, and in His Resurrection. God totally identified us with Christ when we trusted Him for salvation so that when He died on the cross, we died on the cross; when He went to the grave, we went to the grave; and when He rose from the dead, we rose from the dead through our identification with Him.

To understand water baptism properly, the new believer—and all believers as well—must understand God's grace and His work in our lives to make us more Christlike. Being baptized means more than being committed to Christ's lordship, as crucial as that is. Baptism is more than a promise to obey Christ in all our behavior, as imperative as that is. Baptism pictures all God has done and is doing in us through Christ. Baptism means we desire to grow in grace, to say no to the flesh and yes to the Cross every day of our lives. Until new believers are brought into such total identification with Christ and His church through instruction and baptism, they will not grow in Christ. They will be lonely, isolated, and immature. *A Great Commission church teaches all its people what it means to be identified with Christ as the essence of the Christian life.*

Instruction. The Pastoral Epistles tell us that teaching is a pastor's number-one responsibility, but the pastor who thinks this means spending forty hours a week in his study is wrong. We do need to work hard to teach well, but we also need to understand what Jesus means by teaching.

Is teaching a one-way communication of information from the pulpit? Hardly. Jesus didn't teach this way. Teaching is the engaging of learners in developing the skills and practices they must have to accomplish the teacher's purpose. Do we see disciples, reproducers of reproducers, coming from our teaching ministry? If so, we are doing Great Commission teaching. Of course, we must remember we are not the only teachers in our churches. And we must remember that not all teachers develop disciples the same way.

When Jesus taught, He used sermonic instruction, as we see from the Sermon on the Mount, from the parables He told His men, and from His Olivet and Upper Room discourses. But one of His primary means of instruction was involvement, and two of His chief teaching tools with His disciples were bread and boats. Jesus used the incidental experiences of life to teach eternal truths to His followers. He had the wonderful skill of taking a walk through a wheat field, of seeing children at play, or watching people buying and selling in the marketplace and turning these experiences into a life lesson His men never forgot. He took the commonplace, the ordinary, and the everyday, and turned it into the eternal.

What Jesus did most of all, however, was to take His men with Him as He ministered. He was constantly discussing with His learners what they saw in His daily involvement with people. They developed a desire to pray by watching Him pray, they learned to give by hearing His comments on the giving of others, they learned to trust by watching Him trust His Father, and they learned to depend on the Holy Spirit by watching Him depend on the Spirit in all He did. This is teaching, the mix of instruction and training in the midst of life.

For Jesus, teaching meant immersing His disciples in the realities of everyday activity to help them learn vital lessons about their limitations and His resources. They had to grasp these truths before He could release them to disciple others. Teaching was not only information, it was also skill development; not only knowledge, but also wisdom; not just facts, but also faith; not independence, but dependence; not just answers, but living.

Our Lord had a curriculum as well as creative methods when He taught His disciples. When He told us to teach our disciples to observe all He commanded us, He directed us to teach according to those guidelines.

LeRoy Eims suggests thirty ministry training objectives we must accomplish if we are to instruct our disciples in Christ's curriculum.[2]

1. Assurance of salvation	16. Faith
2. The quiet time	17. Love
3. Victory over sin	18. The tongue
4. Separation from sin	19. The use of time
5. Christian fellowship	20. The will of God
6. The Bible	21. Obedience
7. Hearing the Word	22. The Holy Spirit
8. Reading the Word	23. Satan, the enemy
9. Bible study	24. Dealing with sin
10. Scripture memory	25. Assurance of forgiveness
11. Meditation on the Word	26. Second coming of Christ
12. Application of the Word	27. Witnessing
13. Prayer	28. Follow-up
14. Personal testimony	29. Giving
15. Lordship of Christ	30. World vision

A Great Commission church teaches the way Jesus did: from the pulpit and through relationships that turn everyday life experiences into eternal lessons so its people become reproducers of reproducers.

A GREAT COMMISSION CHURCH COUNTS ON CHRIST'S PRESENCE TO ACCOMPLISH ITS PURPOSE

The way to be sure we have Christ's authority is to count on His presence—to be totally dependent on Him at all times. The fact that Jesus promises to be with us is both reassuring and sobering. When we take on the powers of darkness around us, we can be reassured that we can do what He wants us to do because He is with us. Likewise, when we encounter the power of the flesh in human authorities, we can be reassured that we can overcome our opponents because He is with us. Even when it looks as if we are losing—when we face persecution and death—God is still leading us in His triumph in Christ Jesus (2 Cor. 2:14). Christ is with us even when we face a momentary loss because of resistance and injustice, and He will accomplish His purpose for His church. Not even the gates of hell can overcome us. This is the confidence pastors must have as they lead their churches in accomplishing Christ's purpose.

A pastor's central task is to make disciples, that is, to reproduce reproducers. As we shepherd our sheep under Christ, we must be guiding every one of them toward spiritual health and the vision of bringing others to Christ, of helping them mature in Christ, and of teaching them how to do the same thing for those they influence.

WHAT DOES ALL THIS MEAN?

Here are some implications that grow out of our consideration of the church's purpose.

1. *If a ministry doesn't demand Christ's authority to do it, why do it?* Sunday school can't be childcare, fellowship groups can't be holy huddles, seniors groups can't be only potlucks and bus tours. Every ministry program must be a means to accomplish supernatural goals that demand Christ's authority or we're not obeying Him.

2. *All a church does must focus on making disciples.* If a program isn't aimed at making disciples, why do it? Measure everything by whether it contributes to the disciple-making process and retain only those ministries that are helping to develop reproducers of reproducers. Remember, not every individual will excel in reproducing new believers, but every individual must be part of the disciple-making process and must know what part he or she has in this process.

3. *All churches must be structured to make disciples.* The primary task of church leaders is to make disciples as Jesus did. This calls for structuring and organizing the church so that it is free to pursue its true task. Leaders must know how to develop disciples so they can equip others to do the same. When they know how to do this, they will recognize those elements in their ministry that keep others from concentrating on the church's true purpose. Structure must support purpose, not hinder it. Committees and boards that

pursue unfocused ministries keep the church from accomplishing its true aim and must be done away with, no matter how precious they are to those who serve on them. Be gracious, gentle, and kind, but work to help everyone understand how their time and energy can be invested in much better ways.

4. *Every church must have a spirit of intentionality.* All churches must take the initiative to move into their communities to establish a disciple-making presence. The church that does this defines its role in the community as a disciple-making role, choosing to become involved in those things that enable it to bring Christ's life-changing presence to others.

5. *Every church must concentrate on the message of baptism, not just the ritual of baptism.* Through baptism we announce to the watching world that we are under new management because we have been raised to a new life through God's grace. The truths of God's grace and power are at the heart of a disciple-making church. When these emphases are missing, the church creates powerless legalists who make no difference in their community and who misrepresent God as a rule maker, not as a grace giver.

6. *Every church must teach as Jesus taught, through both sermons and life.* People cannot be allowed to think that Christianity is only a matter of the head, and not of the heart and hands as well. Teaching that does not involve life and relationships will never touch the heart or the hands. Listening alone will not make disciples.

7. *Make certain all you are doing depends on Christ's presence.* Jesus would not have promised to be with us if we didn't need Him. We can't possibly overcome the storms of life without Him. So be sure your ministry needs Christ's presence.

8. *The pastor's purpose is to lead a disciple-making church by equipping all leaders for this task.* All we do as pastors must be aimed toward making disciples. If we do anything else, we fail in our task and leave our church stuck in the mud of tradition rather than moving forward in the mission Christ gave us. Our chief role as pastors is to equip others for the work of the ministry (Eph. 4:7–16), and we must focus our energy on this task.

CONCLUSION

Few words in the Bible are more important than the closing words of the Great Commission: "And surely I will be with you always, to the very end of the age." Christ gave the Great Commission and He also made the "Great Commitment." Because Jesus has promised to be with us, we have both His presence and His power to overcome our inadequacies. When He promised to be with us, He made the commitment to empower us to accomplish His commission. As you make disciples, never take Christ's presence and power for granted. Teach others to depend on Him even as you do, and call them to do things that demand His authority. Then your church will accomplish Christ's purpose, and you will accomplish His commission through His commitment.

CHAPTER FIVE

———◆———

WHAT'S A PASTOR FOR, ANYWAY?

WHAT ARE A PASTOR'S RESPONSIBILITIES?
- To visit the sick and encourage the hurting? Yes.
- To strengthen the weak and build up the strong? Yes.
- To greet the visitors and embrace the members? Yes.
- To pursue the wandering and support the faithful? Yes.
- To pray for the fearful and help the needy? Yes.
- To teach the Word and instruct the untaught? Yes.
- To open the doors before all come and to lock up the building after everyone leaves? Doubtful, at best.
- To be the hired "holy man" and do the congregation's religious work? No!

Most people would never bluntly say they expect their pastor to be their hired holy man who does their religious work for them, but that's the practical result of what many think a pastor should do. To some people, pastors are no different from the businessmen in town. There's the insurance agent, the accountant, the lawyer, the doctor, the mortician, the grocer—and the holy man, the one who runs the religious business down on the corner of Second and Main. Every town should have one, of course, whether it needs it or not.

Is this what a pastor is for? If he's not the hired hand running the local religious business, what is he? What does the Bible say a pastor is for?

What is the unique thing a pastor is supposed to do, according to the Scriptures?

Suppose you are a senior pastor who loves to counsel. Every week you spend most of your ministry hours counseling—this is where you get your greatest satisfaction and feel best about yourself. What will you do if someone shows you from the Bible that, as a senior pastor, you should not be spending the majority of your time counseling? Will you change?

Counseling is only one example; you can substitute any of the traditional pastoral practices, things like hospital visitation, evangelism, studying to preach, seeing members in their homes, and raise the same two questions: What if someone shows you from the Bible you should not be spending your time this way? Will you change to do what the Bible says?

Suppose we ask the members of your church the same questions. Perhaps they expect you to counsel, visit, evangelize, or study. What if we show them their expectations are not biblical? Will they change? Changing from the traditional to the biblical can create great struggles, but we must obey the Bible rather than people, even when the people involved are ourselves and the identity we seek is from ministry.

ARE YOU A TASK-DRIVEN OR PURPOSE-DRIVEN PASTOR?

Many pastors appear not to have given this issue much thought. Instead of being purpose-driven, too many pastors are doing their duties as ends in themselves, tasks to be performed because the calendar says it's time to preach or the phone rings with one more problem. When we are task-driven, we treat each task as a stand-alone action with no overarching aim for ourselves and our people. When this is true, we move from preaching to administrating to counseling to visitation and back to counseling with no conscious awareness of why we are doing these things other than the feeling that we should and that we are helping others. But *why* should we do these things, and how are we helping others?

We should be purpose-focused, even during those "hot streaks" when one tragedy after another strikes without warning like a series of earthquakes. Sometimes divorces pile up, physical traumas come one after the other, and the emotional anguish batters us like aftershocks in the night.

Even in those overwhelming times as we serve others, we can have God's purpose in view. Otherwise, the currents of ministry carry us here and there, and we never move successfully toward God's direction for us.

Some pastors don't know where they are going. And unfortunately some of them don't realize they *should* know where they're going. They are prepared for what might happen, but not for what they should make happen by the Holy Spirit's power. Many don't realize they ought to be going somewhere at all times, that they should be pursuing a conscious purpose. They think all they need to do is respond to the needs they confront as they face them. The idea of pursuing a specific purpose is foreign and strange. Those who think this way are like a running back who covers 150 yards running from side to side across the field, but gains only 15 yards running forward. Pastors don't accomplish God's purpose for them by running side to side from one crisis to another. They must move forward toward His aim for them, even in the most difficult crises.

THE PURPOSE-DRIVEN PASTOR

As pastors we must be purpose-driven and Spirit-powered. To be purpose-driven, however, is not the same as drivenness. God's purpose for us is not something we pursue out of the futility of our deficit thinking. It is greater than anything we could ever ask or think (Eph. 3:19), something beyond our empty imaginations, something only God could think of and give us to do. As stated in the previous chapter, our purpose is *to glorify God by making disciples.* And we are to do this by *equipping the saints to do the work of the ministry.* There is no greater privilege than to be God's instruments to help mature His children into effective servants for Him.

Our purpose as pastors is to be disciple-makers, to equip the saints for the work of the ministry so our churches can mature (Eph. 4:7–16). This purpose drives, pushes, and pulls us all at the same time. It fills our thinking, consumes our energy, focuses our time, and turns our lives into a blaze of God's glory.

We can pursue this purpose with certainty because of God's sovereign grace in us and in all others who know Christ. Nothing can stop us from accomplishing God's purpose because it is His will for us. No calamity can stop us because God will turn it to His end. No enemy can stop us because God transforms human wrath into His glory. No evil force can stop us because God defeated all evil forces on Christ's cross. We are the only ones who can stop ourselves from accomplishing God's purpose—if we refuse to pursue this purpose by choosing not to trust Him for it. Never again do you need to treat pastoring as a random series of unrelated events. You can see your pastoring as focused, intentional, and purposeful, no matter what havoc breaks out in your church.

GRACE GIFTS FOR ALL

Tailor-Made Grace

God has given to each of His saints, men and women alike, gifts that suit us exactly for the contribution He wants us to make (Eph. 4:7; see also 1 Cor. 4:7). The word *each* makes it clear no one is left out; each saint has been given one or more spiritual gifts. These gifts are spiritual abilities or capacities that enable us to serve each other. Along with these gifts comes the exact measure of grace we need to minister to each other according to God's sovereign will. Grace is God's enabling power (1 Cor. 15:10), and all of us have all the grace we need to do what God wants. While our spiritual gifts differ, every believer has the exact measure of grace needed to glorify and please Him as He desires. We also have the exact amount of faith we need to trust God to exercise our gifts (the Greek word for "measure" in Rom. 12:3 is also used in Eph. 4:7, NASB). So each saint has received at least one gift with the exact measure of grace and faith needed to serve God and His purposes as fully as He desires.

Our response to this truth should be one of humility, thanksgiving, and confidence. How amazing that God should give some the gift of pastor-teacher. What else can we do but humble ourselves and praise Him for this wonderful though sometimes terrible privilege? And how else can we respond but with confidence? The sovereign God has given us everything we need—gift, grace, and faith. Stop doubting yourself by thinking how young you are or how old you are or how ineffective you are or how you aren't where you expected to be at this point in your life. Thank Him and trust Him to do what He wants you to do. Don't try to be anyone else. Just strive to be the person He graced you to be by the faith He gave you to trust Him. Rejoice; you *are* God's gift to the church, and the church is God's gift to you.

GOD HAS ASCENDED ON HIGH

Why has Christ given each of His saints gifts? Paul answers this by summarizing the message of Psalm 68 in Ephesians 4:8. Psalm 68 pictures God as a king who descends from His throne to lead His troops to triumph in the enemy's territory. Following His triumph, God ascends back to His throne and distributes gifts to those who share His victory with Him. "The essence of the psalm is that a military victor has the right to give gifts to those who are identified with him. Christ, having captivated sinful people by redeeming them, is Victor and gives them as gifts to the Church."[1]

In Ephesians 4:9–10, Paul related this truth to Christ by stating that He entered Satan's domain of death[2] and then returned victoriously with the authority to distribute gifts to those who belong to Him. So, because He defeated His enemies—sin (Rom. 6:1–14), Satan (Heb. 2:14–15), and death (1 Cor. 15:55–56)—at the cross and identified us with Him through redemption, each saint receives grace. Christ gives us gifts in celebration of His triumph at Calvary. To help the church accomplish its purpose of extending Christ's triumph in the world, Christ gave four groups of gifted individuals to serve as its leaders under Him (Eph. 4:11), and one of those groups is pastor-teachers.

EQUIPPING THE SAINTS

Three Ways to Equip the Saints

Christ has given pastors to the church for the equipping of the saints (Eph. 4:12). *Katartizō*, the word for "equip," expresses making something suitable or useful. In classical Greek it meant to put in order, restore, furnish, equip, to make suitable or fitting.[3] It suggests making something work the way it was designed to function, to bring something from a place of ineffectiveness to effectiveness. We equip the saints when we make them ready for service or action, when we bring them to the place where they can do the work of the ministry and help build up Christ's body.

This is what we're all about as pastors: helping people become what God designed them to be by His grace. We do this in three ways, as illustrated by the way the word *katartizō* is used.

First, *katartizō* describes the mending of fishing nets (Matt. 4:21; Mark 1:19). This picture shows us we deal with torn lives, with those who are nonfunctional. If we were to cast them into the sea of ministry, all we would get back is an empty net with holes in it. They are helpless, hopeless people, unable to do anything worthwhile apart from God's grace through us. Our task is to mend torn lives through God's healing love and truth.

Second, *katartizō* is used of restoring a sinning saint (Gal. 6:1). Here is a brother whom sin has taken by surprise. Somehow it caught him when he wasn't listening to the Spirit's cadence, when he listened to a different rhythm and stopped walking by the Spirit. Now he is out of step with the rest of the body of believers, off "doing his own thing," and calling it freedom. Because he is marching to a different drumbeat, he is a danger to himself and others. He needs to be restored to walking by the Spirit, and it is our task to help him do it. As pastors, we are not the only ones responsible to do this, but we may turn out to be the main ones. Therefore we must act with humility to bring a wayward believer back to the Spirit, being as gentle as possible but as firm as necessary.

Third, *katartizō* describes resetting a broken bone. Though not used this way in the New Testament, it does occur with this meaning in extrabiblical Greek. This pictures those whose lives are fractured. Once a broken bone is reset, it is as good as ever, maybe even stronger, since bones are said to be stronger at the point of a break than they were before. This person may be in a time of grief or facing a financial setback. Perhaps his company has laid him off, or perhaps she is a single mother struggling to correct a rebellious child. Maybe there is a moment of failure when all joy is lost, and the future is bleak. The pain is overwhelming, and we are there to comfort, encourage, support, hold accountable, challenge, offer hope— to do what is needed to set the fracture and begin the healing process.

The point is this: We equip the saints for the work of the ministry when we mend the holes in torn lives, restore the sinning to walk by the Spirit, and reset the fractured to wholeness. Apart from Christ, we can do none of these things. But through Christ, we can.

In equipping saints for the work of the ministry, we help make them ready to minister to each other so that believers enter into maturity (Eph. 4:14), spirituality (4:15), and unity (4:16). Equipping is more than discipling, and it is more than training. Equipping is loving, healing, correcting, rebuking, comforting, supporting, encouraging, restoring—whatever it takes to get the saints ready to serve. In a sense, equipping is a one-word job description for pastors.

An Equipping Mind-Set

No matter what situation you face each day, you must consciously be striving to equip others. At times, equipping will be programmed, planned, and organized. On the other hand, equipping may be as informal as it is formal, as incidental as it is intentional. A chance word, a simple question, an off-the-cuff comment—any one of these may be the most significant equipping experience some people ever have with you, and it may change their lives for eternity.

We are to develop leaders on two levels: in competence and in character. Standing by a hospital bed or sitting across the desk in a counseling session, you can be God's instrument to build character into His saints. Through their pain, anger, confusion, fear, or deep struggles, you are equipping even though you are not training them for ministry as such. Years later, when they are able to engage in service to others, they may share the words you spoke that gave them courage to grow. Then people you'll never know will benefit indirectly from your equipping ministry in the life and service of a once torn, wayward, and broken saint.

Having an equipping mind-set means we think of equipping in all we do, whether in purposeful preaching or incidental conversation. There is rarely a time when we should not be helping someone be what God intended him or her to be.

We can't equip everyone personally, even though all saints need to be equipped. Most churches are designed to run programs, but the right way to structure a church is to organize it to equip its members. This may or may not mean a huge organizational change in your church, although it may demand a major mental change. Instead of measuring our success by the number of people who attend, we should measure our effectiveness by the number of people who are equipping others to serve. Ultimately the task of all leaders is to equip others to be leaders.

Since you cannot equip everyone, here are those you must equip: elders and/or deacons, future elders and/or deacons, and your staff. You must concentrate your greatest energies on current and future leaders, both to make them ready for maximum ministry as well as to turn them into equippers who work alongside you in making a difference for Christ.

Make every board meeting a time of equipping. Board meetings must be much more than an agenda racing with the clock. They must be times of concentrated equipping when you train board members to think theologically, to discern their true duties, to make biblical decisions, to shepherd sheep, to lead *God's* way out of God's interests and not man's. *If you are not equipping the saints for the work of ministry, you are not pastoring your church according to God's purpose for you.*

What's a pastor for, anyway? I want to answer this question by developing the pastor's job description of equipping from six vital New Testament words. If your ministry follows this job description, you can be assured you are the kind of equipping pastor-teacher Christ calls you to be.

THE PASTOR'S JOB DESCRIPTION

Presbyteros *(Elder): The Pastor's Qualifications*

The pastor is an *elder* (Greek, *presbyteros*), perhaps the greatest title a man can ever have. An elder is a man of maturity and experience, a man who has been tested and proven in every area of life to have the qualities needed to lead the church under Christ. Elders are men of honor and trust, whose chief responsibility is to model obedience, grace, and spiritual maturity so that everyone in the church knows what an adult Christian is like. A pastor is worthy of his position only if he is striving to model Christlikeness through his ministry.

Episkopos (Overseer): The Pastor's Authority

The pastor is an *overseer* (Greek, *episkopos*), one who reflects Christ's own care for the sheep and who is willing to sacrifice his well-being for others. Although the word *overseer* sounds like a boss, that's not the point at all. The word *episkopos* speaks of looking out for the sheep's concerns, of loving interest, and of active intervention when a sheep is prone to wander. Peter wrote that Jesus is our *episkopos*. "For you were continually straying like sheep, but now you have returned to the Shepherd and Guardian [*episkopos*] of your souls" (1 Pet. 2:25, NASB). What a beautiful way to describe an overseer. As we are Christ's undershepherds, so we are His underguardians to serve with Him in caring for the souls of His sheep. What is our authority as pastors? A proven, loving concern for the sheep's souls. Without this, we are not qualified to be pastors.

Katartizō (To Equip): The Pastor's Process

Equipping is the one word that best describes our specific duties as pastors. This is how we get the job done seven days a week. It means we are up to our necks in developing sheep—our ears full of baas, our noses full of sheep smell, our eyes full of concern, our hands full of gentleness, our hearts full of love, and our souls full of inadequacy. What could compare to pastoring?

Didaskō (To Teach): The Pastor's Task

Didaskō is the one word that best describes a pastor's overall task. Study the Pastoral Epistles, and you will find over and over again that our chief responsibility is to teach God's Word and what it means in daily living. We cannot allow anything to tear us away from it. In 1 Timothy, Paul repeatedly encouraged Timothy to be teaching.
- We are to command others not to teach strange doctrines (1 Tim. 1:3). (The Greek word for "command" in this verse is *parangellō*, a military term, meaning to give strict orders in an authoritative way.)[4]
- We are to call believers to effective prayer (2:1–6).

- We are to tell women how to dress and minister appropriately (2:7–15).
- We are to develop and bring into office qualified elders, deacons, and women leaders (3:1–13).
- **We are to point out the realities of the times and to nourish the people** on "the words of the faith and of the sound doctrine" (4:1–6, NASB).
- We are to prescribe and teach apostolic truths (4:11).
- We are to instruct through the example of our lives (4:12–16).
- We are to establish local-church standards for helping widows, and we are to prescribe *(parangellō)* these things so that all are above reproach (5:3–5, 9–16).
- We are to hold people accountable for how they care for their families (5:8).
- We are to hold elders accountable for the quality of their lives and ministry (5:17–25).
- We are to instruct *(parangellō)* the rich concerning their attitude toward money (6:17–19).[5]

"Teaching" in 1 Timothy means public instruction, as we normally understand it, but it's far more than that. Although we may address all of these issues authoritatively in our sermons, we can't adequately instruct a select group of men and women from the pulpit. Also from the pulpit we can't determine which widows qualify for assistance by the church. Nor can all our counsel about money come from the pulpit.

Our teaching ministry must involve much more than sermons. It calls for small-group instruction and one-on-one direction, as well as pulpit ministry. We can't preach people into being equipped. The only way we can make disciples is to do what Jesus did. To develop His men He used everyday things such as wheat and chaff, boys and girls, olive trees and moneychangers' tables. To equip people we must be with them. We can preach theory to them, but we must live maturely among them if they are to be equipped. Certainly preaching is essential. It is the polar magnet of our ministries, drawing those who are ready to be equipped to us and to others who can guide them in their development. I believe approximately one-third of a pastor's time should be spent in preparing and delivering sermons, but the other two-thirds must be invested in creative equipping, and that means teaching in a variety of settings.

Poimēn *("Shepherd"): The Pastor's Motive*

Several times the Old Testament refers to God as a Shepherd (Gen. 48:15; 49:24; Pss. 23:1; 80:1; Isa. 40:11). "The acknowledgment that Yahweh was the Shepherd of Israel grew out of the living religious experience of the people. . . . In invocation, in praise, in prayer for forgiveness, but also in temptation and despair (Psalm 73), the worshippers know that they are still safe in the care of the God the faithful shepherd (the most beautiful expression of this is Ps. 23)."[6]

God called David to shepherd His people Israel as their king (2 Sam. 5:1;7:7; 1 Chron. 11:2; 17:6; Ezek. 34:23). Jesus, David's Descendant, called Himself the Good Shepherd (John 10:11, 14), and the writer of the Book of Hebrews referred to Him as the Great Shepherd (Heb. 13:20). Then after Jesus was resurrected, He commissioned Peter to tend the Good Shepherd's lambs and to shepherd His sheep. How amazing that the Lord would do this soon after Peter had denied Him three times! And it's just as amazing for us that Peter would pass on this commission of shepherding to future elders (1 Pet. 5:2–4). The title of shepherd elevates the pastorate to the highest honor possible, the honor of being the Good Shepherd's undershepherds.

We are to shepherd the flock of God among us by exercising loving oversight—the same kind of care and concern God exercises over us—willingly, not because we must (5:2). We are to do it unto God eagerly and not for money (5:2). We are to be examples to our flock, not lords over them (5:3). This is what it means to be a shepherd.

The word *poimēn* is closely related to the five other words in this biblical job description. Christ is our *poimēn* (shepherd) and our *episkopos* (overseer; 1 Pet. 2:25), and this is who we are under Him for the benefit of His sheep. As pastor-teachers *(poimēnas kai didaskalous,* Eph. 4:11), we are to *katartizō* ("equip") His saints (4:12). As elders, we are to shepherd the sheep where Christ has put us, in order to make disciples *(manthanō)* of them.

Many people think of shepherding as being a chaplain, a gentle, compassionate, encourager, standing by the hospital bedside or visiting the grieving home. This is certainly true, but this is not all a shepherd is. God called Cyrus, king of Persia, His shepherd (Isa. 44:28). Cyrus was hardly a chaplain standing by a hospital bed. Instead, he was a leader raised up by God to restore His people Israel to their place on earth. In biblical times shepherds were tender, loving providers for their sheep. They were also warriors who protected the sheep from lions and bears. Further, they sought out and disciplined the sheep who strayed. We are to provide for, protect, and discipline the sheep—that's what God did for Israel, what Jesus does for us, and what we do for His sheep. That's being a leader, and that's what a shepherd is.

Manthanō ("To Disciple"): The Pastor's Purpose

Everything in this list of six vital words focuses on one thing: making disciples. Pastors are to make disciples, that is, to reproduce reproducers. You will know you are doing your job well when your team of fellow disciple-makers swells and fills your whole church. When every part of your ministry is filled with disciple-makers, when the hopeless and the helpless have become equippers in your church, then you are fulfilling your purpose as a pastor. When the unlovely and the unlikely grow to become developers of leaders in your church, then you are fulfilling your purpose as a pastor. When your church is lowering the abortion rate in your community and putting drug dealers out of business because they are coming to Christ, and people here, there, and everywhere are discovering Christ, then you know you are doing your job.

Six Vital Words—One Job Description

Based on these six words, here is how we can state the pastor's job description: *The pastor is a qualified overseer who shepherds God's flock by equipping the saints for the work of the ministry through teaching them to know and live God's truth in such a way that they become disciple-makers.* Note the significance of six words in this definition:
- Qualified: having the character traits of an elder
- Overseer: being a loving guardian of the sheep's souls
- Shepherds: providing, protecting, and disciplining the sheep

- Equipping: mending torn lives, restoring sinning saints, fixing fractured souls
- Teaching: modeling, instructing, and motivating the sheep through words and works so that all learn how to lead Christlike lives
- Disciple-making: reproducing reproducers

When we look at this job description, it is strikingly similar in some ways

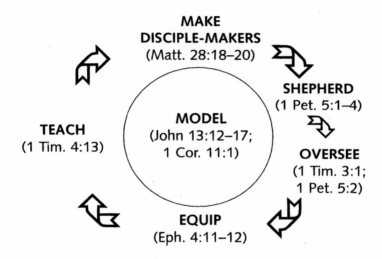

to Christ's own tasks. That's not surprising, since He has made us His undershepherds—He has delegated His task to us. But as Paul asked, "Who is adequate for these things?" (2 Cor. 2:16, NASB). The answer is, no one. The apostle Paul wasn't. When he wrote of all his suffering for the gospel, he topped off his list by speaking of his "concern for all the churches" (11:28). Think of it: Besides his physical difficulties—including lashings, beatings with rods, a stoning, three shipwrecks, danger after danger, labor and hardship, sleeplessness, hunger, thirst, cold, and exposure (11:24–27)—he was burdened for all the churches where he had ministered. If Paul felt so overwhelmed by church demands as to put them on a list like this, is it any wonder we feel overwhelmed and inadequate? Who wouldn't?

On the other hand, we *are* adequate. "Not that we are adequate in ourselves to consider anything as coming from ourselves, but our adequacy is from God, who also made us adequate as servants of a new covenant" (3:5–6, NASB). God has made us adequate to serve His interests as expressed in the New Covenant—the Cross, grace, redemption, sanctification.

This job description humbles and exalts us at the same time. We are not worthy of it, yet He has delegated it to us; we are not adequate for it, yet He has made us adequate; we cannot do it, yet He can do it through us. Never do we need Paul's confidence in Christ more than when we consider the pastor's job description. "I can do all things through Him who strengthens me" (Phil. 4:13, NASB).

So, what is a pastor for? To equip the saints for the work of the ministry so that they become disciple-makers for the glory of God.

PART THREE

THE PASTOR'S PRACTICE

Chapter Six

—◆—

The Order of the Towel

THE CASE OF THE WELL-INTENTIONED RESISTER

FOR TWO YEARS you have been developing a unique leader named Doug Brown. Doug is one of the best people you have ever met and yet one of the most difficult.

Doug is an excellent man. He is energetic, full of drive, willing to do whatever it takes to accomplish the tasks assigned to him. He is faithful and reliable in many ways. He is intelligent, thinks well, able to learn and grow. He is committed, believing in your vision. He is a leader who influences others to live and work with the same passion he has.

On the other hand, Doug has some severe problems. He is self-confident, cocky, certain you are making serious mistakes. He is a controller who constantly resists your leadership in front of your team. He is outspoken and bossy, always saying what he thinks. He uses intimidation to get what he feels is best for the team. He has firmly held opinions that make him unwilling to accept correction.

You have seen a severe flaw of pride in your team that keeps them from serving one another, so you have decided to model what you want them to become. Everyone else on the team is cooperating except for Doug, who is unresponsive to your efforts and who protests that what you are doing is inappropriate for the team.

Take a few minutes to think about the following questions.

- How do you feel toward this valuable but unteachable person?
- What is your natural inclination when you have to lead a person like this?
- How do you respond when he resists you in your team meetings?
- How long would you allow this to happen?
- Would you act to correct this situation or would you avoid doing anything and hope it will go away?
- What if it doesn't go away?
- Would you blow up and fire him?
- Would you consider resigning to get away from him?
- Is he an elder or deacon in your church?
- Is he on your staff?
- Are you Doug Brown?

———◆———

If you feel as I do when I encounter a Doug Brown, you're confused and angry. He is so talented and capable that you love having him on your team. Think of all that energy harnessed and focused on your aims, that excellent mind committed to your vision, influencing others to live with abandon for Christ. Who wouldn't want someone like this man?

But he is also unteachable; asking inappropriate questions or making unreasonable assertions at the wrong time. My natural inclination is to be impatient and think of firing him because he creates such problems. Do you share my feelings? Are you as frustrated as I am by the Doug Browns of the church world?

What keeps me from firing Doug? The example of Jesus in John 13:1–17. You see, Doug Brown is Peter!

Peter was a man of dedication, who gave up many things to follow Jesus. Peter was energetic, full of fury and strength. He was faithful, sticking to his commitment even when others were quitting. Peter was intelligent, knowledgeable, and capable. Peter was a leader, the most influential of his peers.

But Peter had problems. He was bossy, rebuking Jesus when He said things Peter didn't agree with. Think of it—Peter rebuking Jesus (Mark 8:33)! He was self-confident, even cocky, certain he was better than his peers (14:27–31). He was outspoken and controlling, wanting to take over and be in charge. He was so full of his own expectations and understanding that he couldn't hear what his Leader was saying to him.

Yet amazingly, the man I want to fire is the man Jesus wanted to cleanse. Nothing teaches us more about servant leadership than the confrontation between Jesus and Peter when Jesus washed Peter's feet despite his initial resistance. Read John 13:1–17 and think of the following questions.

LEARNING FROM JESUS AND PETER

What do we learn about Jesus' feelings for Peter? How do His feelings about Peter compare to your feelings about men like Doug Brown in your church? Is there a difference? If so, why do you feel about him the way you do in contrast to how Jesus felt? What can you do to change your feelings?

What factors help explain Jesus' feelings and actions? What do you observe about Him that makes Him such a patient, loyal, yet firm Servant?

What steps did Jesus take in responding to Peter?

What lessons do you learn about leadership effectiveness from Jesus' response to Peter?

How do you respond to the idea that leaders must "wash one another's feet?" What does this mean to you? If you wash others' feet, who washes yours?

What have you learned about servant leadership from John 13:1–17? In what ways does a leader serve? In what ways does a servant lead?

Through His interaction with Peter, Christ taught us we are His instruments to help our followers gain freedom from the dirt of sin in their lives. We don't use others for our advantage; instead, we serve by cleansing them through God's Word and God's Spirit to do what He wills. This is servant leadership—getting involved with our followers' dirty feet so they can walk with greater freedom in Him. Servant leaders wash their followers' feet because their first concern in leadership development is to prepare them for what Christ wants done. Servant leaders also must allow their fellow servants wash their feet so they can continue to serve and lead as Christ wills.

SERVANT LEADERSHIP

This leads us to the question, What is servant leadership? This concept may seem confusing because these two words don't seem to go together. When most people hear the word *leadership* they think of things like power, position, influence, visibility, platform—all essential for leaders to be effective. Yet true leadership has another side, a relational, intimate, and often confrontational side that ultimately makes or breaks every leader in the world. This is the servant side of leadership. Leaders can climb to great heights while lacking this dimension, but no leader will stay at great heights without it. Eventually, all leaders collapse in a great Humpty-Dumpty fall without this relational and caring dimension of servant leadership. *As pastors we lead by serving or we don't lead at all.*

Servant leadership demands character to go with our competence and maturity to go with the greatness of our mission. People measure our character and maturity by how we relate, more than by what we accomplish. Relationships tell what we're made of. As pastors, we must have the unique traits of appropriate relationships combined with authority. Our relationships have to be born out of a Christlike commitment to lead those who follow us by serving them. To gain intimacy and authority we must belong to "the Order of the Towel," which Jesus instituted in John 13. This order consists of leaders, both men and women, who are vulnerable and humble through dependence on Christ so He can use them to sanctify others in the leadership development process. We serve others when we lead them into a closeness with God they would never experience any other way, a closeness that results in their spiritual growth and releases them to minister with unparalleled power.

For leadership, our sanctification is more essential than our accomplishments. We are effective servant leaders when our followers are increasingly holier under our leadership than they could have been without us. In ourselves we cannot sanctify anyone, but Christ can use us to call others to holy living, and this is our responsibility under Him. We grow spiritually as we enter into the difficult relationships that call us to be Christ's cleansing agents in the lives of resistant followers. Such tense moments also force us to turn to Christ for our own cleansing and to depend on Him to confront others. These difficult times help prepare us to serve in the Order of the Towel. Leaders in this order have the three marks of Christ's leadership seen in John 13:1–17.

LEADERS IN THE ORDER OF THE TOWEL EXPRESS LOVE

Knowing that the time had come for Jesus to go to the cross, He showed the Twelve "the full extent of His love" (John 13:1) by washing their feet. He knew He would be arrested, scourged, condemned, and crucified, yet He loved His own. The Creator of the universe became the Servant of His creatures because He loved them so greatly. Everything that happened in Jesus' life happened because of His love. Even when He knew His men would deny and desert Him, He still loved them.

Leaders who belong to the Order of the Towel love others because Christ loves through them. Though none of us will face an hour comparable to Christ's, all of us know we have limited time, so we must focus on loving and leading as Christ does. The ultimate measure of our ministry will be loving as Christ loved. The Doug Browns of our world challenge this ideal because of their resistant attitudes and power plays. Their efforts to take over raise massive challenges to our love. After all, when a driven elder decides he can do a better job than we can, we feel threatened. Where, then, can we find the security we need to love a Doug Brown?

The answer to this question is that *we find the security to love through having confidence in God's sovereignty.* Jesus knew that "the Father had put all things under his power" (13:3).

The main reason we fail to love is our lack of security. We are afraid to express our opinion, assert our convictions, verbalize our vision, and in these ways to love others. When we face a resident Doug Brown, we are often insecure and so we can't think objectively and assertively. Certainly we do not think of love in that moment. Too often we ask ourselves, "How can I get rid of Doug Brown?" not "How can I love Doug Brown?" We aim to remove him, not purify him. It takes supernatural security to love the resister, especially when it means giving all we have for the resister's sake.

Think of the kind of men Jesus loved: competitive, selfishly ambitious, insensitive, uncaring, spiritually deaf, disloyal. Does this sound like anyone you know? The men on your board or your church staff? Are any of them self-confident, critical, certain they are right, and utterly overbearing about it? They reach out to take over, and unless we have the security to confront them and call them to cleansing, they *will* take over. Jesus, the man, found His strength and security to serve through confidence in God's sovereignty.

Jesus knew that His past, His future, and His present all came from God's hand, so no matter what He faced in His men or His life, He was totally secure. Whether viewed from the Upper Room, Caiaphas's house, Herod's throne, or Pilate's palace, the assertion that all things were under His power may sound ridiculous. That's because to Caiaphas, Annas, Herod, and Pilate, He was a powerless nobody, and He was virtually condemned, soon to be an afterthought to these busy rulers. In less than twenty-four hours He would be dead, a corpse thrown on the junk heap of history, the victim of heedless, heartless Rome. His followers would deny Him and flee in panic.

God the Father gave Jesus security in three ways, as seen in John 13:3. *First, Jesus knew who possessed true power*, no matter what Rome proclaimed. Rome could drive its chariots, fly its flags, try its accused, crack its whips, and even hammer its nails, but Jesus had power over Pilate, no matter what Pilate thought.[1] Jesus knew He had power from God, and He drew strength from this knowledge to stoop and serve those who were too weak to serve each other. His security in God's sovereignty enabled Him to love one of the biggest collections of Doug Browns in history.

Second, Jesus knew He came from the Father. He was no biological accident, no mere blip on the screen of history—no matter how Caiaphas, Annas, Pilate, or Herod regarded Him. God had sent Him for a specific purpose, and He was about to fulfill it. There is something empowering and defining about knowing where we come from, something that gives us a sense of heritage and purpose.

We also have come from the Father—not in the same way as Jesus, yet for the same purpose. Our past, future, and present come from God, and this is true no matter who resists us. The Son of God came to reach the lost, and in Him we complete His sufferings (Col. 1:24) and carry out that same purpose. We can have the same confidence He had, the confidence of an eternal purpose from God that lifts us above the smallness and the meanness of the many to the glory of the one true God. As pastors we can be bigger in spirit and heart and humility than the Doug Browns of our ministries. We need not be hampered by the invisible shackles of insecurity. We must never lose sight of our origin, because as soon as we do, we lose the security we need to be God's instruments in transforming the Doug Browns of our lives into Peters on the Day of Pentecost.

Third, Jesus knew His destination. He was going back to the Father, not in humiliation, shame, and defeat, but in triumph, power, and glory. What a reunion that was when the Son was restored to the glory He had before the world was and the Father received Him with open arms. Jesus' long self-humiliation was over.

We, too, are going to the Father and we, too, will be exalted in Christ. Only this exaltation matters. We cannot seek our own exaltation or measure ourselves by the number of people who hear us preach, read our books, or recognize our names. Why do we strive for such puny and passing exaltations when our only hope of glory is to be exalted in God's presence by Christ (Col. 1:27), escorted there by the words, "Well done, good and faithful servant"? We'll never hear those words unless we express our love by serving.

LEADERS IN THE ORDER OF THE TOWEL
SERVE OTHERS

What an amazing sight it must have been when Jesus got up from the table to serve His coterie of Doug Browns. What He did was disruptive, startling, even disturbing. No host seated at the Passover meal ever got up, certainly not to serve. Others served him and his guests. The host was responsible to lead them in the meal, to guide them in their worship of God, and to focus them on the meal's meaning. All Twelve were reclining on couches at a low table, resting on their left elbows, heads toward the table, feet away from it, their hands available to reach for food. There were three men at each side of the table, apparently with Judas on one side of Jesus and John on the other, while Peter was some distance away

(John 13:22–24).[2] The scene was an intimate one since the men were both physically and emotionally close to one another, with John resting on Jesus' chest at times during the meal.

Suddenly Jesus stood, disrupting both John and Judas, creating a stir around the table. Then He did the unthinkable: He took off his outer garment, wrapped a slave's towel around His waist, and poured water into a basin. Startled, the disciples had to wonder what He was doing; yet no one said a word. His point soon became clear—He was going to wash their feet. Incredibly, later that same night the disciples got into an argument over who among them was the greatest. They had no desire to serve the Doug Browns around that table—*they* were the Doug Browns around that table!

Like Jesus, as servant leaders we must choose to humble ourselves and do things our followers may be too proud to do. Of course, this includes menial tasks—everything from being at the church on workdays to picking up gum wrappers strewn on the lawn. But everyone does this, and these things are easy to do—we don't need personal security to do them. There's far more to servant leadership than this.

In the Upper Room servant leadership is relational—it has to do with people, not things—more specifically proud people, not pleasant people. Servant leadership is serving people we don't want to bother with, people who create problems for us.

This means servant leadership must be humble because proud people serve only for what they get out of it. Humble people serve for the sake of those being served, not for their own sake. We can mow the lawn and be proud while we're doing it; we can paint walls and be proud while we're doing it; we can set up cribs in the nursery and be proud while we're doing it. But there is no way we can honestly serve a Doug Brown and be proud while we're doing it. Can we truly serve a man who is out to fire us, without humbling ourselves? Can we truly serve an ambitious staff member who has cultivated a following that threatens to eclipse our own, and be proud while we're doing it? We may have proud thoughts afterward, but not while we're doing it. It takes a conscious decision of the will for us to choose to humble ourselves, gird ourselves with a towel, and wash the feet of the proud, the insensitive, and the uncaring. Only this kind of leader becomes Christ's instrument to cleanse others. Any leader who does not become one of the Lord's cleansing instruments does not lead effectively for Him.

LEADERS IN THE ORDER OF THE TOWEL CALL OTHERS TO CLEANSING FROM SIN

Imagine what it was like to see the sovereign Lord stripped to His waist, on His knees washing His disciples' feet. Stunned, silent, shamed, confused, all they could do was submit to His service, that is, until He came to Simon Peter. Peter always did things no other disciple would, and he was not a disappointment on this night. Now Doug Brown showed up. Peter interrupted the shocked, deadly silence with a word of strong protest. "*You* wash my feet? No way!" Jesus responded with a patient explanation. He said, in essence, "You can't understand what I'm doing now, but you will later." Then Peter protested again: "You shall *never* wash my feet" (John 13:6–8, italics added).

What did the Servant Leader do now? Did He do what Peter wanted? Was that serving Peter? Was He serving only—or even primarily—Peter? No, he was serving God. And we are not serving only the Doug Browns of our churches. We are serving the Lord Jesus, and we must serve others the way He served Peter. Jesus, the Servant Leader, told Peter exactly what he needed to hear, not what he wanted to hear. "Either I wash your feet or you have no part in what I am doing because you are useless to Me. I cannot have an uncleansed man leading My cause. My atoning death is the only thing that will cleanse you. Accept it, or you have nothing to do with Me. Others will participate with Me, but you won't. The choice is yours" (13:8, author's expanded paraphrase).

Until now we have seen that *the servant leader leads by serving or he doesn't lead at all.* Now we learn another truth about servant leadership: *The servant leader serves by leading or he doesn't serve at all.* Jesus showed us this in the way He addressed Peter's next response. Peter then went to the opposite extreme. He went from never to now, from nothing to everything. "Not just my feet, but all of me." Though it sounds humble, Peter was still reaching for power. Once again the Servant Leader responded firmly to His resistant follower, since doing more than the Lord wants is no better than doing less. The issue is obedience. Jesus told Peter he was already clean all over; his only problem was his feet (13:10). In other words, salvation totally cleanses believers, but our feet become contaminated by our daily walk through the streets of sin, and they need to be cleansed.

Then Jesus washed Peter's feet, serving him by doing what He planned to do all along. He listened to Peter's protests, responded patiently to his resistance, answered only what Peter could understand, and did exactly as He determined He would from the beginning. Servant leaders serve by leading, and by leading with authority and direction. Jesus served Peter by leading him to see the need for cleansing.

The only reason we humble ourselves and serve proud, angry, controlling, demanding people is because we love God with all our might and our neighbor as ourselves. Servant leadership is relational (people, not things), humble (self-giving, while expecting nothing in return), and loving (seeking only what is best for those it serves out of love for God). This means that servant leadership, while being gentle and compassionate, is also firm, strong, determined, directive, and demanding. When we meet that standard, we become models for others to follow, exactly what we are to be as servant leaders.

MODELING TRUE SERVANT LEADERSHIP

As pastors, we are to follow Christ's example and minister as He did. Of course, it is He who does the ministry through us as we abide in Him (John 15:1–11). In the Upper Room Jesus did three things in motivating His disciples to lead as He led (13:12–17).

First, Jesus affirmed His identity and established His authority. After washing their feet, He asked them a thought-provoking question: "Do you understand what I have done to you?" (13:12). Then He said, in essence, "You recognize My authority over you by calling Me Teacher and Lord, and you are correct in this because that's who I am. I am your Teacher and your Lord; I have authority over you" (13:13).

Many pastors struggle to understand the nature of their authority as servant leaders. Often they are afraid to assume authority lest they become arrogant or presumptuous. Yet godly servant leaders in the Bible did not have this fear. For example, Paul expressed no doubts about his authority when in 2 Corinthians he asserted it with great energy and emotion. The same is true in Galatians where he defended the gospel and asserted his authority to define the truth. Paul also directed Timothy, a pastor, to exercise authority when he told him to determine which widows deserved the church's support (1 Tim. 5:3–16) and how to go about rebuking elders (5:19–20). The Scriptures include many other examples of leaders exercising authority under the Lord.

Servant leaders have authority, but their authority does not come from themselves. It comes from Christ, who has all authority. Pastors have authority as elders, but positional authority is not enough to lead the church. Unless pastors grow as servants of Christ, they will not have the relationships they need to lead with authority.

Second, Jesus affirmed Himself as our Example by telling us to wash each other's feet. His words are simple and clear. "Now that I, your Lord and Teacher, have washed your feet, you also should wash one another's feet. I have set you an example that you should do as I have done for you" (John 13:14–15). This command describes a debt, an ethical obligation that we must fulfill.[3] We are certainly no better than Christ; if He washed feet, can we expect to do any less? We are to follow His example by humbly ministering to others. And as we do, we become true servants and true leaders.

Third, Jesus gave a special blessing to those who obey this command (13:17). All commands are given to be obeyed, but this command brings with it a special blessing. What is more difficult than humbling ourselves in front of our peers and serving them in ways we want to be served? We have thoughts like, "I should be doing this myself rather than helping him do it. I'm better than he is at this." Or, "How did he get where he is? I was a better student than he was in seminary." Competitive thoughts cloud our thinking, lock our knees, and paralyze our hands. We don't want to wash each other's feet. We leave the basin empty, the towel hanging on the wall. "We would gladly wash the feet of our Divine Lord; but He disconcertingly insists on washing ours, and bids us wash our neighbor's feet."[4] Yet there is a blessing in this; it is the blessing of obeying Jesus, of growing more like Him, of gaining freedom from our pride and fear, of making a difference in the lives of those we serve.

This calls for us to be involved with others at the deepest level of their needs, whether for salvation or sanctification. Servant leadership means we serve others by becoming involved in the messes they make of their lives in order to help bring about their deliverance from sin so they can participate in Christ's purpose for them. This is vital to our identity as pastors.

Servant leaders are not passive. They work to help untrained and untrusting elders understand how to grow in faith so they can make decisions that build the church rather than destroy it. Servant leaders join the Order of the Towel and stoop down to wash their followers' feet, telling them they need to submit to the cleansing of their souls. In other words, servant leaders confront prideful and controlling saints whenever necessary. There is nothing easy about this, but there is everything supernatural about it.

Recently I heard about a man who had to step aside from leading a ministry because he could not confront those who needed to be cleansed. When a pastor can't confront, inevitably there will be dissension, division, and unfairness on the staff.

When this occurs, there is a breakdown in servant leadership. The leader refuses to serve by cleansing the dirt off his followers' feet, so they track it all over the ministry, usually right after someone else has just cleaned the floor. The one who cleaned the floor screams at the one who tracks dirt all over the clean ministry. The one who tracks dirt screams back at the one who has cleaned the floor, accusing him of being uptight or telling him to mind his own business and not be such a busybody. Anger and resentment get out of hand, and the unity of the ministry is destroyed. Jesus did not allow this to happen among His disciples, and the leader who does, while presenting himself as a servant leader, is in fact a passive coward without the courage to confront. The heart of servant leadership is dependent courage, the courage to rely on Christ to be His instrument in cleansing others.

One of the greatest needs in many churches today is for true servant leadership born of love, established through sovereign security, and carried out by following Christ, our ultimate Example. Servant leaders do what

Jesus did—they wash feet. But He didn't simply wash feet; He cleansed souls. We become servant leaders when Jesus cleanses souls through us by making our hands His hands. This is why gently but firmly confronting others is involved in servant leadership.

Of course, by ourselves we can't cleanse people of their sin, but He can do so *through* us. If we refuse to correct others with gentleness, patience, and firmness as Jesus did Peter, we will fail as pastors. We are legitimately afraid when we recognize that we are not worthy of the task. But we are illegitimately afraid when we fear the way others will respond when we face them. Christ has called us to this task. We must have humble hearts and loose shoelaces, always ready to have our "feet washed." At times Christ calls on those who serve with us to wash our feet, even as He calls us to wash theirs. We must humbly submit to them, even if it means we hear unjust criticism or have our feet washed by people who hurt more than they help. As pastors we are not above sinning, and we are not above receiving cleansing through the hands of other men and women.

Today's church cries out for this to be done. God's Word cries out for this to be done. Every Scripture verse that calls for spiritual restoration cries out for this to be done (Gal. 6:1). Every passage that calls for church discipline cries out for this to be done (Matt. 18:15–20; 1 Cor. 5:1–13). Every verse that calls for the correction of false teachers cries out for this to be done (1 Tim. 1:3–7). To refuse to do these things is to cower in the fears of the flesh, more concerned about our careers and our images than about Christ's command to be His cleansing agents. We are His instruments, and He acts when we act. This is the awfulness of our responsibility for those whom God bought with His own blood (Acts 20:28).

Commenting on John 13:1–17, C. K. Barrett wrote, "The apostles, the disciples and servants of Jesus who is the teacher and lord, must follow His example: they must show the same humility, must, in fact, take up the cross and follow Jesus. So far as they do so, they share His authority. . . . The church is the responsible envoy of Christ, sharing His dignity and obliged to copy His humility and service."[5]

Servant leaders do more than act as Christ's cleansing servants in the lives of the sheep He entrusts to us. We preach God's truth, we hear the hurt of the brokenhearted, we develop organizational structures so the church can grow together as a body, and we serve people by helping them develop their gifts. What an amazing trust it is to be a difference maker in human lives, used by God as His instruments to bring others into conformity to Christ's image. No privilege is greater than this.

We join with Jesus in a twofold effort to build believers. We seek to develop competence, that is, to focus on the believers' doing. But in the process of developing competent servant leaders, we must face the flawed foundations of their characters. Jesus did exactly this with Peter. Only if we are willing to rebuild a flawed foundation can we see ultimate effectiveness in the Doug Browns we seek to develop. This is why we focus on the character of those who follow us, as well as help develop their competencies. Once we develop competence and stabilize character, the maturing believer is ready for Christ's commission, the commission to lead others by serving them, just as Jesus did. *This is what we are to be about as pastors: developing character and competence so those we serve can carry out Christ's commission.*

On the central quad of the campus of Dallas Theological Seminary stands a life-size bronze sculpture of Jesus washing Peter's feet. Few things have influenced me more than this sculpture. I have been so deeply affected by it I have often taken my classes to study it by asking them what they see so they can better understand what servant leadership is. In this sculpture Peter is a hulk of a man, big-boned and exuding strength, with veins bulging and incredulous eyes, amazed that Jesus would wash his feet. He can't believe what Jesus is doing. Peter would stop Him at once if he could. Jesus is stripped to His waist with a towel around His middle, down on His knees, left hand firmly holding Peter's right ankle, right hand holding the end of the towel with Peter's foot in the basin. His back muscles ripple with strength and determination to wash Peter's feet. Jesus is serving God—and Peter— by doing the Father's will and going against Peter's initial will. This is servant leadership: doing what God wants at all costs, even at the price of resistance and confrontation from those whom we serve by leading. One of the ways we function as servant leaders is when we go against the will of others in order to accomplish God's will in their lives. Only those who belong to the Order of the Towel are true servant leaders. The rest are either dominators or avoiders. Which are you?

CHAPTER SEVEN

SERVING GOD, LEADING OTHERS

SEVERAL YEARS AGO I met a young pastor who had started a church in one of the least responsive areas of the United States. It was his first ministry after seminary, and it went so well that within eighteen months 150 people were attending. They outgrew their facility and faced the happy problem of having to move. The pastor and the elders discussed the situation, and the pastor felt the best step for the church was to rent a building larger than their income could presently justify, supported with the expectation that new growth would generate new funds.

The elders resisted this conclusion. What would happen if growth didn't occur and the money didn't come in? Their thinking was understandable, but God had met all their needs without fail. Surely He wouldn't stop now. However, the pastor thought of himself more as a servant than as a leader, so he didn't assert himself or take a stand. He expressed his opinion, but didn't do anything to persuade the elders. Because he felt he was their servant, he thought he should let the elders make the decision and serve them by doing what they wanted. He failed to understand that serving the elders meant helping them grow in faith by trusting the Lord to do what He had consistently done all along, namely, to meet their needs as they depended on Him.

So the elders made the decision and chose to rent a facility they could afford, but one that was not big enough for them. The result? The church shriveled, shrank, and eventually ceased to exist. The elders went the "safe" route rather than the "trust" route, and the people lost confidence in them. The people sensed that the elders lacked the vision and courage to lead. When I met the young pastor he was out of the ministry, feeling God and man had let him down.

Did God and man let him down? Or did he fail to understand what servant leadership is? Was this pastor a servant leader? No. Unfortunately he was neither a servant nor a leader when measured by Jesus' model in John 13:1–17. No passive pastor is a servant leader, even though he looks like a servant by doing what others want him to do. In that sense, he is the servant—*their* servant—but not God's.

When we respond as this man did (and many of us do), we fail as servants because we don't wash our followers' feet of their fears and unbelief in order to move them forward in a growing faith in God. We act as a subordinate among superiors rather than as a leader among leaders. A study of servant leaders both in the Bible and throughout history will show that they don't dominate, but they don't abdicate either. They serve so their followers become holier people because of their leadership. Followers find freedom from fear and a new confidence in God's grace when they respond to a true servant of God.

When we don't step forward and provide direction for our sheep, we fail as leaders because we don't lead them in a vision that gives them a bigger view of God's power and what He can do through them. They continue to live fearful lives of uncertainty instead of faithful lives of security in the Lord. Because we fail as leaders, they continue in their small view of God and do not see what He can do through them.

We also fail as leaders when we don't prepare our sheep for the changes they must make to serve God in a radically different culture from the one we've known and wish were still here. Often we don't understand how to guide followers through the change process. Perhaps no one has even told us there is such a thing as a change process, and we don't know enough about leadership to understand change and people's response to it.

Further, we fail as leaders when we don't have the courage to define direction, communicate conviction, and call others to follow us as we follow Christ. Perhaps we lack confidence that we are following Christ. Sometimes we wait for our followers to confirm our vision before we lead them toward it.

When we fail to step forward and lead, we have a breakdown in character and competence. We lack character because we lack courage. We lack competence because we fail to recognize our vital role in developing vision, in communicating that vision, and in preparing our followers for change. As a result, we leave our sheep unchallenged and unchanged. No wonder, in the case of the pastor described previously, the church shrank to nonexistence. What was the tragedy in all of this? This pastor thought he was doing what a servant leader does because no one had ever taught him how to serve by leading. He thought teaching God's Word was enough. He had no idea that being a servant leader meant he had to join the Order of the Towel and become involved in the sanctification process of those he shepherded. Nor did he understand that sanctification for them involved taking the risk of trusting God to provide for their building needs as a church as well as to reach for an ever-developing vision of God's will. This is what it means to be a servant leader.

Let's take a quiz to test your understanding of servant leadership before I present my thinking to you in the following pages.

DO SERVANT LEADERS SERVE OR LEAD?

- Whom do servant leaders serve?
- Whom do servant leaders lead?
- What makes some pastors hesitate to be leaders? Is it their humility, their confusion about leadership, or their fear of leading?
- What are the requirements for someone to be a servant leader?
- What's the difference between servant leadership and other forms of leadership?
- What should I do if I'm afraid to lead because I know my motives are mixed?
- Should the emphasis in servant leadership be on serving or leading?

- How can a servant leader serve and still be a leader? Does a servant leader serve others by doing what they want?
- How can a servant leader exercise authority and still love others? Can a servant be a leader if he refuses to assert authority? Can a leader who asserts authority still be a servant?
- How does a servant leader lead? What does a servant leader do as a servant? How can a leader serve and still be a leader?
- How can a leader do what others want and still be a leader?

Servant leaders serve by leading or they don't serve at all. Poor leadership makes us poor servants. When we refuse to provide direction and refuse to call on others to follow us, we fail to serve them and help them grow in faith to become more like Christ. I hope answers to the following questions will help clarify this subject and will motivate us to lead by serving so we can serve by leading.

WHOM DO SERVANT LEADERS SERVE?

Servant leaders serve God first and then those who follow Him. Just as Jesus, the Servant of the Lord, served only God the Father's interests, so servant leaders must have the same attitude (Phil. 2:4–11). This attitude calls for us to humble ourselves by obeying God and becoming His slaves, leaving our exaltation in His hands. To serve God we must turn from serving ourselves.

Paul answered this question best when he told the Corinthians, "For we do not preach ourselves, but Christ Jesus the Lord, and ourselves your bondservants for Jesus' sake" (2 Cor. 4:5). Paul identified himself as a slave to the Corinthians, but he was their slave for Jesus' sake, that is, when he served them, he did only what Christ wanted him to do for them, not what they wanted him to do. They didn't want him to address publicly their failure to keep their word about contributing to the Jerusalem church's financial needs; they didn't want him to correct them about their failure in church discipline; they didn't want him to rebuke them for resisting his authority. But he did all of these things because Christ wanted him to. We serve the followers God gives us in light of His interests in their lives, even when they resist us.

WHOM DO SERVANT LEADERS LEAD?

Servant leaders lead *God's* followers, who are Christ's sheep purchased with His blood. They lead by calling others to follow Christ, by equipping His followers with the skills they need to become servant leaders themselves, by holding them accountable for their hardened hearts and selfish expectations, and by sending them forth according to Christ's commission to reach, teach, and send others.

WHAT ARE THE REQUIREMENTS TO BECOME A SERVANT LEADER?

There are at least four requirements: (1) a love for God that spills over in a love for His followers marked by genuine care and concern for their well-being, (2) a mature, broken, and humble heart that is growing in commitment to God and His interests, (3) a spirit of Christlike self-sacrifice that calls servant leaders away from their own interests to God's alone, (4) a dependent courage—that is, a courage that depends on Christ for its wisdom, strength, love, and fruit—that enables servant leaders to stand for God's interests at all times against resistance and rejection.

HOW DO SERVANT LEADERS LEAD?

Servant leaders lead by doing the following: (1) Servant leaders put forth a vision that attracts others and takes them into a better future. (2) Servant leaders develop their followers' gifts. (3) Servant leaders recruit, delegate, orient, evaluate, hold accountable, bring about change, instruct in areas of ignorance, empower—they do everything we call leadership. (4) Servant leaders raise and develop human, financial, and physical resources. (5) Servant leaders reproduce the abilities they have in those who follow them so they can do the same thing, with the result that generations of leaders spring up after them.

One vital difference between servant leaders and other leaders is that servant leaders lead with a different set of motives than most, as well as from a different position, because servant leaders are followers of *the* Leader and serve for His glory. At the very core of their beings, servant leaders know they are always followers and will never be more than that, no matter what heights they reach. After all, what greater ministry is there than being a servant of the Lord?

WHAT IS THE DIFFERENCE BETWEEN SERVANT LEADERSHIP AND OTHER FORMS OF LEADERSHIP?

Jesus never said His servants shouldn't lead. He never said we shouldn't call others to a great vision or hold others accountable or rebuke them for their sin or demand changes in them and their behavior or correct their failures or discipline them in their disobedience. If He did, Paul sinned in 2 Corinthians when he firmly corrected the church at Corinth for its challenges to his authority. He also sinned when he corrected the church in Galatia for its distortion of grace. He further sinned when in 1 Corinthians 5 he commanded all church leaders who came after him to exercise church discipline. Servant leaders exercise authority, but they do so with motives, focus, values, and methods that differ from those of other leaders. The servant leader exercises authority motivated by a love for Christ, a focus on His interests, the values of the Cross, and the courage to wash the feet of those who follow Christ with him.

Much of the confusion over servant leadership comes from a misunderstanding of Matthew 20:20–28 and Mark 10:35–45. In these passages our Lord said we cannot lead as the gentile rulers lead, by lording it over others and by exercising authority over them. What does He mean by this? We find the answer to this question by considering three Greek words found in both passages.

The first word, "ruler" (*archōn*), describes those who govern the Gentiles. This word drips with dominance and is filled with force. It describes those with power and authority, whether in politics, the military, religion, or over demonic forces. Those rulers exercise power at the highest levels, including the celestial.[1] No Christian leader is ever called a ruler. Even Jesus is called a ruler only once (Rev. 1:5), though not with the negative connotations associated with the word.

The next two key words are "lord it over" (*katakyreuō*) and "exercise authority over" (*katexousiazō*); (Matt. 20:25; Mark. 10:42). Leaders who act as lords misuse their power for selfish ends.[2] "The prefix καТα . . . implies that the princes exercise their rule to their own advantage and contrary to the interests and well being of the people."[3] Peter used the word *katakyreuō* to tell his fellow elders to shepherd the flock without thought for their own interests and without lording over them (1 Pet. 5:3).

Katexousiazō speaks of the exercise of authority over others and refers to the misuse of official authority. It can convey the idea of exercising authority perhaps to tyrannize others,[4] or to play the tyrant.[5] "The compound prep[osition *kata*] in the verb gives the sense of using lordship over people to their disadvantage and to one's own advantage."[6] Alford notes that this prefix signifies "subjugation and oppression."[7]

The problem in these verses is not in exercising leadership but in exercising lordship. When a leader's motive is to subject others to himself and control them for his advantage, that leader becomes a tyrant. However, when a pastor seeks to serve others for their good no matter what demands he must make of them, he becomes a servant.

We see Jesus telling His men He doesn't have the authority to give them the seats on His right and His left in the kingdom (Matt. 20:23; Mark 10:40). We see Jesus giving His life as a ransom for many (Matt. 20:28; Mark 10:45). We know Jesus gave up all independent use of His attributes and veiled His glory when He enslaved Himself to His Father's will (Phil. 2:4–11).

However, Jesus rebuked Peter, calling him Satan (Mark 8:33). Again, Jesus spoke emphatically to Peter when the apostle claimed He would never fall away (14:30). We have seen His response when Peter first refused to have his feet washed; after explaining His purpose, Jesus washed his feet anyway. Clearly, servant leaders hold God's followers accountable, exercising an authority in their lives that releases them from their pride and blindness and sets them free to live God's way.

Likewise Paul taught us what a servant leader is. He spoke of his willingness to give all he had to others (1 Thess. 2:1–12), even to being like a nursing mother to them (2:7). He raised Timothy as a child in the faith (1 Tim. 1:2). Yet, though he was like a nursing mother and a faithful father, he was also a forceful leader, as seen when he addressed the Corinthians who were challenging his authority (2 Cor. 10:1–18). For Timothy to speak to some unusually sensitive issues, as Paul encouraged him to do, would be to act as a servant only if he had God's interests at heart.

IS THE EMPHASIS IN SERVANT LEADERSHIP ON SERVING OR LEADING?

The answer is both. Servant leaders serve God and others by sacrificing themselves and their interests for God's sake. Just as Jesus gave Himself for His followers' sake, so servant leaders give their lives—their energy, their strength, their wills—to accomplish God's purposes. Servant leaders earn the right to lead God's followers when they serve them in this way. If this requires strong words, specific direction, rebuke, correction, or confrontation, then this is what must be done. If this requires a challenge to commitment, a call to vision, or an exhortation to risk everything for Christ, then this is what a servant leader must do. Servant leaders don't make demands of others for their egos' sake; they speak strongly to others only out of God's interests. Their aim is not to come down on others, but to lift others up. This is the Order of the Towel.

HOW CAN A SERVANT LEADER SERVE AND STILL BE A LEADER?

The only way a leader can truly lead as a servant is by properly understanding what serving is. True serving is doing what God wants, not what people want. A servant leader serves others by doing what God wants done in their lives—holding up His holy standard by holding forth His holy Word and by holding his followers accountable to obey God.

HOW CAN A SERVANT LEADER EXERCISE AUTHORITY AND STILL LOVE OTHERS?

A servant exercises authority in the lives of others and still loves them by doing what Jesus did when He washed Peter's feet. A servant leader loves others by getting involved in their struggles and their confusion, by confronting their pride and their fear, by guiding them to deliverance from their failures to restoration and new influence for Christ. No one who lacks authority can do this. Anyone with authority who fails to do this neither serves nor leads.

CAN A SERVANT LEADER WHO REFUSES TO ASSERT AUTHORITY WHEN NEEDED BE A LEADER?

What if Jesus had refused to assert His authority over Peter and wash his feet? Where would Peter have been? Jesus answered that question Himself when He said to Peter, "If I do not wash you, you have no part with me" (John 13:8). Would Jesus have been a leader if He had allowed Peter to remain unwashed and unusable to Him? Of course not. When a leader refuses to exercise appropriate authority in a follower's life, he leaves the follower unqualified to serve Christ. There can be no greater leadership failure than this.

CAN A LEADER WHO ASSERTS AUTHORITY BE A SERVANT OR IS HE JUST A CONTROLLER?

The answer to this question depends on the leader's motive and method. If a leader seeks to serve God by leading Christ's followers in God's way, that leader has innate authority. Christ will act through him for the followers' good. Further, if a leader's methods release followers from sin's daily dirt and make them ready to serve Christ, that leader has appropriately exercised authority.

CONCLUSION

Servant leaders serve, or they don't lead at all. As pastors, we earn respect and trust when we humble ourselves by seeking the good of those who do not seek our good. So we do the mundane tasks no one else will do. We also do the unwanted things by becoming Christ's hands in cleansing the feet of those who follow Him through us, even when they protest strongly.

Servant leaders lead, or they don't serve at all. As pastors, we earn respect and trust when we step forward and go before the sheep into new and uncharted territory. We lead when we exercise dependent courage through Christ and call followers to new risks and new trust so they grow in Christ and make their lives count for eternity.

Servant leaders serve, or they don't lead at all. And servant leaders lead, or they don't serve at all. Stated another way, *servant leaders lead by serving and serve by leading.*

CHAPTER EIGHT

THE PASTOR'S AUTHORITY

Ray Stedman is coming! These words flashed across the campus of Dallas Seminary in midwinter 1964. Ray Stedman was coming to speak at a retreat for Dallas Seminary students. Almost everyone was going, everyone except me. All the hype turned me off. It sounded to me as if Stedman was the answer to everything. If we just went to hear him, we would be guaranteed a lifetime of ministry success. I didn't trust anyone who had all the answers, so I wasn't going.

But that changed.

The Friday afternoon of the retreat I saw Ray and Elaine Stedman coming along the cloistered walkway toward Stearns Hall on the Dallas Seminary campus. It took only one look for me to realize Ray was not a man who claimed to have all the answers. I've never had another experience like that, but I could see in his face he was a man I wanted to know. Immediately I called my best friend and said, "We need to go to this retreat." One hour later I was on my way to a life-making experience.

I fought everything Ray said that weekend, but afterward I knew I wanted to intern with him, which I did, first for a summer, and then, three years later, for a year. I saw him in action, and I saw a man who exercised pastoral authority in wise and effective ways. He was a man who had innate personal authority. When he spoke, people listened, but he spoke only when he felt it was necessary. He also listened to others who differed with him, even when they were lowly interns. I learned more about pastoral authority from Ray Stedman than from anyone else, before or since.

I learned from him that pastoral authority does not demand control or power, and that a pastor who exercises authority does several things. He

- takes risks
- is not afraid to make mistakes
- listens
- doesn't need to have all the answers
- develops and exalts others
- is humble
- is patient
- earns respect and trust by giving respect and trust.

No wonder that retreat was a life-making experience for me.

Pastors *must* have authority—no one can pastor without it—and we must not be afraid to exercise that authority. The responsibilities Scripture assigns to us require that we have authority to accomplish them:

- teaching God's truth
- selecting, leading, and developing elders
- equipping the saints
- exercising church discipline
- confronting false teachers.

Where do we get the authority to shepherd a church under the headship of Jesus Christ?

WE HAVE NO AUTHORITY IN OURSELVES

All pastoral authority is derived authority. In fact even Jesus' authority was delegated authority. He said, "All authority has been given to Me [by God the Father] in heaven and on earth" (Matt. 28:18). Authority is not ours, it is Christ's, and we have authority only as He exercises it through us. Our right to do anything rests in His hands; so unless our hands become His hands, we are empty-handed. Through dependence on Him, we have all the authority we need to do whatever He wants, and this makes authority a spiritual concern.

If we don't rely on Him alone, we may have the title of pastor, but not the authority. We may have the power to make others do what we want, but we will lack the moral leverage and respect that calls others to follow us. They won't have the commitment to serve with us, forgive us when we sin, or comfort us when we fail. We may have control for a short time, but we will never have genuine authority. Being a pastor does not bestow authority on us; instead it gives us opportunity for divinely given authority to be recognized. We either walk with Christ or we fall on our faces.

How then do we get authority?

WE GET AUTHORITY FROM CHRIST

Our authority comes from the Lord Jesus. When others know we are subordinate and obedient to Him, they more willingly follow our leadership as their shepherds. His authority over our lives gives us authority in their lives. We gain authority the same way Christ did, through vulnerability, love, and self-sacrifice, but we can be like this only through Him.

WE GET AUTHORITY FROM BEING LIKE CHRIST

We also get authority from who we are, because knowing Christ makes us more like Him. Our authority comes from our person more than our position, from trust earned more than from power delegated or control exercised. We gain authority as we grow in Christlikeness.

Christ's sheep in our flock know His voice and recognize it when they hear Him speak. If they hear His voice through us, their confidence in us grows and their trust in us deepens. They can tell, however, when we use Christ's name to mask our own interests, and then they will resist our authority at every turn. There are always some, of course, who don't want to subject themselves to Christ. Therefore the more our Lord speaks through us the more they will resist us. Although their resistance seems personal to us, it isn't. We receive their anger only because Christ is in us, and to them we sound like Him. Eventually their response works to our advantage and increases our authority because others see our true commitment to Christ and His character in us as they watch us endure opposition. Ultimately our authority comes from our character tested over time in the intensity of public relationships and the intimacy of private relationships.

WE GET AUTHORITY FROM WHAT WE DO

We get authority not only from the One we know and from who we are. People also grant us authority based on what we do. A spiritual man of high moral character who won't act when he should will not earn authority from followers. No one will follow someone who isn't going anywhere.

Therefore a pastor's authority comes from excellence in his ministry, which includes the following:

- caring for people
- meeting people's needs
- leading people to obey God and His Word
- calling people to take a stand for Christ
- calling people to be accountable before God
- organizing people to work together

If we are to have authority, we must minister competently. *After character, competence is essential to authority.*

WE GET AUTHORITY FROM
THE PURITY OF OUR MOTIVES

Motives make the difference when we seek to earn authority, as Peter wrote in 1 Peter 5:1–4. In calling us to "shepherd the flock of God," Peter, with apostolic authority, appealed to us as peers, as a fellow elder. What an outstanding example he became as he issued a call for us to be examples to the flock, and not to use compulsion or seek sordid gain. We are not to lord it over others, but we are to exercise oversight of them. Many people think exercising oversight means establishing control over others. But nothing could be further from the truth.

The overseer (Greek, *episkopos*, from the related verb *episkopeō*) means "one who cares for" as well as "one who oversees or has oversight." The overseer cares for his sheep; he encourages growth; he doesn't exercise control. Even when we must discipline the sheep, our concern for them should be care rather than punishment. We are motivated to nurture, not to overpower. Peter's plea is a call to leadership—*servant* leadership.

Our primary concern is accountability, not authority, because our Chief Shepherd (5:4) may return at any moment. When He returns, we will give an accounting to Him of how well we carried out the stewardship He delegated to us. He is the owner and He will be concerned about the way we treated His sheep. Did we *provide* green grass and still waters for them when they were hungry? Did we *protect* them from wild animals and thieves in the darkness of the night? Did we *pursue* them, as He would, when they wandered off? If we did, we will receive His reward for us (5:4). We are to care for them as Jesus cares for us. As Peter wrote, "For you were like sheep going astray, but now you have returned to the Shepherd and Overseer of your souls" (2:25). "Oversight means loving care and concern, a responsibility willingly shouldered; it can never be used for personal aggrandizement. Its meaning here is to be seen in Christ's selfless service which was moved by concern for the salvation of men."[1]

WE LOSE AUTHORITY WHEN WE SEEK POWER AND CONTROL

Authority is *not* power and control. Power and control are domination, which may work over the short term but will eventually fail. We can distinguish between the two in the following way.

Power is the use of gift, position, and opportunity to control others so that they serve the pastor and his aims. Often pastors claim their power is from God, and they seek to justify it by well-meaning claims, but their claims are marked by destructive attitudes that bring great hurt to our Lord's sheep.

Authority, on the other hand, is the use of gift, position, and opportunity to release others at the right time so that pastor and people serve Christ together. We do exercise control over people, but not for our sake. We do it because of our concern for their maturity and growth. This demands a maturity and humility that comes only through the Cross, the grave, and resurrection.

Power is something pastors must turn from, whereas authority is something pastors must have. Henri Nouwen expresses profound insight into the dangers of power.

> One of the greatest ironies of . . . Christianity is that its leaders constantly gave in to the temptation of power. . . . The temptation to consider power an apt instrument for the proclamation of the Gospel is the greatest of all. . . .
>
> What makes the temptation of power so seemingly irresistible? Maybe it is that power offers an easy substitute for the hard task of love. It seems easier to be God than to love God, easier to control people than to love people . . . the temptation of power is greatest when intimacy is a threat. Much Christian leadership is exercised by people who do not know how to develop healthy, intimate relationships and have opted for power and control instead. Many Christian empire-builders have been people unable to give and receive love.[2]

Concerning the need for the Cross, Nouwen observes, "The way of the Christian leader is not the way of upward mobility . . . but the way of downward mobility ending on the cross. . . . The most important quality of Christian leadership . . . is not a leadership of power and control, but a leadership of powerlessness and humility in which the suffering servant of God, Jesus Christ, is made manifest."[3]

Some years ago I attempted to bring about reconciliation between a fired pastor and his former church. This man loved his church and wanted the best for it, but he had no idea his inappropriate control was so destructive. He thought he was doing what was best for the people. Across the years several elders talked with the pastor about his control, but every time he convinced each of them it was the elder's problem, not his. However, later each elder, thinking about what happened, became angry because he realized the pastor had talked him out of the truth. When this happened to several elders, they understood the pastor was controlling them, not leading them. So one evening the elders fired the pastor. It was painful and shocking for him, but inevitable, and he never recovered from this experience.

One of two things happens when a pastor attempts to gain authority through power and domination. Either he succeeds and the ministry shrivels and dies, choked to death by his controlling grip, or the leaders do what these elders did—rebel and remove the pastor. After this they go through a period of reaction until they are ready to respond to healthy leadership once again and to seek a mature pastor to serve them. However, some elders will never follow another pastor after having experienced excessive control.

WE SEEK SHEPHERD AUTHORITY, NOT COMMAND AUTHORITY

A pastor is to be more like a husband or a father within a family than an executive over a corporation. Pastors are shepherds, not powerbrokers. Although a pastor has biblical authority, he is to use influence, friendship, patience, and persuasion, except when he must respond to issues such as church discipline or aspects of staff management and is forced to take an authoritative stand. Pastors gain authority through healthy relationships and long-term faithfulness. Those who pursue appropriate intimacy, approachability, vulnerability, and humility earn the confidence they need from others to act with authority.

Many fail to realize that pastors enhance their authority through confession of sin, acknowledgment of needed growth, and acceptance of help from others. When pastors project a protective wall to keep others away, they undermine their own leadership. Some seminaries teach pastors to create distance between themselves and their sheep in order to be safe, but I believe this is poor advice. Granted, there is a need for wisdom, testing, and timing before entering into deep trust with others, but no shepherd can serve God's sheep from behind a wall.

Shepherding is dangerous because sheep are dumb and they force shepherds to take great risk, as Jesus showed (Luke 15:3–6). Sheep do things that send us out into the night, scrambling and stumbling through briar patches and along precipitous cliffs—or in our times, along dangerous city streets—looking for those missing from the fold. Shepherding is not a telecommuting task. We can't call in our gentle care and compassionate concern from home via e-mail.

Executives and generals operate with command authority. If followers don't obey orders, they are fired or court-martialed. However, pastors do not exercise this kind of authority over subordinates. Some may have learned to their deep regret that they cannot do this in the local church. They are to be shepherds involved in loving relationships with volunteers. Pastors have shepherd authority rather than command authority, an authority that comes not from position and power but from service resulting in trust.

WE GAIN AUTHORITY THROUGH
THE COURAGE TO CONFRONT

Shepherd authority includes direction and confrontation. We fear times of confrontation because they make us uncomfortable; yet we cannot avoid them if we are to develop disciples, as Jesus showed in His relationship with Peter. Think of the way He confronted him: When Peter attempted to correct Jesus, He called him "Satan." Jesus also warned him that he would betray Him, and when His warning came true He looked out of Caiaphas's window at Peter (Luke 22:61). When Peter was broken and struggling, Jesus pressed him by asking him three times, "Do you love me?" Jesus loved Peter so much that He confronted him in direct and unavoidable ways.

Many pastors see their authority break down because they lack the courage to confront. They can't face the criticism or stand the anger that confrontation brings from those who don't want to hear Christ speaking through them. They try to please everyone because they think this pleases the Lord. Nothing could be further from the truth. Washing the feet of kicking sheep is often the key to respect and trust, which is the essence of authority and one of the greatest tests pastors face.

THE ULTIMATE AUTHORITY QUESTION:
PASTOR OR BOARD?

Who has the authority to lead the church, the pastor or the board? The answer is neither. All authority belongs to Christ. And He exercises His authority through those who rely on Him and serve Him with competence. This means that those who don't rely on Him don't have legitimate authority, no matter what office they hold. Nevertheless the invisible Lord must express His authority in visible, tangible ways, and He does so through those whom He chooses to represent Him. This issue involves the pastor's authority in relation to the lay leaders in the local church.

- What authority does the pastor have in relation to the lay leaders?
- Does he have authority as *the* leader?
- Is he one leader among many?
- Is he an employee subordinate to the lay leadership?
- Can he be subordinate to, equal with, and leader of the lay leadership, all at the same time?

These questions demand answers because they define the pastor's leadership role in the local church. How does the pastor lead? Does he set the pace for the church, or do the lay leaders? In a multiple staff situation who is responsible to hire, develop, and monitor the staff? If we don't answer these questions, we will live with constant frustration and confusion.

I believe there must be responsible leadership among men who differ in spiritual gifts and who have equal but delegated authority under Christ. Jesus Christ is the church's Head, and no one will replace Him (Matt. 16:18; Eph. 1:22; Col. 1:18). Under His headship elders are always plural in number (Acts 11:30; 14:23; 20:17; Phil. 1:1; 1 Tim. 3:1–8; 5:17–25; Titus 1:5; James 5:14–15; 1 Pet. 1:1; 5:1).

Further, elders serve as brothers who are equal, not as superiors in a chain of command. Jesus does not deny leadership, but He does denounce dominance. Practices such as planning, organizing, training, evaluating, and establishing accountability are all critical for pastors. However, anytime anyone in God's family lords it over others, he is disobeying Christ's command. When we hold others accountable by rebuking, correcting, or disciplining, we do not have to dominate them.

Because we are brothers, we must lead as brothers and not as corporate executives (Matt. 23:8). Brothers are men with a common heritage and a common dependence, and the father is the one who has authority in the family. As brothers we serve in the family according to our different abilities as assigned by the Father. One administers, another exhorts, while another creates. In a family that lives and works well together, the father assigns the brothers and sisters to do what they do best and delegates authority to them as their abilities and positions require and their character permits. Competition and control do not scar good families, and this certainly must be true in God's family. No one is superior to the rest or has authority to dominate the church. Each of us has unique abilities and perspectives for serving the family, and we must support one another in our service. All believers are equal in value and significance, but not all are equal in capacity, maturity, or authority. However, equality with each other does not deny accountability to one another, so let's not get into squabbles and arguments over who's the greatest. Character, gifts, maturity, and proven ministry determine our roles in the local church.

The heart of the authority issue for pastors is our character. All the qualifying traits of elders are moral qualifications (1 Tim. 3:1–7; Titus 1:5–9). No one can be a legitimate Christian leader who does not have a tested and proven Christian character. The position of elder depends on character, while the function of each elder depends on the capacities the Holy Spirit has given him. A pastor who can teach, develop vision, and lead will be a leader among equals.

No human venture gets done without human leadership. The two extremes of collective leadership and dominant leadership are not effective. Collective leadership (no established human authority) has rarely been productive over a long period of time, and there is no model of it in the Bible. If God wanted us to pursue this format, He would have given a clear enough model for us to know how to minister in such a situation. Just as there is no model of collective leadership in the Bible, there is also no model of dominant leadership in Scripture. We see many individual leaders in the Word (Moses, Joshua, Samuel, David, Daniel, Paul), but none of these leaders dominated their followers. If there is no constituted and recognized human leadership among the elders, usually a dominant individual assumes leadership over the rest of the board, but this is not biblical.

THE SOLUTION: THREE-IN-ONE

How then does the pastor exercise authority among the elders? The answer is threefold: The pastor is subordinate to the elders, equal with the elders, and a leader of the elders—and all are subordinate to Christ.[4]

The Pastor as Subordinate to the Elders

The pastor is subordinate to the elders as an employee. They determine his salary, work hours, work setting, vacation schedule, weeks of conference, study breaks, standards for evaluating his job performance, and whether he remains as pastor. The pastor should have a voice in all these concerns, but he must always be under the authority of the elders as an employee and must communicate the respect and accountability due them, as the Bible requires.

The Pastor as a Peer with the Elders

At the same time, the pastor is an equal of the elders because he is a fellow elder. Apart from his responsibilities as an employee, the pastor is a brother among the elders. As a brother, he shares a mutual accountability to Christ with the rest of the elders, since together they are responsible to Him for all they do. In his shepherding, overseeing, and teaching task, he is an equal of the elders, and they of him.

The Pastor as a Leader of Leaders

The pastor is also the leader among the elders. In this sense he is the first among equals. He is responsible to lead out in vision, in teaching the Word, and in being a model of all Christ expects them to be (1 Tim. 3:12–16).

The following charts illustrate these three positions. As an employee, the pastor is subordinate to the elders.

Christ

Elders

Pastor

As a fellow elder, the pastor is equal with the elders. They are brothers together, as this illustrates:

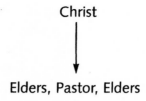

Christ

Elders, Pastor, Elders

And as first among equals, the pastor is the leader of the elders.

Christ

Pastor

Elders

Thus the pastor subordinates himself to the elders as those who have the authority to define his task, evaluate his character, and develop him as a man. He is one with the elders in that he is as qualified in character to serve as all the others are. He is the leader of the elders, the first among equals, because his character, training, gifts, and experience qualify him for this task.

Pastor and Staff

The pastor leads the staff, and, under the oversight of the elders, he directs them in pursuing the church's vision. Staff shepherding and leadership is draining for the pastor who seeks to build elders, stay in touch with the congregation, develop vision, plan and evaluate the ministry, as well as serve his family effectively. In view of these demands, the pastor needs to be protected from losing vital study and sermon preparation time by excessive administrative demands. When the church is large enough, a pastor can protect his central functions of preaching and leadership while fulfilling his pastoral duties by delegating staff management to a trusted associate or executive pastor subject to the elders' approval. This trusted associate must be worthy of the task and compatible with the pastor in every way. Even when the senior pastor has an executive leader, he cannot totally delegate his accountability for the staff's ministry, development, and growth because he continues to be accountable to oversee these ministry tasks.

Elders must agree that the pastor is the leader of the staff and is responsible to lead in implementing the church's vision. There can be no competition between the pastor and the elders in staff management and other leadership responsibilities in the church. You cannot take a pastor's call, training, gifts, experience, and proven effectiveness and put that aside so a group of men with limited time, training, experience, and a different call can lead the church. Neither elder nor pastor should deny each other their God-given shepherding roles.

Church Bosses

A major problem occurs when a church becomes a place where some laymen exercise power they can't get anywhere else. Instead of serving others they attempt to satisfy an unfulfilled drive for power. Still others use a top-down authority, which is appropriate in the business world but totally inappropriate in the church. When either of these kinds of men exercise power on the board, they cease to be brothers and start to be bosses, but there is no place for a boss on any board, whether he is a pastor or an elder. Unless the pastor is willing to confront, teach, and disciple such men in how to lead, they will constantly tell him what to do, even though they have neither the qualifications, the experience, nor the character to do so. Many pastors also seek to fulfill ego needs through ministry, and when they do that they are just as wrong as the laymen.

The issue of the pastor's authority may be the thorniest one in the body of Christ today. Churches everywhere are splitting over it as apparently godly men of integrity divide in anger with fellowship fractured, friendships shattered, and hearts broken. The problem seems to have two causes. First, it appears to be the unintended result of giving the ministry to the saints. Clericalism was convenient. When you have a "holy man" who is superior to others, there's no doubt about who's in charge. However, when all the saints are gifted and everyone is a minister, questions about leadership and authority inevitably arise. The church's shepherding structure is unnatural for some men who are accustomed to the gentile model, and it takes much grace from God to lead His way. Many of us will have to pass through some deeply humbling experiences before we stop striving for control and start serving Christ's way.

The other factor is the lust for power. When our sinful desires find a way to justify themselves theologically, confusion reigns supreme. Power, whether used by a pastor to force his way to the top of the heap or used by elders to pull him back down and exalt themselves, is wrong. In fact it's an evil of the lowest and most destructive kind.

WHAT CAN WE DO?

No words in a book can guarantee a solution to pastor-elder conflicts. Still, it is worthwhile to list some specific steps a pastor can take to avoid some of the more terrible thickets. The following suggestions are not fail-safe, but they can help get you started in the right direction.

- Define the board structure and role clearly and succinctly in the church constitution.
- Define the pastor's *core* responsibilities clearly and succinctly in the church by-laws (you can't be comprehensive because time, churches, culture, and human needs change, so you must be careful not to lock yourself into an unchangeable job description). Make sure there is no conflict or confusion between the elders' role and the pastor's core responsibilities.
- Define pastor/board responsibilities clearly in the pastor's job description.
- Build in pastor/board responsibilities in the annual evaluations of the pastor and the elders, and hold all accountable for their stated tasks.
- Review and adjust these accountability descriptions at least once every three years.

- Establish lines of authority and accountability, and then do everything you can to avoid having to exercise that authority.

A MATRIX OF TRUST

These steps may be helpful, but no words on paper are strong enough to overcome the flesh when it reaches for selfish ambition or grabs for power. Because of this, the only way to maintain an authority balance between the pastor and the board of elders is through *a matrix of trust established by the Holy Spirit in the context of competency and compatibility.*

A matrix is an organizational structure designed to get tasks done that centers on leadership responsibilities and relationships, not authority. In a matrix, people with needed skills are brought together under the guidance of a leader. They commit to a voluntary submission for the sake of the task, and relationships lie at the heart of a matrix. This is exactly the way a human body works. In a healthy body, all the parts work together in relationship to each other and no one part dominates. Among elders and pastor, the most vital relationship we have is with the Holy Spirit, since He is the One who holds all relationships together.

Three elements tie pastors and elders together when they function as a matrix rather than as a power structure: trust, competency, and compatibility.

Trust—confidence in the motives, abilities, and character of each other—is the lifeblood of a group. Trust enables them to work together without doubt or conflict. Without trust, no constitution or job description can hold board and pastor together. I have already presented numerous ways a pastor can earn trust from a board, but I now add several steps we can take to honor the legitimate authority requirements a board makes of us. If we do these things while doing our job well, most authority tensions will never develop.

- Do what you're asked to do or give a careful and thorough explanation of why you can't. If your explanation is not accepted, do what the board wants or see if they will wait while you seek to help them understand your point of view.
- Have no hidden agendas. Hidden agendas destroy trust. By a hidden agenda I mean an undisclosed plan to get what you want for

your advantage. I am not talking about a beneficial aim for which the church is not yet ready. Many times you will have hopes and plans for the future you cannot and should not disclose. Jesus Himself did not tell His disciples all He had in mind because they weren't ready to know it (John 16:12). Also do not try to sneak in changes by manipulation and deception. Nothing will get you fired more quickly.

- Be totally open about your motives and methods. Never leave the elders guessing about what you're doing, why you're doing it, and the way you're doing it. Tell them these three things consistently, and they'll trust you every time.
- Pursue constant communication. Tell the elders everything you can and don't worry about overcommunicating. You cannot communicate too much of the right kind of information.
- Don't avoid elders who intimidate you. Some pastors try to isolate themselves from some board members by spending time with only those who make them feel comfortable. But avoiding them can get you fired when you least expect it. Stay in touch with them no matter how unnerving it is. Learn to talk with them peer-to-peer and you will discover they respect you and are not a threat to you. Or you will discover they are a threat to you and you can act to prevent their intended harm.
- Invest time. It takes time to build trust, so give all the time you can to being with members of your board. Time with elders is like bread on the water—it will come back to you after many days.

Competency and Compatibility

Competency means being good at what you do. Compatibility means you and your board are in agreement in four ways: biblically, philosophically, methodologically, and governmentally.

You and your board have *biblical compatibility* when you have theological agreement, are not divided over what the Bible teaches, and also agree on what are primary and secondary issues.

You and your board have *philosophical compatibility* when you agree on your purpose and core values and are not divided over what you're working to do. Everyone on the board knows your purpose and is committed to it.

You and your board have *methodological compatibility* when you are agreed on how you get things done and are not divided over ministry practices.

You and your board have *governmental compatibility* when you're agreed on how your church is structured and are not divided over how it operates.

If you seek to make a change in any one of these areas without careful planning and wise actions, the chances are very high that you will be the one making the biggest change—to a new ministry.

Bipolar Churches

A bipolar church is one in which leaders are competing with each other, and the people are split over whom they will follow. Frequently a senior pastor has labored long and hard to bring the ministry to the place where it is well established and well funded with excellent facilities. He hires a bright, talented young man who soon attracts large numbers of "generation Xers" who fill the facilities with claps of joy and shouts of praise. Then comparisons arise and a Corinthian kind of competition looms on the horizon. The church is now bipolar, and the senior pastor's role and authority can be thrown into doubt. Perhaps the senior pastor is threatened by the younger man's success and creates the problem himself. Perhaps the younger man is ambitious. Perhaps the people are Corinthian in their attitude, and they help bring on the problem.

In any case the younger man has a free ride—he leads no elders, he hired few if any staff peers, he built no buildings, he raised no funds. He's been given too much opportunity and too little responsibility, a destructive formula for an untested young man. He may be like a twenty-one-year-old whose parents give him a million dollars—he's unable to appreciate what's been provided for him. A church within a church may be like a baby within a mother who is permanently pregnant: Something has to happen.

What's the solution? The answer is not one person's exclusive control over "a church within a church." Instead, create preaching teams and make certain the pastor and the younger man or men trade congregations several times a year. Be sure there is a clear line of authority and accountability along with mutual trust, respect, and submission between senior pastor and the younger man or men. It may be difficult at times, but their shared presence in the services will prevent a party spirit from developing to undermine the senior pastor's authority and bring him to a Humpty-Dumpty fall. You can have generation-focused ministries without becoming a bipolar church if you recognize the dangers and make plans to overcome them.

CONCLUSION

How does a pastor gain authority? By serving his Lord and tending His sheep. And he does this by doing the following:

- serving out of genuine care for the sheep, not out of self-interest or for self-promotion;
- being open, vulnerable, touchable, a shepherd who, like Jesus, shows he has been tested and tempted the same way the sheep have;
- being quick to let his feet be washed because, unlike Jesus, he is sinful;
- being teachable, quick to hear when others make suggestions;
- keeping his word, showing respect and regard for others;
- being gentle with everyone, especially his critics;
- submitting to human authority when he must, even against his will;
- resisting human authority when he must in God's will;
- taking calculated and supportive risks with others;
- developing and exalting others;
- having the courage to protect and correct the sheep;
- humbling himself before God in dependence on the Lord.

It was these and many more lessons I learned from Ray Stedman more than thirty years ago that I continue to apply as I pursue my shepherd's task in these days. I invite you to join with me in earning authority as pastors, an authority we can earn only as we trust our Good and Chief Shepherd, the Lord Jesus Christ.

CHAPTER NINE

DEVELOPING TRUST ON A CHURCH BOARD

SOME OF THE GREATEST moments of my life have occurred during church elder board meetings. This may seem strange since board meetings have such a negative reputation, but it's true. They have been some of the richest experiences I have ever known.

Before I began pastoring, I had seen two models of pastor-board relationships. The first was a large city pastor with whom I interned early in my seminary studies. The night I arrived to begin my internship I was invited to a board meeting. However, I was asked to wait in an adjacent room while the board discussed a sensitive matter over which they and the pastor differed. The pastor spoke with such volume and force I heard every word and knew exactly what was going on. I might as well have been in the room. In that board I saw tension, efforts at control from both sides, and meetings that were more draining than energizing. The problem wasn't that there was tension between the pastor and the board— every board faces tension sometime or other—but that the pastor and the board had never established a relational basis for resolving conflicts.

The other model I saw was a church that showed me the essence of pastoral authority. The pastor and the elders worked together as a team, not as adversaries, and trusted each other implicitly. Relationships were at the heart of this board. It was these values that I worked to establish in our new ministry at South Hills Community Church, in San Jose, California.

I was so naive about leadership when we started South Hills that I didn't even consciously think about building trust with the elders. We took four months in planning to plant the church and another five months to get it started. Our time of praying and planning brought us together and helped us build trust in each other. Although we had moments of tension and disappointment, we never lost the trust God gave us in the very beginning.

TRUST DEFINED

When I speak of trust I mean *confidence earned from others through an intimate observation of our character and actions over an extended period of time.* People know us, and know us well because we enter into relationships with them that allow them to see us with our families, in private, in public, in one-on-one settings, as well as with large groups. They observe us in just about every way possible: when our guard is up and when our guard is down, when we're fresh and when we're fatigued, when we're encouraged and when we're discouraged, day in and day out.

The more consistent we are in our behavior over time, the more other people of integrity will know they can count on us. They will know

- when we respond and when we react,
- when we are predictable and when we are unpredictable,
- how to approach us and when to avoid us,
- when we care and when we don't.

Ultimately they will know whether we are worthy of trust, and they will give us exactly the amount of trust we earn.

Much of what they learn about us will come in the elders' meetings when they see us in those small-group settings. During these times we can't hide our true selves since they will know we are hiding, and this will cost us trust. Nothing is hidden from the elders in the intimate settings of our meetings with them. Since this is true, elders' meetings become one of the most important times in our ministries when we either build or lose trust.

TRUST LEARNED

Love God and Work Together

I'm sure your meetings are like ours were—often fatiguing as we came together after a long, hard day's work. Still our meetings were almost never draining. The ideas, vision, time of prayer, time in the Word, time of waiting for God to bring about resolution of differences, working toward unanimity—these things showed what a group of men who love God and each other looked like when they were working together. This is why I say some of my life's greatest experiences were elder board meetings.

We learned to trust each other *in times of decision*—to start South Hills Community Church, to hire staff, to build a building, and so many more decisions that took time and energy but always built relationships.

We learned to trust each other *through times of prayer*—for a widow who lacked funds and was raising her granddaughter, for the anointing of a woman diagnosed with leukemia, for a family in terrible trauma because of a murder, for effective ministry Sunday by Sunday, for all the supernatural needs of a church.

We learned to trust each other *during times of risk*—for struggles leading to church discipline, for the carrying out of church discipline when we wrestled with its impact on the church, for the restoration of broken marriages, for financial resources.

In all these situations our relationships were strengthened through our common dependence on God, and our trust in each other continued to grow.

There were other times, too, when I enjoyed refreshing fellowship with the elders:

- when I sought advice on how to deal with a particularly difficult, situation with my parents and received wisdom from the elders,
- when elders wept over strikes in the businesses they managed,
- when they had to fire incompetent employees,
- when elders struggled with harsh bosses,
- when an elder's wife faced cancer,
- when recently I had the privilege of going back to San Jose to speak at the memorial service of one of our founding elders.

These were moments of trust and support when men loved each other deeply. There were also times when I heard true words of rebuke that caused me to weep with a Romans 7 helplessness in the elders' presence.

Build on the Bible

What brought about such trust and love? This came because the elders were committed to the Lord and to studying the Bible and praying together; taking risks together in obeying God publicly and privately; ministering together in everything from information meetings to church discipline; and opening up our lives to each other in times of mutual evaluation.

How did this come about? Why was my experience so great when the experience of others has been so difficult? I don't fully know, though trust came as we carried out the following principles.

Commit to Serve

The elders and their wives were committed to serving Christ. Their families were Christ-centered, and the elders were totally supported by their wives, who teamed together with them. Among the board members there was a broad span of careers and temperaments that ranged from the highly relational to the highly technical, yet none of that got in the way.

Give the Ministry to the Saints

I believe the ministry belongs to the saints, so I gave it to them. The elders were my peers, and I was theirs. There was no distance between us in terms of position or power; I submitted myself to them, and they to me. We mutually evaluated each other annually not only as employer/ employee but also as brothers in Christ growing together. Sometimes what they said to me hurt, but it was mostly true and always said in love. I needed them to pray with me, and I told them so. In response they came every Sunday morning at eight o'clock to pray with and for me. I did not attempt to control the elders to get what I wanted. I didn't and don't have enough political savvy to pull that off. Instead we talked together about our hopes, our dreams, our thinking, and our plans.

We were not well managed—we got things done, but if I had been a better manager and leader, we would have accomplished a lot more. We did make many good decisions and at least one bad one—not to build a building. Initially that cost us, but we recovered and moved forward. We had some hard moments, times when some felt alienated and chose to resign. Part of that was my fault. In those days I did not know how to tell men I loved them nor did I know enough about temperament differences to appreciate them or communicate how much I needed those who were different from me.

Center Your Meetings on God

In our meetings we focused on three things: the Word of God, prayer to God, and ministry for God.

Every meeting began with Bible study, and each elder took his turn alphabetically. When we got to the L's, I led a study just as everyone else did. We prayed real prayers, personal prayers with tears in our eyes as we cared for one another. Boards are like families. The board that prays together stays together, but the prayers have to be real and personal, not some sort of official words elders are supposed to say. Over a period of time Bible study and prayer create a vulnerability that comes because of love and trust in God's presence. In fact, if there is anything I would say that is essential to building trust between a pastor and the board, it is that they spend as much time together as possible in God's presence.

Serve Together

We ministered together frequently as we gave accountability to the church for our decisions, taught the new members' class, or led other ministries, always in elder/staff teams. Every elder had a ministry in the church, and we attempted to meet biblical standards for everyone who became an elder. I'm not sure we always met these standards. And I'm sure I wasn't as qualified in those days as I should have been. Hindsight always gives you

20/20 insight into your immaturities, and I'm sure there were areas in my life that were not worthy of the title "elder."

Do the Hard Thing

We faced painful decisions together in relation to church discipline and when it was necessary to confront people with their sin, we did so in teams of two. We anointed and prayed for the sick. We struggled through tragedies of many kinds. We celebrated when God demonstrated His power through us. We wrestled together when I was offered a faculty position at Dallas Seminary and went through the resignation process, a decision I never expected to make.

TRUST EARNED

As pastors we must earn trust from a board. We do this in two ways, through competence and character.

Competence: Be Good at What You Do

Leaders respect—and expect—excellence in other leaders. The least you can expect from any leader, especially one who leads in Christ, is competence. Trust begins with competence. Each of us as pastors has a leadership trust account in our churches, an unseen but real level of trust that releases us to lead. The more we keep in our leadership trust account through competence, the greater our freedom to lead. Competence alone is not enough to maintain trust, but it gives you a significant start, because confidence from others begins with your competence. There are several areas in which you must be competent in order to gain trust from your board.

Competence in your family. Give your wife honor and respect at all times. Be gentle in nurturing and admonishing your children so they do not develop anger toward you that eventually undermines your ministry. When our three sons were very young, Lynna and I took them to dinner one night. While we waited for our food we talked with them and did activities together. Just before we left the restaurant, a man whom I had never seen before nor since walked over to our booth and said, "I have heard sermons before, but tonight I've seen one." I don't know who he was, but I'm grateful that the sovereign God protected me that night, because people did not always see sermons when I was with my wife and children. Occasionally my wife reminds me to be careful what I say when we are standing in line at church dinners or some other event. She knows we are being watched, and trust depends on the incidental and unnoticed ways we relate in unguarded moments.

Competence in the pulpit. As I work with pastors, I am amazed at the absence of excellence in their preaching. It's as if they never took a homiletics course, yet I know that many of them had some of the finest homiletical training available anywhere in the world. On graduation from seminary, however, they seem to decide that nothing is more irrelevant to the effectiveness of their ministry than preaching. As a result, they are disorganized, boring, and they often mishandle the biblical text. Pastoring is the only job I know of in which your impact depends on a thirty- to thirty-five-minute speech delivered the same time every week. With that much at stake, you'd think we would strive for the highest level of competence and excellence possible in our preaching, yet few do. To earn trust from your board, as well as from your church, seek to be the best you can in your preaching.

Competence in your relationships. Many of us are afraid of people because we don't know how to connect with them, so we distance ourselves and create barriers between us and others. Who can trust a long-distance shepherd? As Christ enables us, we must take the risk to relate and to become caring leaders. To gain trust in our relationships, pursue these steps:

- Learn to understand others. Stop demanding that everybody else be like you. Seek to understand others before you expect them to understand you.
- Learn to weep with those who weep, and laugh with those who laugh. Be real among your people.
- Learn to be teachable. You will have plenty of opportunities to develop this skill, since many critics will be generous in exercising their gifts of insight on your behalf.

- Learn to be vulnerable. Be willing to take risks and to admit your needs.

Competence in your service. You demonstrate care for your members through a willingness to support and encourage them in times of need. I'm sure many of you have had experiences similar to mine when I left South Hills Community Church to join the faculty of Dallas Seminary. The people gave us a large album of letters expressing their appreciation for what we had done during our twelve years there. Most mentioned some event of pain or joy in their lives when I served them. I had forgotten many of those occasions, but they hadn't. What mattered most was that I came. That builds trust.

I was not always successful in building relationships. I will never forget a conversation I had with a man who eventually became an elder in our church. It was the first time we spent time together, and we hit it off in ways neither of us expected. We visited over lunch for four hours. At one point this rather large man leaned across the table and said to me, "You know the question about you, Lawrence, is not, 'Can you preach?' The question about you, Lawrence, is, 'Can you relate?'" That was very penetrating. It was, in fact, the very question I had about myself when I finished seminary and entered the pastorate. I will never claim to be a truly capable "relater," but I will say that I am seeking through Christ to do all I can to grow in this area. Visiting with that man twenty-five years later, I reminded him of our conversation. He responded by saying, "You have learned how to relate." That's encouraging, and I hope it is increasingly true.

Competence in your management. You show leadership competence in how you manage. The way you manage your office, the way you manage money, the way you manage meetings, the way you answer questions and concerns from the flock you serve—all these reflect your level of effectiveness as leaders. Competence earns respect, and respect brings trust.

Seven Actions Guaranteed to Earn Trust

Be on time for all appointments. Punctuality says many things about personal competence. It tells others that we have the discipline and self-management to leave on time for an appointment without trying to get "just one more thing done"; we have exercised forethought in planning before the appointment, so we come prepared to use the time well; we don't think we are more important than others; we respect other people because we recognize their time is as valuable as ours; and we care for them enough to be interested in their concerns and to value what's on their calendars.

The simple discipline of being on time says far more about us than we recognize and earns us greater trust than we realize.

If you make a promise, keep it. When you do what you say you will, you show you are a man of your word. Few things build more trust than reliability and faithfulness. Think of those people you know who consistently keep their word. You never have to worry that they will let you down or offer you useless excuses because they couldn't deliver. When you want something done, they're the first people you call, aren't they?

Do you know where this trait shows up most consistently? In the so-called "small things" like returning phone calls, answering letters, remembering appointments, and responding to requests. Try to return every phone call on the day you receive it, even if only to set up a time when you can talk longer.

Make every effort to handle each piece of paper once. Sometime ago I learned an acronym for handling paper that has helped me immensely. It's the word *TRASH*, and it goes like this. You can do one of five things with every piece of paper you get.

- *T: Throw it away.* Before you throw a piece of paper away, ask yourself two questions: Who else has this information that I can call on when I need it? What will happen if I don't keep this paper? If the information on the paper is easily obtained from someone else responsible to keep track of it or if nothing harmful will happen if you don't keep it, throw it away.
- *R: Reroute it* to someone else who needs it more than you do.
- *A: Act on it* by doing whatever it calls for in accord with your assigned tasks.
- *S: Save it* by putting it in a place where you can retrieve it easily.
- *H: Halt it.* If you have no need for this piece of paper, notify whoever sent it to you not to do so again.

You will be amazed how much trust the proper handling of paper will earn you from elders and everyone else. A volunteer or administrative assistant can help you in responding to telephone calls, letters, and memos. Try to find someone who can draft letters for you; then you can add your own finishing touches. This person will not only make you more responsive to mail, you will also save time since writing letters can be one of the most time-consuming tasks many of us face. Work in every way possible to do what you say you will do.

If you start something, finish it. This shows that you can plan, implement, and deliver, that you do not make false starts, and are not marked by empty talk. It shows that you can be counted on not to quit when you run into some discouraging and confusing difficulties. No doubt after you've completed a difficult task, someone has said to you, "I really respect you because you stayed with the task when others would have quit." That's when the competence of finishing what you start earns trust.

Remember to say Please and Thank you. These simple good manners show respect and honor for others. They express a kindness that demonstrates regard for those who help you, since inevitably we say Please and Thank you to people who are assisting us in some way. This shows we do not have a demanding or assuming attitude toward others.

Spend time together. One of the most significant ways to build trust is to spend time together with elders. Besides the board meetings, spend time in things like retreats, lunches, breakfasts, recreation, and other activities that contribute to building relationships. The most significant thing we can do to have efficiency in our boards is to build relationships that create a web of trust which becomes virtually unbreakable. Have social events that bring everyone together. In my church, after every elders retreat the group, including myself, had dinner with their wives in order to help them understand why they were left home with the children and the lists of chores that remained unfinished for yet another week. We also invited the wives to meet with us once a quarter for a potluck dinner and a discussion of some topic. We never broke confidence concerning the private things we knew, but we involved our wives as much as possible, and they appreciated it greatly. In fact, it was amazing to see how their resistance to some of our meetings dissipated when they understood more fully what we were doing.

Focus on purpose. People trust each other when they know they are all going together in the same direction and along the same route to an agreed-on destination. New board members may have a different understanding and expectation of what the elders should be doing. They may attribute wrong motives to other board members or to us as pastors because they measure us by inappropriate standards. We need to work with new board members in orientation experiences so that they understand the church's purpose, values, and vision and don't attempt to take us places we do not want to go. This is especially true as older members are rotated off the board and newer and/or younger members come on.

Build faith memories. We earn trust each time we commemorate God's doing something for us that is special and unique. Perhaps we stack a pile of rocks near the driveway as a memorial to God's miraculous provision for a new building. Perhaps we have a special celebration event for some unusual thing God did. Whatever it is, we need to build "faith memories" so people around the church are saying, "Remember when...." Then we are trusting God together, and this builds trust in each other, a trust that will continue long after you are gone. Remember, when God acts through you, people trust you. For this reason, we all need to make sure it is God who is working through us.

Character: Be Good at Who You Are

Grow in character. To become better at what we do, we need to become better at who we are. If we become competent in the areas I just described, we will grow in character and show others who we truly are. Doing and being are intrinsically connected because the public and the private can't be separated in anyone's life. If we love our wives, others will see we are sacrificing ourselves for them and will recognize our caring character. If we nurture our children in gentleness and encouragement, we demonstrate self-control, patience, understanding, and compassion. But we can be good fathers only if we are good men.

Sometimes we are poor at what we do because of a character flaw. There is a direct correlation between character and competence. We fail to prepare on time because of character; we fail to delegate because of character; we fail to make difficult phone calls because of character; we fail to be available to others because of character; we strive to control others because of character. *To be good at what we do, we have to be good at who we are.*

Deal with character flaws. Consider the relationship between preaching and character. What keeps us from being vulnerable in our preaching? Fear in our character. What keeps some of us from preparing to preach well? Fear that we'll fail or even that we'll succeed and have to live up to it next week. If we preach poorly, we attempt to make up for it in other areas like visitation, counseling, or administration. However, nothing can really make up for poor preaching. What keeps us from finding good illustrations for our preaching? Often it's laziness. What makes us overprepare our sermon content and underprepare our applications? Many times it's because we fear we'll be wrong in something we say. As a result we overload people with information and don't show them a way to connect the truth to their lives.

Phillips Brooks defined preaching as "truth through personality." In our personalities—that is, our characters—we must strive to be as true as the Word we preach. Of course, this is not possible, but we can make a genuine effort with the Lord's enabling to grow toward this standard. Our listeners will recognize our desires and trust us accordingly.

True competence grows out of true character. If we strive to be competent in our families, our preaching, our relationships, and our leadership, it won't be long until we run into huge barriers in our character. Then we are forced to choose between laziness and discipline, fear and faith, control and trust. Then we are forced to face our character flaws before we can grow in competence, or we'll have to try to cover up what is obvious to all. The commitment to grow in competence brings us face to face with the realities of our character. The elders around us know this. That is why they respect and trust us when they see us make a determined effort to be good at what we do and who we are.

Live the truth. One of the most significant ways we earn trust as Christian leaders is through our conduct. Consider the way our wives and children respond to us. If they show respect for us, this will earn immense trust from others. No matter how hard we try to cover up the tensions and stresses in our homes, sooner or later the truth will emerge in the faces and body language of our wives and children. This is why 1 Timothy 3 calls for elders to have wholesome families.

Confess and be humble. We earn trust as we confess sin when someone points out disobedience in our lives. Remember, we must have loose shoelaces and stand at the head of the line when it comes to foot-washing time. We don't have to accept everything others say about us, but we do have to be prepared to consider seriously any comments made about our character, especially by an elder.

Love and serve. Another way we earn trust is in caring for and serving others. The more interest you show in your board members' personal lives, the more they will trust you. The more concern you have for their families, their business needs, and their fun activities, the more they will trust you. Remember the needs they tell you about and ask them how they are doing. Call them when you have a minute or two just to say, "I'm thinking of you." If possible, visit them at their place of employment. Send them notes and letters. Do things with them. Let them know you, just as you seek to know them.

Ask for help. Trust comes by asking for help from elders, and we gain trust when we extend trust by seeking assistance from others. One of the elders in our church was a manager for a local utility company. One winter Sunday afternoon the pilot light in my furnace went out, and I could not figure out how to get it lit, so I called him. This elder and I have entirely different temperaments, and I'm not sure he always felt comfortable with me, but I knew he was my friend, and I needed help. About fifteen minutes later he appeared at my front door in his jumpsuit with his tools, and that manager of hundreds of people got down on his hands and knees and worked until my pilot light was lit. I was probably the only person in all of San Jose to get a house call from the district manager of our utility company.

Months later he told me how good he felt when I asked him to help me. Because I gave him trust, he trusted me more and that strengthened our relationship.

Draw on board members' gifts. Ask elders to carry out ministry tasks in line with their gifts. One of our elders was a true shepherd, a man who cared for people and would do anything to help them. Often when a church member was in the hospital, I called and asked him to stop on the way home and minister to that person in need. I did this because I knew his visit would be a great encouragement to hurting people. It made him feel good to be asked, and he knew I trusted him. This built a relationship with him that continues to this day.

Lead well. One way we build trust is by leading the board in appropriate ways. When we work hard and demonstrate our competence, we build trust. When we communicate our vision in appropriate ways and do not have hidden agendas, which reflect a self-serving power play on our part, we build trust. When we don't manipulate but instead are openhanded in all we say and do, we build trust.

Without trust a church board will rapidly spin out of control and find itself broken and shattered at the bottom of a ravine. Although you as the pastor are not the only trust builder on the board, you are vital to the process. You will never earn trust unless you take the risk of giving trust— and giving trust is a huge risk. If you refuse to take that risk, you will end up angry, isolated, and cut off from your board. If you take that risk, you run the possibility of being misunderstood, confused, and wounded— and that's how you will earn trust.

Ultimately your ability to earn trust depends on your competence and your character. What you *do* and who you *are* establish the trust climate on your board. Take the trust risk; it's the only way to serve effectively.

CHAPTER TEN

———

FEED THE WIDOWS AND
STARVE THE CHURCH

MANY LEADERS feel church board meetings are a waste of time. Board meetings often lack a sense of direction and of defined goals. Church boards tend to concentrate on what comes next, and they rarely view the larger picture. If anyone asks, "What are we doing and why are we doing it?" few have answers. Those who do raise questions are often labeled unspiritual and unqualified to be members of the board. This is why many energetic and creative leaders choose not to serve on church boards.

Church board meetings don't have to be, and should not be, a waste of time. Church boards must become what I call "Q2 boards."

I'll explain later what "Q2" means. But we need to note first that a Q2 board is one that concentrates on the core of the church's ministry and delegates everything else to qualified men and women who serve with care and excellence. Q2 boards consist of leaders like those in Acts 6 who focus on purpose and core values based on a clear understanding of who they are and where they are going in God's will. In Acts 6:1–6 the apostles faced a fivefold dilemma as real as anything we meet in today's world.[1] There were issues of language, economic status, race, gender, and age. What could be more difficult to untangle? What could more legitimately demand a church board's attention? How could a board not get involved with this problem?

Many church boards choose not to be involved and to seek to find ways to avoid problems like this. Pretending the problems aren't there, they continue on their oblivious way until the church explodes, splits, and loses its testimony. This occurs because a board has no sense of its true task or courage to pursue God's purposes. One reason boards don't act on vital issues like those in Acts 6 is that they don't understand their purpose and core values. If they do become involved in such issues, they feel they alone must solve the problems, which means they fail to delegate properly and they become overinvolved. Boards must turn from both avoidance and excessive control. Otherwise, they spend their time on secondary concerns and miss what God is calling them and their church to do. Rather than invest their time, they will waste it, and the church will miss its mission.

The Jerusalem church was riding the crest of a Spirit-inspired wave. Three thousand people spontaneously responded to the gospel on the Day of Pentecost (Acts 2:41) and another five thousand came to Christ because of Peter and John's witness following the healing of the lame man at the temple gate (4:4). Although the initial thunderheads of persecution had appeared on the horizon, the first real difficulties the church faced came from inner stress rather than outer storms. The early church was made up of two kinds of Jews, those who came from Israel and those who were dispersed throughout the Roman Empire. The latter were called Greek (Hellenistic) Jews. There were radical differences among them, especially their languages, since the Grecian Jews did not speak Aramaic, the everyday language of Israel at that time. Throughout the Jewish world tensions existed between the Grecian Jews and the Aramaic Jews, and these strains stepped right into the early church with the early believers.[2]

The Jerusalem church assumed responsibility for its widows by meeting their daily needs. This ministry created tension because the Grecian Jews were ignored in the daily distribution of bread (6:1). Immediately we see issues of language (Aramaic versus many other languages), race (home-grown versus Grecian-born), gender (widows), economic class (these widows were poor), and age (most widows are older women).

How did the leaders deal with this problem? They had to solve it because the church's testimony rested on their love and sacrifice for one another (2:42–47, especially v. 45; see also 4:32–35). They neither avoided the problem nor made the mistake of becoming overly involved in meeting the needs. In this the leaders showed the courage of Q2 men leading in a Q2 way because they knew who they were and what they needed to do.

They based their decision on two key words, "right" and "neglect" (6:2). They defined what was right in light of God's purpose, and they refused to turn from His will no matter what pressure they felt. Their primary contribution to God and His people came through knowing, living, and teaching His Word, and they could not neglect obeying Him. The Greek word for neglect *(kataleipō)* means "to set to one side."[3] The point the apostles made was that they could not set the Scriptures aside, even when widows were at stake. The apostles understood their limited time and grasped what God wanted them to do because they knew their purpose and their core values. This is what made them Q2 men, and boards who follow their example become Q2 boards.

QUADRANT 2

When I speak of Q2 boards, I am taking what Stephen Covey calls Quadrant II in his time-management matrix and applying it to church boards. Covey developed these concepts in two of his books, *The Seven Habits of Highly Effective People* and *First Things First.*[4] Most of us evaluate time in terms of priorities rather than purpose. So if we are good time managers, we tackle the items of most importance, leaving the rest until later. Since there is never enough time for the rest, we tend to wait until they become pressing priorities, usually based on the impending doom of a deadline. We are getting things done, but we aren't able to measure the value of what we are doing. Without clear purpose and core values we cannot determine what things are truly first. Deadlines are a deadly way of deciding what should come first because deadlines are time muggers that subject us to the tyranny of the urgent and rob us of the important. These time muggers are one of the things that make church board meetings so ineffective.

Most church boards have no means of defining priorities because they rarely have stated their purpose and core values. As a result, they spend much of their time in Quadrants 1, 2, and 4. Often they focus on things others should be doing or on things no one should be doing. Either way, most important items never get on their agenda, let alone to the central place in their time and thinking.

We can divide everything we do into one of four quadrants based on importance and urgency. All activities are either important and urgent, important and not urgent, not important but urgent, or not important and not urgent. We see this through Covey's time-management matrix.[5] I have adapted Covey's chart significantly in order to relate it to the responsibilities of a church board.

	Urgent	Not Urgent
Important	**Quadrant 1**	**Quadrant 2**
	• Crises such as life-threatening illnesses, tragic physical traumas and deaths, church discipline, unexpected financial emergencies • Pressing problems, such as an unexpected resignation, city zoning concerns, staff or board tensions • Deadline-driven projects, meetings, preparations (for example, getting ready for the quarterly or annual congregational meeting)	• Bible study, theological concerns underlying evangelism, ministry and financial considerations • Prayer for the needs and future of the church • Contemporary cultural concerns and needs • Purpose definition • Values clarification • Financial practices designed to accomplish the church's vision and its values • Ministry development • Long-term planning for staff expansion and building projects • Policies for preventing damaging practices • Building of relationships
Unimportant	**Quadrant 3**	**Quadrant 4**
	• Interruptions to the stated agenda • Some reports • Some meetings • Many immediate and pressing matters • Physical repairs	• Trivia, busywork • Time waters, rabbit trails • "Escape" talk • Irrelevant topics

QUADRANTS 3 AND 4: TIME WASTED

Which quadrant on the chart do you think should receive most of a board's attention? I have already stated my answer when I call for Q2 boards, boards that focus on important but not urgent matters. Perhaps a better question is, Which quadrants on this chart get most of the attention in a typical church board? Of course the answer is Quadrants 1, 3, and 4. Quadrant 1 often deserves attention because we must attend to crises and pressing problems, as we see in Acts 6. Far too many boards spend their time in Quadrant 3 and even in Quadrant 4, and much of their activity in Quadrant 1 would never need to happen if they were focused on Quadrant 2. Adequate preparation, long-term planning, and relationship building will keep most crises from occurring and will iron out many pressing problems before they approach the struggle stage.

Likewise, if we think ahead we can avoid many of the stresses brought on by unnecessary deadlines. Some deadlines belong in Quadrant 2, but these deadlines will be anticipated, planned, and met in the normal course of board activity. They will not become tyrants, enslaving the board to the demands of the immediate instead of releasing it to the opportunities of the ultimate. A board that leads in the light of eternal purpose and core values focuses on the important before it becomes urgent.

Consider the time and energy lost in Quadrants 3 and 4. Just thinking about this is boring and fatiguing. The meeting is moving along, maybe even headed for an early ending, when someone brings up an unplanned item. It may be urgent, but it is trivial at this point or it would be on the agenda. The topic is unplanned, unevaluated, moves nothing forward, and is of little current value; yet the chairman and others tolerate it and chime in on the discussion. Now the meeting is stopped in its tracks and all hope of finishing at a decent hour is lost. Before the night is out, tempers may flare and many may leave frustrated and confused.

It could be a planned item, a report somehow made urgent by someone's pressing concern, but completely unimportant to the true needs of the moment. All reports should be short with a one-page preview, then distributed to the board ahead of time and read by all before the meeting in order for them to make the best use of time. Unless the board is dealing with administrative policies (either Quadrant 1 or Quadrant 2), all administration should be implemented outside their meetings by those authorized to do so. The board should delegate these concerns to trusted, qualified, and capable leaders as modeled by the Twelve in Acts 6.

Think, too, of the time that boards waste talking about physical repairs—the leaky roof, the stained carpet, lost keys, broken pipes, or the color of the walls in the third-grade room. Why do board members do this? Because this is what they think they are supposed to do—they feel secure dealing with such things. However, none of this belongs in any board meeting. Urgency makes very few concerns important. Unless a topic is important in its own right, as defined by the purpose and core values of the ministry, that topic has no right to demand the attention and time of all board members.

QUADRANTS 1 AND 2: TIME INVESTED

Quadrants 1 and 2, on the other hand, are legitimate concerns of all boards, and the more time a board spends there, the more productive that board becomes. Quadrant 1 is both important and urgent. As we see from Acts 6, many crises cannot be avoided because they demand immediate attention lest they escalate into divisive and destructive storms in the church.

All of us have experienced the awful and unpreventable force of tragic events running randomly and uncontrollably through our churches. There was nothing I could do to anticipate six simultaneous divorces in our church. Or the tragic death of a nineteen-year-old Olympic hopeful. Or the near death of a young father in his twenties. Or life-threatening cancer in an elder's wife. Or three key leaders moving to another city when we were in the midst of our building program. All of these occurred in a matter of months. These tragedies and difficulties made exhausting demands on all our leaders. These problems appeared on the scene like bandits out of the dark, and all we could do was give ourselves to fighting these intruders as long as they lasted.

Likewise, we may not be able to prevent the sudden resignation of a staff member, the bothersome resistance of the city zoning board to a new building, or petty and irritating tensions among church leaders. Perhaps we could have seen these things coming, but most postmortems are autopsies of the obvious—we did the best we could. Often Quadrant 1 *just is,* and we can't avoid it.

Even when we can prepare for certain events (for example, the quarterly congregational meeting), there is only so much we can do ahead of time. All information must be current, so we can't write up the final financial report until we count and deposit last Sunday's offering. Since this probably happens Monday morning and congregational meetings are often on Wednesday evenings, we cannot prevent a late Tuesday night for someone to get the report in final form. So boards must care about Quadrant 1 with its important and immediate demands. However, without a primary focus on Quadrant 2 and clear convictions about the church's purpose and core values, far too much time is spent in the other quadrants.

QUADRANT 2: TIME MULTIPLIED

Quadrant 2 is the area where boards can invest their most important time and energy. Yet few ever get there because so many Quadrant 2 concerns can be ignored with little evident loss. Ignoring Quadrant 2 is like skipping your annual physical; it may take a long time for the results to show up, but when they do, they are devastating. The real loss resulting from such dereliction of duty is insurmountable. What if the Twelve in Acts 6 had not measured the problem by Quadrant 2 standards? Weren't the widows' needs more important and immediate than studying Scripture? How could the apostles turn away from active involvement in the economic, racial, age, and gender injustices the widows faced? Yet they did, because the study of Scripture and the resolution of theological issues is the lifeblood of the church. Pursuing the apostles' teaching stands at the head of healthy church practices in Acts 2:42, showing that the knowledge of truth must precede the practice of ministry. If the Twelve had ignored the study of Scripture and the theological concerns that underlie evangelism, ministry, and financial considerations, they would have been feeding the widows but the church would have starved spiritually. Could anything have been more tragic?

QUADRANT 2: ATTENTION BEFORE ACTION

For the early church leaders the issue of justice in meeting widows' needs was a Quadrant-1 concern, a crisis worthy of their attention but not of their action. Instead they dealt with the issue by calling for the selection of seven godly men. The seven all had Greek names, suggesting they were trusted members of the Grecian Jewish community. They were the best men to meet the need, and in this way, the apostles maintained their true priorities while solving the problem. Without a Quadrant-2 mentality, the Twelve would have led the church into ineffectiveness and failure, but they didn't. What was Quadrant 1 for the apostles was Quadrant 2 for Stephen and his band. They were able to lead the church into greater spiritual prosperity while meeting the pressing physical needs they faced. They also kept their testimony and expanded their witness (Acts 6:7). What could have been wiser?

But how many church boards commit themselves to a Quadrant-2 mentality? How much time does the typical church board spend studying God's Word, considering the theological foundations underlying evangelism, ministry, and financial matters? How many church boards spend significant blocks of time in prayer, seeking God's direction for their ministry? Far too many boards open their meetings with a cursory prayer designed to baptize their deliberations, and then they "get right down to work." In other words, they sink immediately and completely into the quagmires of Quadrants 3 and 4. Little wonder, isn't it, that so few churches make the spiritually powerful impact the Jerusalem church made in its early history?

In fact, the Jerusalem church eventually lost its influence because their Quadrant-2 mentality was too limited to give them a vision for the whole world. Even though they were Quadrant-2 leaders, their quadrant wasn't big enough to include the Great Commission because they did not have a heart for Gentiles. As a result God scattered them throughout the Roman world. Then He used a nameless collection of Christians in Antioch to break through the cultural blinders of Jewish self-centeredness and reach the first Gentiles (11:19–30). All too often, contemporary Christians wear the same set of self-centered blinders and live with a Quadrant-3 commitment to their own security and prosperity rather than with a Quadrant-2 vision for the success of the gospel, no matter what it costs.

Definitions of Key Terms

These are definitions of terms used on the following pages.[6]

Purpose: The unique reason why an organization exists, the one thing it must accomplish, no matter what. The purpose, when properly understood and biblically founded, never changes.

Universal value: A value a ministry shares with the body of Christ at large which makes that ministry Christian, but does not distinguish it from other ministries in the body of Christ. Examples of universal values are commitment to the glory of God, the Word of God, prayer, dependence on the Holy Spirit, and the pursuit of the Great Commission.

Core value: A principle, standard, or quality to which a ministry unalterably commits itself, that lies at the heart of what it is and defines its identity. Ministries must be so committed to their core values that they would go out of existence rather than break a core value. As with the concept of purpose, core values, properly understood and biblically founded, rarely change.

Vision: A preferred picture of the future which guides the ministry toward the accomplishment of its purpose, while honoring its core values by means of implementing ministries.

Implementing ministry: A practice or program through which a ministry pursues its purpose and expresses its core values.

A vision is the sum total of an organization's or a person's purpose, universal values, core values, and implementing ministries.

BECOMING A Q2 BOARD

What must we do to have a Q2 board, a board that pursues the most important issues in the church and doesn't get lost in the jungle of nonessentials? To have a Q2 board we must take three steps.

Q2 Steps

1. Concentrate all board activities on your church's purpose, core values, vision, statement, and current implementing ministries.
2. Make all agendas Q2 agendas.
3. Keep all meetings focused and on target.

Let's look at each of these steps and consider how to implement them.

Concentrate All Board Activities on Your Church's Purpose, Core Values, Vision Statement, and Current Implementing Ministries

To accomplish this step, do the following:

Know your purpose. Make sure you know what your purpose, core values, and vision are. If you don't, you will have no measuring standard to use when making decisions about the direction and activities of your board. Without this your board members will frantically pursue many unimportant but urgent considerations that leave them exhausted and further behind than ever. At the end of their meetings their tempers will be frayed, their emotions on edge, their bodies worn out, and their time wasted, even though they have worked and worked and worked. Good people will not stay long in such frustrating situations. Unless you help the board focus on what really matters, you will never get to what really matters.

Know the difference between a core value and an implementing ministry. A core value is a timeless tenet, principle, standard, or quality to which the ministry is unalterably committed that lies at the heart of what it is and defines its identity. An implementing ministry is a practice or program through which a ministry pursues its purpose and expresses its core values. Many people, however, are confused about this distinction. For example, in many churches fewer and fewer people come to Wednesday night prayer meetings, often for good reasons. They live too far from the church to get there in the middle of the week, they travel in their jobs, both spouses work and have long commutes, and their children have demanding school schedules and other activities. Wednesday night is not a good night for many families to be out, so they don't come to prayer meeting.

Those who come conclude, "No one wants to pray anymore!" Is that true? What if Monday night were a better night or Sunday night or Saturday afternoon at five o'clock? What if homes in the neighborhood were more convenient places to meet for prayer? Does God hear people pray only when they're at a church building on Wednesday nights? Of course not, but some people seem to think so. They fail to understand the difference between a core value (prayer) and an implementing ministry (midweek prayer meeting at the church).

In the case of midweek prayer meetings the core value is the principle that prayer is central to the health of the church; the time and place when and where it occurs are unimportant. Our object is to get as many people as possible engaged in prayer. When we ask which is better, twenty people praying in one place on Wednesday night or eighty people praying throughout the community during the week, the answer is obvious. Prayer is the value; time and place are the implementing ministry. We must keep this straight, despite the fact that many people confuse these concepts. As a pastor, you know what is timeless (a core value) and what is timely (an implementing ministry). Lead so as to preserve the timeless and change the timely.

Be biblical. Be sure your purpose and core values come from the Bible, because this is the heart of Q2 board thinking. Biblical realities are always important, but not everyone recognizes them as urgent. Often there are more pressing items for the board to consider—squeaky doors, unmowed lawns, or someone's complaint about why the first-grade room wasn't open when children started to arrive last week. All these important items press on us with legitimate urgency, but they're not the primary concern of a board of elders. Biblical truth is far more important than these things; it just doesn't carry the same urgency. Yet the Bible is the one authority all of us recognize, the one authority to which we all must submit our thinking. Unless the Bible lies at the heart of everything the elders consider and do, the church will begin to drift from the eternal to the temporal, then to the banal.

In developing and leading your board, do not appeal only or primarily to church-growth principles, business practices, or organizational gurus.

Appeal instead to Scripture. If church-growth principles, business practices, or organizational gurus agree with Scripture, use them in a support role, but never replace the Bible with lesser authorities. It's tough enough getting the elders to submit themselves to Scripture; don't waste your time and energy with anything else until all are unified around the Bible.

Follow four steps in developing your purpose and core values. If you have never developed a common understanding of your church's purpose and core values, here are some suggestions to help you and your elders accomplish this.

- *Don't think for your board.* Help them consider difficult questions that will mature them and bring them together around God's truth. Don't let your mind be the only mind working on your board. No matter how bright we are, we all need more brain power than our own.

Early in my pastoring I wrote a paper on the purpose of our church. It was long and comprehensive and included every important biblical passage I could think of. My aim was to motivate the elders to become more "Great Commission conscious." After I finished writing it, I handed it out at a meeting. I can still see one of the elders put that paper down and look at me as if to say, "Okay, we're finished with that; what's next on your agenda?"

I realized I had made a terrible mistake. The paper did not relate to the elders because they had not considered the issue and had no sense of need for what I had prepared. In their minds it was not relevant to us as a church. I had not succeeded in making them more "Great Commission conscious"; instead I had treated them as if they did not know how to think for themselves in studying God's Word.

I learned from that elder's look that I needed to respect them by working with them rather than by thinking for them. I also realized I was still in my seminary mode—write the paper, hand it in, and you're finished. That's not how life works with elders. I never did that again.

- *Don't lecture your board.* As pastors we're used to giving lectures and thinking our job is finished. If Israel didn't listen to God when He spoke, why should our elders listen to us when we speak? We do not change our board members' minds by lecturing them. We may bore, anger, or turn them against us, but we rarely get them to think with us through lectures. We get our best results when we involve them in the process, but this takes longer than we want to take. The question is, Which is better, to lecture and lose them, or to involve them and get to our destination together?

- *Don't assume an authoritative position over your board.* We do this when we think for them, lecture them, boss them, or make demands of them. There are times when we need to issue challenges to the board, but these challenges should be as rare as a healthy person's need for major surgery. Serve your board by modeling godliness and by leading them by example into the greatest privilege possible—becoming like Christ and helping a church do the same.
- *Teach your elders to think for themselves biblically.* Show them respect by teaching them how to arrive at biblical answers to church problems. Suppose you want to determine your church's purpose according to the Scriptures. Follow the seven steps in this box.

HOW TO DETERMINE A CHURCH'S PURPOSE ACCORDING TO THE SCRIPTURES

1. Select the vital biblical passages that enable all of you to arrive together at what the purpose of the church should be.
2. Develop questions about each passage that will guide the elders' thinking toward this purpose.
3. Respect the elders throughout the process by encouraging them to think for themselves in the text. (Somewhere along the way you need to teach them Bible study methods so they are able to think and study independently.)
4. Select a date when the study of each passage is due and lead a discussion in the board meeting about the assigned portion. If one of the elders can lead the discussion effectively, ask him to do so.
5. Draw their conclusions together in a series of observations and ask each of them to write a purpose statement for your church.
6. Discuss each one's thinking and work together until you arrive at a mutually agreed-on purpose statement.
7. Be sure their conclusions are biblical. Guide them as necessary in the process so that they don't reach an unbiblical conclusion.

Don't be afraid to lead the elders or feel you are manipulating them. If you are manipulating them, stop, and then start leading them. They want your leadership and won't resent it if they trust your motives. Tell them what you are doing up front, so they know you are not hiding anything. Say something like this: "We need to understand God's purpose for our church. I have chosen several key biblical passages to help us understand this vital truth and I am giving you questions to guide you in your thinking. You're not limited to these passages or these questions, but they are the ones that will help us come together around the truths we need to grasp."

By doing this, you have told them exactly what you want them to do, how they can do it, and what they will have when they finish. You have also given them permission to think for themselves. Further, you have been up front in every way. Nothing could be more honest. This is leadership, and your board will thank you for it. If someone suggests an additional passage and it's appropriate, thank him and add it to the list for a future time. If it's inappropriate, either explain why in the meeting or ask if you can talk about it with him later and tell him why you don't feel it fits at this point in the conversation. Perhaps it will fit in when you consider another topic. Most elders will accept your leadership; boards want to be led more than many pastors realize.

Make All Agendas Q2 Agendas

Use a two-step filter. In planning an agenda, you need to run every potential item through a two-step filter. The first filter makes sure that every agenda item without exception relates to your purpose, core values, vision, and implementing ministries. If an item does not contribute to these elements, why is it on your agenda? Once an item has passed through this filter, you are ready for the second one, the Quadrant-2 filter.

The question here is, Into what quadrant does each item fall? Is the topic both urgent and important? Then it fits in Quadrant 1 and may belong on your agenda. If it's important, but not urgent, it's Quadrant 2 and definitely belongs on your agenda. If it's urgent but not important for the board, it doesn't belong in the meeting. However, if it's important to your church's ministry it belongs on someone else's agenda. It may be both urgent and important for the youth ministry, the worship committee, or the missions task force, but not for the board. Delegate this item to the right place, and keep it off the board's agenda. If you have items that are neither urgent nor important, be sure to keep them off your agenda. Those topics should not be taking the board's time.

One way to determine what belongs on the board's agenda is to create a Quadrant chart and write each item in the appropriate space. By doing this you will be able to decide quickly whether an item belongs in the board meeting. Of course, you should consider other factors such as timing and the treatment of a topic when planning board agendas.

Keep All Meetings Focused and on Target

Stay on target. There is one way to stay on target: Stick with the prepared agenda. Don't let anyone take the board away from the agenda; allow only essential exceptions. There might be a last-minute shepherding need, a potential church-discipline issue, an unexpected resignation, or a churchwide trauma—things that legitimately preempt a planned board agenda. There could also be a personal need in one of the elders' lives requiring prayer and support from the rest of the elders. However, unless there is a need of near-titanic proportions, stick with the agenda.

Don't allow idea chasing. In the course of a meeting many important topics can develop that draw the board away from the prepared agenda. The board needs to have some means of keeping track of these items by summarizing them at the end of the meeting and by including them in the minutes either as assigned items or as potential agenda topics for a later time.

Don't let anyone take you down a rabbit trail. Never become so involved in idea chasing that you knock the board off target. Some may object that you are so tightly controlled that God Himself couldn't get a word in edgewise. However, if you sense that God is moving you from your agenda to His, go with God. But usually agenda drift is due to our lack of discipline, not God's interruption.

Save time for God. The aim of all agenda planning is to be sure we are discerning God's direction for us and guiding the meeting in productive ways. The first and last step in every agenda planning session is prayer. Good agenda planning also treats church business efficiently. When you do this well, there will be time to concentrate on listening to God to hear what He has to say to the church. The better you administer the board, the more time you have to invest in unhurried prayer, Bible study, and relationship building among elders. This means fewer tensions in meetings, better trust among members, and less stress for everyone. Good agenda planning makes this happen.

Q2 BOARDS MAKE A DIFFERENCE

Quadrant 2 boards invest significant time in prayer, studying the Scriptures, and wrestling with theological issues of the day. They strive to break free from their own selfish concerns in order to understand the forces around them that are blinding unbelievers to Christ and His love. These boards lead their churches in defining God's vision for them and in living according to the values that demonstrate God's love to the unbelievers, just as the Jerusalem church did. They design financial practices to release the truth rather than restrict it. Their hands develop ministries that build believers and turn them from fearing unbelievers into those who love and reach the unsaved through God's irresistible power. Their knees bow before the sovereign God in praise of His grace and hope of His blessing. Their eyes look into the future as they plan to make a difference in generations to come. Their minds think in terms of expanding staff and building facilities that attract the committed and train them in ministries that glorify God. Their hearts grow in a love for each other that models care for all the church to see. This is the impact of a Q2 board. What could be more exciting?

CHAPTER ELEVEN

VISION OR VACUUM

WE LIVE in one of the most significant eras in history. Many people see this as a threatening time when all we believe in is being pushed aside by a horde of barbarian ideas thundering against us. They are tearing down our walls of protection and exposing us to frightening concepts we never thought we would see in our society. Therefore many of us are paralyzed and don't know what to do.

However, I believe we are living in a time of unparalleled opportunity. True, times are threatening, but God is still sovereign, and because He is with us we are living in some of the greatest moments in history. Consider what is happening:

- The children of divorce are growing up and deciding they want stable families.
- There is more overt interest in spirituality in our society than ever before.
- Evangelicals are more visible in our culture, inviting the highest level of scrutiny we have faced.
- The sexual revolution has proven itself deadly, and emptiness and futility are on the rise.

All these present us with great opportunities for ministry.

In the midst of the battle for the soul of our society, opportunities abound, but often we don't see them or commit to pursue them. To see opportunities we must have vision. It is here that our churches have a major choice—the choice between vision or vacuum.

Too often there is a vacuum in our churches, and we must fill the vacuum with a vision from God's Word. Many times the vacuum consists of a federation of church fiefdoms held in place by tradition and the influence of the people who lead them. Many churches do the same thing week after week with little or no understanding of what they are doing or why. They pursue a collection of tasks with no reason or purpose because they lack a unifying biblical vision that propels them into the future toward greater accomplishments. They erect no standards to measure their progress. They have no goals to guide them forward, no North Star to help them determine where they are going. They are lost, adrift, and don't even know it.

Such churches could be called treadmill churches. They think they are making progress; after all, they are working hard and perspiring greatly. The incline is getting steeper, but the impact is less than ever before. They are like a treadmill, a collection of moving parts all working together to tire everyone out while getting nowhere. "People don't seem to care the way they used to," they say. But people do care. They just don't care about churches that make no difference in their lives. Where there should be a vision propelling the church forward, there is a vacuum waiting to be filled.

To overcome our own isolationism and irrelevance, we need to develop a vision that not only protects the purity of our truth but also enables us to penetrate the world around us with our values. As defined in the previous chapter, a vision is a picture of the future which guides our ministry toward accomplishing our purpose. When we call men and women to serve as leaders, we must call them to the risk of an impacting vision, not to the safety of self-centered service. Our purpose is to change lives—first by changing those who are part of our fellowship and then, through them, those who do not know Christ. We must attract our people to a gripping dream, not a grinding job. Leaders grow into vision; those who have no vision grope in the dark for a reason to be alive. When tasks become tiring, our vision can enliven us to continue on. Unless we challenge the lethargic, they will remain lifeless and inert. But when we call them to new opportunities, the potential for new life is present.

The intensity of a vision combined with the magnetic pull of commitment makes it the fire of leadership. Vision is what ignites people's interest in following a leader. It creates a sense of confidence and significance in others, the awareness that they are undertaking a great task which, to some measure, depends on them for its accomplishment. As John Haggai put it, "Leadership begins when a vision emerges."[1]

All leaders must provide direction. Those who are effective at doing this possess five key traits.

- *Visionary*: The ability to create a picture of the desired state of affairs that inspires people to perform.
- *Communicative*: The ability to portray the vision clearly and in a way that enlists the support of others.
- *Persistent*: The ability to stay on course regardless of the obstacles encountered.
- *Empowering*: The ability to create a structure that harnesses the energies of others to achieve the desired result.
- *Organizational*: The ability to monitor the activities of the group, learn from mistakes, and use the resulting knowledge to improve the performance of the organization.

Although some people naturally seem to have several of these capacities to a certain degree, very few have all of them. However, they can be learned by anyone who is willing to work at developing them. Not everyone will be equally adept, but anyone who is in a leadership position is obligated to work at learning these traits. If you don't possess these capacities naturally, you must work to gain at least minimal skill in each area. Your effectiveness depends on this, since a pastor can't delegate the responsibility of developing and leading others toward vision.

It takes pastors of vision to guide a church off the treadmill and onto the pathway of impact. What is needed to replace a vacuum in the church with a vision from God? Three things: a proper understanding of what vision is, including the distinction between vision and a visionary; a proper understanding of the pastor's role in developing and implementing vision; a proper understanding of how to implement a vision, which includes patience, timing, and persistence.

Often I have felt as if I were in a treadmill situation, sometimes justifiably so, but many times because of my own personal dissatisfaction with myself. I've seen my frustration and inner anger soar as I wrestled with feelings of failure and resentment. How many times have we as pastors become bitter and lamented, "My people won't follow me"? That may be the case, but we must consider what vision actually drives us.

At times what drove me were career concerns, masked in "God words" rather than an absolute commitment to exalt Christ. As we begin to talk about vision, we need to step back from the fantasies that exalt us to positions of success and fame, and seek to know Christ more than ever. For too many of us, vision means our glory. But accomplishments are not to be for our benefit; Christ in us is our only hope of glory (Col. 1:27). Don't allow the concept of vision to move you from your great purpose: to know and glorify Christ by bringing others to know Him in the same way you do.

TRAITS OF VISION

Vision Is Future-Focused

This is so obvious it almost goes without saying, but vision cannot be thought of as moving the past into the future. If what we have always done is good enough for our future, we don't have vision; we have memories we are trying to live again. The Bible has a future focus that forces us to look ahead and that demands we develop ways to make a difference in the coming generations. Our task is to take advantage of the opportunities before us.

Vision Is Purpose-Centered

Purpose is why we exist; vision is a broad statement of how we plan to pursue our purpose and how we will implement it over the next three to five years. Purpose never changes; but vision changes as frequently as every year because needs and opportunities change that rapidly.

Vision Is Need-Driven

Vision starts with needs and moves to fulfillment. Vision is not smoke and mirrors, dreams in the night, or sudden revelations from God. Vision grows out of an awareness of the needs that surround the ministry and provide it with opportunities to make an impact. Vision sees needs as opportunities and responds accordingly. Further, vision describes what we will do to meet those needs by showing how we plan to go about serving those with the need. Besides having an overall purpose, we can have a vision for each dimension of our ministry.

Vision Is Realistic in Light of Available Resources

Wise leaders do not take on needs they can't meet, no matter how important or enticing the needs may be. Any leader who uses up resources he doesn't have loses the confidence of his people; they withdraw their trust. This means wise leaders are patient when pursuing vision. They work to achieve small wins and move their ministries forward toward their ultimate aims. Our resources consist of:

- finances
- people
- believers' spiritual gifts
- people's varying levels of personal stability
- people's varying levels of spiritual maturity
- physical property.

Wise leaders preserve their resources and invest them wisely.

Vision Motivates Others

Our vision must be attractive to our people. It has to grab their attention and make them want to be involved. The desirability of pursuing the vision motivates people; their confidence in the leader motivates people; the challenge of doing something greater than what has been done before motivates people. The vision-development process itself generates excitement as people see what they can do through Christ. Their anticipation of personal growth through the effort makes them want to be involved in both developing and implementing the vision.

Vision Empowers Followers

Vision empowers followers because it releases their gifts and motivates their service by showing them what they can do to make a difference for the Lord. They see an opportunity to do something with their lives that is bigger and more satisfying than anything they have ever seen before. As a result, they don't need guilt, shame, or rebuke to motivate them. Instead they have a challenge that has the ring of spiritual reality and lifts people above the smallness of the flesh.

THE RESULTS OF VISION

Vision Provides a Focus and Direction for a Ministry

Through vision the church gets off the treadmill and onto the pathway of glorifying God and impacting others. People now know why they do what they do. They also have something to aim for that is bigger than anything they are or anything they ever thought they could do. They feel that the status quo is no longer acceptable.

Vision Motivates People to Trust God

Vision motivates followers because there is something for them to do, a demand to which they can commit. It releases the energy of many spiritual gifts that may suddenly explode on the scene when followers see the vision for what it is and realize the leaders truly intend to accomplish it. People who have been held back by lack of opportunity are delivered from passivity to become engaged in ways they never dreamed possible.

Vision Unifies

People come together in a unifying commitment to the vision. At first there may be division, anger, even resistance when people discover you are serious and intend to accomplish the things you have been talking about. Yet if you communicate the vision properly, you will attract new people and awaken long-term members to the wonderful and challenging opportunities the vision presents.

Vision Measures Progress

A vision enables you to have a better idea of how you are doing, whether you are on the treadmill of futility or the pathway to fruitfulness. By having a vision you have provided a measure of objectivity and accountability that enables everyone to grasp where they are going.

Vision Helps Make Decisions

When vision aligns with purpose and values, it is much easier for the church to make decisions about what kind of ministry it will have, about how it should spend its money, about how it will engage people in the congregation in service. Such decisions are difficult when favorite ministries are at stake, but that makes vision even more essential.

THE DIFFERENCE BETWEEN A VISIONARY AND VISION

Having vision is a special ability, but it is also a process anyone can learn. Like the spiritual gifts of faith, giving, and evangelism, vision is something all of us must pursue. People with the gift of evangelism are more effective evangelists than those who don't have that gift, yet all are commanded to spread the gospel. Those with the gift of giving are more effective at giving than those who don't have it, yet all are commanded to give. All of us have faith, but some have a special measure of faith that enables them to trust God for things the rest of us would never dream of. Likewise, all of us can have vision; it's just that some will be more effective at it than others. As all pastors must do the work of an evangelist, so all pastors must do the work of a visionary.

Remember this: A visionary is not one who just talks vision; he is one who does vision. The talker has ideas; the doer has results. Don't be swayed by those who simply talk vision; seek to learn from those who do vision.

Also don't try to copy what others do just because they are visionaries. You are most effective when you are yourself, not when you become a copy of someone else. Study the process they followed, not the product they developed. Try to understand their mind. Think about how they thought when they developed their vision.

- What questions did they ask?
- How do they evaluate what they do?
- What observations did they make of their cultural setting?
- What kind of people did they involve in their approach?
- What did they do to determine the needs around them and to define their opportunities?
- How did they decide what not to do as well as what to do?
- How did they get their people to commit and become engaged in their vision?

Develop your process to arrive at your unique vision. Though all Christian visions will have many common components, not all will do the same thing, because the settings, needs, opportunities, and resources differ. That's why you can't do what others are doing in the same way; you must do it your way.

Don't resist learning from someone because his church is bigger than yours. Have you ever said, "I have a small church, he has a big church, and I can't do what a big church can do"? Of course you can't. You don't have the same number of people, the same amount of money, the same diversity of gifts, or the same opportunities. That doesn't mean you can't learn from a larger church. The underlying principles that pastor employed to develop and implement his vision are more important than the size of his church. Learn to discern his principles and to translate them into your setting. Creativity comes through the discipline of learning to implement the process, not through the laziness of copying someone else's success or the insecurity of refusing to learn because his church is bigger than yours.

THE PASTOR'S ROLE IN DEVELOPING VISION

Most often the pastor is the initiator and developer of the process, the one who involves others in the study of the Word, the study of the culture, and the development of the opportunities. But the pastor cannot be the exclusive developer of the vision. When I tried that, the elders watched me do the work. They had no real understanding of what I was trying to accomplish. Why? Because I didn't invite them to become involved with me. They didn't stop me; they just didn't get behind me when I tried to push the wagon up the hill. The fault was mine because I didn't bring them along with me, not because they didn't get engaged.

If we are to be effective in attracting others to develop a vision, we need to be willing to listen to them, hear their concerns, note their interests, and talk through their ideas with them, even when we know their thinking is not as good as ours. We may be able to do it better, but we'll end up doing it alone, and nothing we can do alone will be as effective as what the whole church does together. Even though we may need to slow our plan down in order to involve others, we cannot abdicate leadership. We are responsible to the Lord Himself for the health, ministry, and ongoing effectiveness of the church. Remember our Lord's warnings to the angels of Revelation 2 and 3. Although it is not specifically stated, it appears that when He spoke to the "angels" of the churches He was speaking to pastors or other significant leaders of those churches. The warnings show we must call our churches to vision and action.

Some pastors want to teach without leading toward vision, but they won't step aside for someone who can and will. They become a bottleneck and either shrink the church down to their comfort zone or control zone, or they end up fired and confused. If you are a pastor who has neither interest nor inclination in developing vision, then let someone else initiate the vision and you implement it in accord with your gifts. This would be better than losing out entirely because of fear or insecurity. We gain far more respect when we recognize our limitations and make room for others to exercise their strengths than we do when we seek to limit everyone to the sphere of our strengths.

FIVE GUIDING QUESTIONS IN THE VISION PROCESS

What Should We Be Doing? God's Commands

With this question we look at the biblical issue of what God wants us to do, the place to start when thinking about vision. Any vision that doesn't begin with God's revealed will cannot be a biblical vision. We must agree on at least two points. First, our target is the world, as Matthew 28:18–20 tells us. Second, our task is to equip the saints, as stated in Ephesians 4:11–16 and 2 Timothy 2:2. Everything we envision must include equipping the saints to reach some part of the lost world. If this is not part of the core, the vision lacks biblical support.

What Could We Do? The Culture

Our culture reveals our opportunities for serving Christ by answering the question, What are the evident needs for the gospel in this society? When we look through the lens of the gospel at the media, education, politics, and the private and public sectors of our culture, we see people hungering for identity, longing for integrity, lacking leadership, and experiencing false spirituality—all evidences that our culture is seeking spiritual answers to life's biggest questions.

What Can We Do? Our Church

Now we are ready to consider what we *can* do among all the things we *could* do. Here we introduce the realities of resources, the fact that our limitations allow us to meet only a few of the needs we want to meet. We are obedient when we reach as far as our resources will allow and then trust God to supply additional resources so we can take advantage of more opportunities.

What Will We Do? Our Commitment

At this point we make our commitment to pursue the vision we can accomplish through trust in God's presence and power. We are investing all of our resources and praying for more when we commit ourselves to the vision we have developed. Now we are counting on God to keep His promise that He will never leave us nor forsake us.

How Will We Do It? Our Conviction

From the vision we move to specific goals and steps that will transform it from an idea on paper to an accomplishment written on hearts. When we are convinced God wants us to carry out our vision, this conviction will give us strength to endure, no matter what obstacles we face. We are obeying God in a great work, and nothing will stop a committed church once the Holy Spirit's conviction grips it.

FOUR QUESTIONS ANSWERED BY VISION

Where Are We Going?

Our clearly defined and developed vision tells us where we are going by giving us direction and destination. Through this vision we know where we plan to be the next three to five years, as God enables. Of course God can change our direction, but at least we are now in motion. God can redirect us if He so chooses, but He is no longer working to get us started.

Who Is Taking Us There?

A good vision identifies the leaders who will be implementing the plan. The leaders don't have to be mentioned by name, but their positions and responsibilities must be defined in the plan. When appropriate, the church can have a voice in identifying these leaders. Most frequently, however, the staff and elders will know best who the key leaders are, and they should make these appointments.

How Will We Get There?

The vision tells the participants what specific steps should be taken. Will you be starting a new ministry? Your vision will tell you that. Will you be evaluating an old ministry? Your vision will tell you that. Will you be adding staff? Your vision will tell you that. Will you be increasing your budget? Your vision will tell you that too. A good vision helps everyone see how you will seek to get from where you are to where you want to be.

How Will We Know When We Arrive?

A good vision helps everyone involved understand what the ministries will look like when the vision is carried out. Many changes may come between now and then, but everyone knows exactly what you are aiming for. Because this is true everyone can

- pray about these aims,
- consider financial responsibility for these aims,
- understand how physical and financial resources will be invested to accomplish these aims,
- perceive what his or her role is in pursuing the vision,
- know what the church will look like when the vision is completed.

THE VISION-DEVELOPMENT PROCESS

Step 1: Pray

To avoid human presumption, pursue dependence on God. You do not want a plan you have dreamed up with goals that are not from God. Nor do you want to design your own desires and then "baptize" them as God's will. Therefore you must pray before, during, and after you develop the vision, as well as throughout the entire implementation process.

Step 2: Start with the Bible

The Bible must define your vision. To be biblical build your vision around four core factors: edification, exaltation, equipping, and evangelism. If these four elements are absent, it will be impossible for you to have a biblically based vision.

Step 3: Look at the Community around You

Define the needs you see around you and begin to discover opportunities God has for you. Look at your present situation by asking yourself the question, "What are our current circumstances?" This question gives rise to several others.

- What opportunities (needs) do we see now in our community?

- What resources must we have to meet these needs?
- What are our most obvious strengths?
- What are our most obvious weaknesses?
- What limits do we have that keep us from doing more to meet the needs around us?
- How long will it take for us to fill our internal needs so we can grow to meet our external opportunities?

The present state of your community demands research in order to determine what kinds of needs those around you have that you can meet. Perhaps you have some in your church who are particularly gifted in understanding the current culture. If so, they can be helpful to you in discerning the opportunities you have but may not see. Be sure to include youth and adults of various age-groups when you discuss societal needs. Young people give you important insights into the frontiers of our time. Don't forget to include senior citizens, the fastest-growing population group in the United States. Perhaps you will discover some exciting ways to reach octogenarians!

Step 4: Look at Your Resources

Determine the resources you need to develop the kinds of ministries you are thinking about.

- What kind of people do we need in terms of spiritual gifts and temperaments?
- How should we put these people together in teams so they can be most productive?
- What sort of physical facilities will we need to develop these kinds of ministries?
- What will it cost us to pay for these ministries?
- What kind of staff will we need to accomplish the vision?
- What kind of resistance will we face from people within the church who will not feel comfortable with the vision we are developing?
- What is the wisest way we can respond to the opposition both in and out of the church so we don't lose and/or alienate people unnecessarily?

Step 5: Look at Yourselves

Start with your past. Just as people are extensions of their past, so also are churches. Look especially at how the church got started. The vision of the founders often permeates the thinking of the church years later in unstated ways. The ideas you are developing may actually be at odds with the vision of those who started the church. If this is so, be aware of it because you need to understand you are departing from the original nature of the church. If you have good reasons to do so, go ahead. Perhaps you will discover your church was started to teach the Word, but what that really meant was head knowledge and not a burden for changed lives. If you are motivated by changing lives, you need to know you may be headed for resistance from some of the old-timers in the church. Ask yourselves questions like this: How did we get where we are? What have we achieved up until now? How did we achieve this? What helped us accomplish what we've done? What has hindered us from achieving more?

Research the past in order to gain insight into your origin, to understand God's past faithfulness, and to understand the influence of the past on the present, all of which will impact the future.

Stories about God's faithfulness from the past, especially in times of vision expansion, will help encourage the doubtful and the fearful. God, who has been faithful in the past, will certainly be faithful in the future.

Step 6: Look to God

Often we want to start with what we want to do, rather than starting with who God is and what He can and will do. When developing vision, always start with who God is and what He can do, never with what we can't do, or what we want to do. Take some time in the vision-development process to worship and praise God, remembering His faithfulness in the past, His promises for the future, and praying to Him about the opportunities you have for making a difference in your community.

This is especially important to do, even though you have already prayed and spent some time in the Word. It's easy in this process to forget about God and get caught up in what you're doing. This is a good time to reflect on who He is and to remember that He's in charge.

Especially look at what God is doing that you may not even be aware of. Ask the following questions:

- What is God doing in and through our church that we have missed?
- What stories can we share with each other about God's amazing power through us in our community?
- What does God want us to do to meet the needs around us, as expressed in His Word? (This is a review of the biblical question raised at the beginning of the process.)
- What is His capacity for accomplishing His purpose? (This gives you time to pause and consider the greatness of God, so that the size of the task doesn't overwhelm you.)
- What has He said in His Word and done in our past to assure us that we can do what He wants us to do? (Once again, a review of God's past faithfulness as well as a reminder of His future faithfulness from His Word will be encouraging.)

Step 7: Develop Your Vision

Define the parameters of your vision. In the early stages the most the leaders should do is establish the broad outlines of the vision. Do not do all the work for the church and then expect them to own the vision. People must be given an opportunity to participate in the process as much as possible, even when this may slow the process down. In the long run this will make for much greater ownership and therefore much greater participation.

Make certain, however, that these parameters include total obedience to God. People should participate in deciding *how* they will obey God, not whether they will or will not obey Him. There is no choice about this, although many will resist obedience because it forces them out of their comfort zone. They may also resist obedience because they are hearing things they never heard before or because they are learning new approaches they never saw previously.

Get people to "own" the vision. You help establish ownership of the vision by opening up a way for a large number of people in various church ministries to participate in the vision development. Be sure potentially competitive interests are represented in all phases of the planning. Never leave a group of "problem" people out of the process. Bringing people of differing opinions together in a unified way may tax your leaders' ability, but it will help unite the church around the final vision. Once you have done this, you will see your church moving forward with greater excitement, unity, and impact than ever before. The key leaders must set the pace and guide the process, but the more people you get involved, the greater will be their commitment to the vision. Once you have defined how you want the people involved, follow through with your plan, keep it moving, make it happen.

State your vision. After developing the vision, work to put it in the best language possible, using words that most accurately and effectively represent your conclusions.

Plan to accomplish your vision. After the vision is stated and accepted, develop a plan that will enable you to make your vision a reality. You do this when you establish the steps to be taken, assign the leadership you must have, recruit the participants required, and define the accountability needed. Make accountability specific according to the calendar and the budget.

Communicate your vision. Communicate your vision in as many ways as possible:

- from the pulpit;
- through interviews in Sunday school classes;
- through written materials;
- through specially called fellowships such as banquets, potlucks, desserts;
- through slogans and banners;
- through creative videos and dramas.

Communicate the vision in a variety of ways. Anything that people don't hear at least once a month will not be part of their thinking. So don't be afraid of overcommunicating your vision.

Structure to accomplish your vision. Once you have a new vision, you may have to redefine your organization so it will accomplish your plan. Design your organization to create relationships, communication, and unity. A good organization energizes people by being as flexible and nondemanding as possible so those involved can concentrate on what they're called to do together rather than fight their way through unnecessary barriers. Too often structure weighs people down because it takes so much just to keep it going.

Don't allow your plan to be limited by some structural sacred cow left over from days of long ago and given a biblical label it doesn't deserve. No form of church structure should be allowed to become permanent unless it is truly anchored in Scripture. *Biblical structure is always simple, flexible, vision-focused, and gift-releasing.* Remember that elders and deacons can fit into a lot of structures. Make sure your form follows the functions that your vision now calls you to accomplish.

Pursue your vision. Go after your vision with all your energy. Look ahead. Don't look back. Put your heart where you put your hands. Pray earnestly and often. Worship God. Trust Him. Don't question in the dark what you decided in the light. Go back to His Word again and again— especially in times of doubt, confusion, or uncertainty.

Evaluate your vision. Vision can and should change. You might make a mistake during the planning process. If you did, correct it. If it's time to change, change. Do not allow the vision to become a shackle that keeps you from moving toward fresh opportunities. But be sure the change you make is from God and not because of a lack of discipline or an unwillingness to follow through.

Occasionally review your vision to discern how appropriate it continues to be. Be sure it is doing what you thought it would do. If it isn't, change it. Keep going after the burden God put on your heart when you prayed, looked at the Word, considered what you felt He could do, looked at society, determined what you needed to do, and moved to do it.

Update your vision. Once you've evaluated your vision, keep improving it to make it more and more effective. Remember that the process of developing and implementing a vision is never finished. The needs of the world around us will never go away, and the opportunities to meet these needs will never decrease. In fact, needs and opportunities will constantly change. Therefore we must always be evaluating our vision to keep it as strong and clear as possible.

A RIVER RAN THROUGH IT

I end this chapter with a parable.

Once upon a time, there was a beautiful town, precious to all who knew it. A wonderful place to live. Families worshiped there. Children learned there. Businesses were successful there. Men and women loved to live there.

A river ran through that town, giving the community water to drink, irrigation for crops, fishing holes for dads and kids to be together, and beaches where families could swim, picnic, and have fun. In the wintertime when the river froze, there was ice-skating and ice-fishing. It was a wonderful town, thriving alongside its shimmering river.

But one day some dads took their children fishing and discovered the river was drying up. Their favorite fishing hole was gone because the river had receded from the banks. Then they noticed their swimming holes were not as deep as they used to be. Word went out across the town that their river was dying and their lives would be changed forever.

The city fathers met and determined something should be done. One said, "Let's go to the mouth of the river to see what's causing it to dry up." So they set out walking along the banks of the river, tracing it across the valley and into the mountains nearby, until finally they came to its source, a mountain spring. There they saw trees and rocks and brush blocking the spring and shutting down its flow. Immediately they cleared away the brush, and the spring began to flow freely once again. Near the spring there was a cabin. Some of the men went into the cabin and found an old man slumped dead across his kitchen table. They never knew this old man was the keeper of the spring—that the life of joy and delight their river brought them was a gift from the keeper of the spring. They had seen him come to town occasionally, buying supplies and driving off toward the mountain in an old pickup truck. Little did they know they owed their town to this old man, the keeper of the spring.[2]

As pastors, you are the keepers of the spring that gives life to your church—the spring of vision from God and His Word. Don't let the underbrush of tradition, the fallen trees of inflexible structure, and the rocks of willful disobedience hinder your church from bringing the Water of

Life to your city. Keep the river of vision flowing through your church and into your community so children can learn of God, so neighborhoods can be reached, and so families can worship. Then your church will bring the Water of Life to all.

CHAPTER TWELVE

PLANNING FOR NONPLANNERS

EARLY IN MY MINISTRY I was influenced by a church that resisted planning. The founders of this ministry had come out of well-structured but powerless churches that were held in a death grip of tradition. Their plans served as braces to support them, but their paralyzed perspective kept them from making more than a crippled effort to serve God. In contrast, the ministry they started was marked by a spiritual dynamic I had never seen before, and I was attracted to them because of the life-changing power I saw working in and through them. So when they said that not planning was one of the keys to their power, I said "amen" and did likewise. Eventually I realized the key to their power was not their lack of planning but their unadulterated dependence on Christ. I was caught in the tension between God's sovereignty and my responsibility as a pastor and I found this tension difficult to overcome.

IT'S THE HOLY SPIRIT, NOT THE PLAN

How do we live with the tension between planning and faith? There is an innate stress between making plans and trusting God, and some of us have never understood when our planning gets in God's way or when it guides us into God's will. Many argue that planning is wrong because when we plan we attempt to do what God alone can do. I regret I once believed this, because such thinking cost me greatly as a pastor. Many of the things I could and should have done did not get done, and I became frustrated in what was a satisfying and fruitful ministry.

Through this experience I discovered if we substitute anything for Christ in us, whether planning or not planning, we are powerless. It's just that people who don't plan are powerless in a disorganized way, while people who do plan are powerless in an organized way. What's the difference? When the power plug is pulled because we don't depend on the Holy Spirit, nothing happens, whether we do or don't plan.

Planning can get in the way of the Holy Spirit, but so can the failure to plan. We saw this in Acts 6:1–6, where we noted that widows were treated unjustly because no one thought to organize the daily distribution of food to them. When people go physically hungry because we don't plan, we act to correct the problem with a plan. Should we not do the same when people go spiritually hungry? Isn't it amazing how we credit a secondary issue such as not planning for our spiritual success when the Holy Spirit is our only source of success? As pastors, we must stop crediting secondary factors with primary impact. *What we need to do is learn how to plan so we don't get in the Spirit's way.*

Some argue that planning gets in the way of relying on the Spirit because we depend on our plans rather than on God, so we're better off not planning. Well, we depend on money for ministry, don't we? We also depend on all kinds of physical resources such as buildings, telephones, and computers. Would we be better off without these things? These are all means, tools, that God uses to accomplish His purposes. Interesting, isn't it, how some planning doesn't get in the way of the Holy Spirit while other planning does? We don't think retirement planning gets in the Spirit's way, but many think ministry planning does. That's a strange way of thinking for leaders who have the greatest stewardship in the world in their hands. The answer is not to get rid of planning, but to plan in a way that leaves us dependent on Christ.

MORE BAD THAN GOOD

One of the reasons I responded to the idea of not planning is that I am not a planner by nature. My natural bent is to feel my way along, make decisions on the run, keep moving, and make things happen. This approach works well in some situations, but not in most. It doesn't work in the pastorate because it doesn't move a church toward its most effective impact. Too many good ideas end up as words lost in space because no one ever suits them up, puts a rocket under them, and launches them toward a goal. More bad than good happens when we fail to plan. The following are some of the reasons we don't plan.

We Don't Know Where We're Going

For one thing, we're never sure where we're going. We seem to be headed in one direction, then suddenly we change to another. People can't figure out what's happening; communication breaks down; followers end up going in two or three different directions at the same time; tempers rise; confusion reigns; key leaders quit; we are left with those who don't mind being lost and going nowhere. As a result, we watch while other pastors do what we thought of but couldn't implement because we failed to plan.

We Don't Know Where We Are

Because we don't know where we're going, we never know where we are. How can we know whether we're on course if we don't have a course to be on? Because of this, we tend to put our hand to whatever comes along without evaluating it in any way since we have no standards by which to measure our decisions.

We Start Too Much and Finish Too Little

For most pastors, the failure to plan will mean many things started, few things finished, no dreams fulfilled—and much blame for all. We complain that the staff isn't supportive, the elders don't deliver, the deacons can't decide, the congregation won't cooperate. But the real problem is that the pastor won't plan a course of action that all can see and support.

We Don't Make Commitments

One of the advantages of not planning (if we can call this an advantage) is that we don't have to make any commitments. Many pastors refuse to plan because planning means they must give up control and trust others. Planning demands commitment to the goals that the plan develops; otherwise, planning is a useless waste of time. Goals make us accountable to others, and accountability demands mutual trust. When I lead a team that has a plan, I know their goals, and they know mine. We become mutually accountable, so trust must become mutual as well. Just as I know when they're accomplishing their goals, they know when I'm accomplishing mine. Each week as we discuss our progress, I must report to them how I'm doing just as they must report to me how they are doing. I have to lead in giving accountability and extending trust or I fail as a leader. Planning makes the same demands of both leaders and followers.

Planning helps reduce the superior/subordinate difference and helps us see that in the body of Christ we are brothers and sisters. For some pastors, accountability is fine for everyone but themselves. They have no intention of entrusting themselves to anyone, so they resist planning because it demands accountability and trust. Of course, none of us admits this. We just use spiritual words to cover up our fear.

We Aren't Willing to Pay the Price

Other pastors don't plan because they don't have the discipline it takes to stick with the process and produce the results required once the plan is outlined. Planning is a grinding process in which you look at every possible option, decide which is best in light of your purpose, values, opportunities, and resources, and then lay out your proposed aims over the next three to five years. It takes time and it takes effort. It is demanding and frustrating, and many pastors aren't willing to pay the price either to plan or to implement the plan. They, too, cover up their flaws with spiritual words.

We Have Character Shortcomings

It's amazing how much the issue of character lies at the root of our resistance to plan and delegate. So much of what we do or don't do relates directly to who we are, and so many of our high-sounding reasons for not doing something really come from some low-driven motives.

Neither the issue of excessive control nor the lack of discipline is a skill issue; both are issues of pride and tests of character. Pastors can overcome both of these issues by choosing to trust the Spirit and humble themselves before the Lord. I have found there are others on our team who are better strategic thinkers than I am, so I have had to give them the responsibility to lead in this area even though organizationally they report to me. Leaders can't drive the car everywhere it goes. We earn respect and attract the most talented people to our teams when we are willing to acknowledge our gift limitations and character flaws.

When it comes to limitations, we should strive to recruit workers who can complete our deficiencies, while we focus on what we do best. For those of us who are not strong strategic planners, this means we search for others who are and let them lead the way in this area. On the other hand, when it comes to character flaws, we must confess them and grow in freedom through the Holy Spirit's power and the help of others. This calls for humility and accountability from us even as it does from all believers. Though this is painful, we should confess our sin quickly with genuine humility because, no matter how painful this is, it doesn't compare with the pain of having our ministries fall apart around us or of being fired.

The point of this discussion is that we must learn to live within the tension between divine sovereignty and human responsibility in all aspects of our lives, including planning. Certainly there are many biblical examples of planners. Let's look at some of them, starting with God Himself.

PLANNERS IN THE BIBLE

God

God is a planner—He has planned all of time and eternity. Since we are made in His image, we, too, must be planners. Of course we can't plan our lives in every way. Only the sovereign God has the power to do that; only the omniscient God has the knowledge to do that; only the holy and loving God has the right to do that. God's sovereignty always includes human means such as planning and praying.

God reserves the right to redirect any human plan with His own unforeseen twists and turns. These twists and turns are often confusing to us, but time usually clarifies them and shows them to be part of a plan that is better than ours. As we plan, we must remember the somber warning God issued to the people of Judah through Isaiah. "'Woe to the obstinate children,' declares the LORD, 'to those who carry out plans that are not mine, forming an alliance, but not by my Spirit'" (Isa. 30:1). This passage tells us God has plans, and this means our task in planning is to strive to do His will and make His plans our plans.

Moses

While visiting his son-in-law Moses in the wilderness, Jethro observed Moses acting as the sole judge in Israel (Exod. 18:13–14). Jethro saw immediately that Moses was overwhelmed by the number of cases he had to hear, so he suggested a court system that established judges at every level of the nation (18:17–23). Moses still dealt with the most difficult cases, but he had the help he needed to bring justice to the people fairly and quickly without ever turning from his primary leadership responsibilities. Isn't it interesting that there was no justice without a plan? The same was true in Acts 6:1–6.

Joshua

Joshua, like his mentor Moses, was a planner. He planned battles, sometimes with God's input, as at Jericho and Ai, but frequently with no specific direction from God, as in the battle with the kings of southern Canaan (Josh. 10:1–11). In this instance God gave Joshua the assurance of victory, but He did not give a complete plan (as at Jericho; 6:2–5) or a partial plan (as at Ai; 8:1–2). Apparently Joshua devised the battle plan in this and other situations when he had no direct revelation from God, although he learned from both the sin of Achan (7:1–26) and the deception of the Gibeonites (9:1–27) how risky it was to plan without consulting God in prayer.

Nehemiah

Confession, planning, and prayer form a great pattern for planners. Nehemiah had to plan or he could never have rebuilt the walls of Jerusalem in fifty-two days (Neh. 6:15). But his plan was bathed in prayer. In fact Nehemiah told us of his intense prayer—"I beseech thee, O LORD God of heaven, the great and terrible God"—as he cried out for Jerusalem's restoration (1:5, NASB). This leader called out to God in confession, then planned, and then prayed for grace when asking the king for the help he needed. Nehemiah 2:4 tells us of his "quickie prayer," an aside he silently spoke to God before he answered the king's inquiry about what concerned him.

We can be certain Nehemiah had a plan in mind when he spoke to the king because he asked God to make him successful in gaining compassion from Artaxerxes (1:11), and because he had a definite time in mind for how long it would take him to rebuild Jerusalem's walls (2:6). Later he prayed when he and his workers faced opposition while they were building the wall (4:5–6). Each time Nehemiah faced a new crisis of opposition, he planned and prayed, until he prevailed against his enemies. Few men planned better or prayed more than Nehemiah.

Jesus

Jesus had a plan to develop His disciples, which becomes evident as the Gospels unfold His identity and His purpose. Although His plan is never stated in specific detail, no one can deny the fact that such a plan existed in His thinking.[1]

- He summoned His disciples to a specific task (to become fishers of men).
- He taught and trained them in preparation for a specific assignment (to go out and speak His words and minister two by two).
- He called them to trust Him more as He prepared them for His departure (the feeding of the five thousand and the walking on water).
- He revealed the Cross to them only after they acknowledged His true identity as the Christ, the Son of the living God.

- He told them of His expectation for the future. (They would eat the Passover meal with Him when they would all be together again in the Millennium.)
- He prepared them for His resurrection (by telling them to meet Him in Galilee).
- He commissioned them to go into all the world.
- He promised them He would come back.

Paul

Paul, too, planned diligently at every turn. His specific strategy included the following:

- He went only to key urban centers.
- He started in synagogues or with a handful of Jews if he could find no synagogue.
- He established churches made up of those who trusted Jesus as their Savior.
- After a period of time he appointed elders and brought the church to a place where it could be self-sustaining.
- When he stayed for an extended period of time, as in Corinth and Ephesus, he built up the church so it reached others in its city and also planted churches in neighboring cities.
- He stayed in touch with all the churches he planted, sometimes returning for follow-up visits or writing an epistle to encourage a particular church or to call it to purity in doctrine and practice.

Each of these biblical leaders (including the Son of God) had a plan and implemented it under God's hand. This shows us not only that planning is right but also that planning is essential. The key is to plan the right way, and that means relying on God in all our planning.

HOW DO WE RELY ON GOD WHEN WE PLAN?

We can answer this question by discussing some guiding principles to help us turn from our own selfish interests and to focus on God's interests when planning. Though we must make every effort to turn from self-interest, we must also realize that we can never fully overcome our hardened hearts. For some, this is reason enough not to plan. Such people seem to think that by doing nothing they do no wrong, but that idea is false! Apparently they forget Jesus' words to the servant who did nothing with the talents his master gave him. He lost what little he had to the servant who went out, planned, implemented his plan, and made the most profit (Matt. 25:18, 24–28). The problem with many people who resist planning is that they use spiritual excuses to mask their real motives: laziness, fear, and a passion for comfort in their lives. The need is for the right kind of planning, and this begins with a plan for planning.

PLAN TO PLAN

Plan to Obey

Because we are committed to loving Christ and because we love Him when we keep His commandments (John 15:9–10), our first aim in planning must always be to obey Him. All obedience to Christ comes down to two things: loving God with all our heart, mind, and soul, and loving our neighbors as ourselves (Matt. 22:36–40). To do this, be certain all your plans help others love God and each other more. If this is not the case, you have a poor plan, no matter how good it may look on paper. We should not plan events that enhance people's careers at the expense of their obedience to Christ, nor should we allow those who serve with us to plan activities that build their budgets or their egos instead of building believers to obey Christ. Further, our churches should not plan functions that establish their reputations more than they establish their members in the faith. All such plans are unbiblical and ungodly and accomplish nothing for God.

Our plans must encourage relationships, not use people or wear them out because of the demands we place on them. For this reason, when you plan, have a Bible in one hand, pen and pad in the other, and both knees on the floor. If we can't demonstrate that what we are planning will enable those who follow us to love God more fully, obey Him more completely, and serve others more effectively, we must revise our plan. Plans must not focus only on programs and activities. Plans must also focus on structures that bring people together in loving relationships and enable them to carry out ministries of care and concern for others.

Further, in view of Christ's commission for the church, every plan we develop must contribute in some way to bringing others to Christ, whether directly or indirectly. Not everything we plan will reach unbelievers directly, but every plan has to accomplish something that advances the gospel, whether it is discipling believers so they represent Christ more effectively, or helping others worship so they know Christ more deeply, or teaching others truth so they speak for Christ more accurately.

Pray While You Plan

Our best planning occurs on our knees. An open Bible and a bent knee represent the two most vital elements for effective planning. Because we know this is true, we must pray before we plan, while we plan, when we implement our steps, when we evaluate the results, and when we redefine our plan. A truly good plan becomes our prayer list of all we are asking God to do through us.

Remember how thoroughly Nehemiah integrated planning and praying? We must do the same. Paul also pursued this practice. No one could have been a more effective planner than Paul, yet he prayed. He prayed for direction as to whether he should leave Antioch (Acts 13:1–2); he prayed for growth in the believers whom he had established (Eph. 1:15–23); he requested prayer for himself and his efforts to reach others for Christ (Col. 4:3–4). Prayer and planning are not separated in the Scriptures; they are inseparable twins for God's biblical leaders.

Certainly this was the case in Jesus' ministry. He prayed at the beginning of His ministry (Mark 1:35), in the middle of His ministry (6:46), and at the end of His ministry (Matt. 26:36–45; John 17:1–26). Jesus knew God would accomplish His plan because He is sovereign; yet Jesus took time on the night of His arrest—when He had very little time—to pray about things that were already part of God's will.

He asked God the Father to keep believers secure through God's name (John 17:11); make us one even as the Father and the Son are one (17:11); give us the same joy He had (17:13); keep us from the evil one's control

(17:15); sanctify us through God's Word (17:17); and have us with Him to behold His glory (17:24).

Since Jesus knew God the Father would accomplish His plan, why did He pray what He, the Father, and the Spirit had already purposed together to do? Because God's sovereign plan includes human means. God has chosen not to accomplish His plan without including our planning and our praying. Rarely in Scripture do we see planning without prayer. What we plan we should pray for, and what we pray for we should plan, until we reach the end of our ability to implement our plans. Then the plan becomes waiting for the Lord to move us toward what we are to do next. While we are waiting, our plan should include such things as considering alternatives, consulting with others, studying Scripture, and praying for the strength and courage to endure. We move forward in God's purposes by taking these steps, even while we stand still. Never plan without planning to pray.

Plan with a Spirit of Humility

One of our greatest fears when planning is that we will do what we want rather than what God wills. We are right to be concerned, but we don't solve the problem by choosing not to plan; selfish factors can be just as much involved in the decision not to plan as in the decision to plan. The problem is not with planning; the problem is with us. Therefore we must plan with a sense of humility before God.

We have already taken some big steps toward planning with humility when we decide to immerse all our planning in prayer. By doing this we have determined to do nothing except what God wants done and to do everything the way He wants it done. In addition, we have to bring our egos to God and acknowledge that we may be driven by desires that bring more glory to us than to Him.

We may also be confused by mixed motives—some for God's glory and some for ours. Or we may be shackled by fears that blind our eyes and limit our hands. Fear is a part of ego, although we don't always realize this. When we are afraid to take steps to go against one of the power players in our church, the underlying concern is often for our egos. After all, what will it look like to my seminary professors or my pastoral colleagues if I get fired? Or what will people think of me at next year's denominational convention when they find out I'm selling insurance to feed my family while I look for a new position? Both selfish ambition and fear distort our plans and turn us into self-centered security seekers rather than self-sacrificing servants.

For this reason we must humble ourselves before God. Proper preparation for planning demands a conscious self-searching through which we strive to purify ourselves of every wrong motive. Of course, we'll never be certain of doing that, for, as Paul wrote, "My conscience is clear, but that does not make me innocent" (1 Cor. 4:4). However, we are responsible to take every step we can to purify ourselves before God (2 Cor. 7:1). After that, it's up to Him to show us our motives and use us as He desires. God will convict us when we are proud and use us when we are humble if we seek His heart when we pray and plan.

Plan to Depend on Christ

Jesus said, "Without me you can do nothing" (John 15:5), and this includes planning. This reality takes us back to prayer and then on to a conscious awareness that Jesus must be the One who plans with and through us. We are dependent on Him to do all He wants done through us. He is the Vine, and we, the branches, are the means by which He expresses Himself in our world. We are involved in the process of fruit-bearing, but it is His life and His energy through us that produces fruit in us and others.

What did Jesus mean when He said we can do nothing without Him? Actually, we can produce a number of things without Christ. For example, we can produce sermons, counseling centers, organizations, and committees without relying on Him at all. But what we plan and do amounts to *nothing* if we are not dependent on Him. Plans we develop independently of Christ may have the appearance of life since churches may attract large crowds of excited people who look alive, but their impact ends as soon as the event is over. By contrast, what we do when we depend on

Him lasts because it has His stamp of resurrection life on it. As a result we bring Christ's life to all who are involved; people are refreshed and encouraged; they grow in confidence and the certainty that God is for them; they are built up and energized, not worn out and used up.

Therefore when we plan we must declare our dependence on Christ and confess our desperate need for Him to guide and empower us. Failure here means our plans are condemned even before we pour the foundation for them, let alone erect anything on them. Good planning makes us more dependent on Christ, not less, because good planning aims to bring His life to others who desperately need it.

THE PLANNING PROCESS

Plan with Your Purpose in View

Now that we have looked at the preliminary factors involved in planning and are ready to begin the process itself, the first thing to consider is what we should include in our plans. The controlling elements in all our planning are our purpose and our core values because without these we have no idea how to decide what we should do. Our purpose and core values give us our measuring standard for every planning decision we make. If the opportunity is not in keeping with our purpose or violates even one of our core values, we must not do it.

One thing to remember is that the planning process and the vision process are similar. This makes sense because once you get past the initial stages of developing a vision, you start to plan how you will implement that vision.

When you plan, sit down with your purpose and core values and measure every action you are considering. You should do nothing, no matter how profitable it appears, unless it furthers your purpose and expresses your values. Otherwise you are going against your God-given conscience as a pastor and a church, and this demands a higher price than you can afford to pay. By focusing on your purpose, you will preserve your resources for just the right actions and not drift off course, drawn away from the best by the good.

Plan with Reality in Mind

One of the greatest temptations we face when we plan is to reach for more than we can grasp. God can do far more than we could ever ask or think (Eph. 3:20), and we need to plan things that are worthy of His greatness.

However, arrogant presumption is a sure way to bring hurt to others and shame to ourselves. A church of one hundred members is not likely to be a church of two thousand in three years; a church with a budget of $200,000 a year is not likely to have a budget of two million dollars in the near future. Although this could occur on rare occasions, we should not presume this will happen in our ministries unless we are looking at some extraordinary circumstances. Otherwise, we will be like the king who led his troops into war against a stronger army without considering what these superior numbers would mean to him and his subjects (Luke 14:31). What it meant was death and the loss of his kingdom, even as it will mean failure for us.

Evaluate Resources

Realistic planning demands we evaluate our resources thoroughly once we know what we want to do. Of the resources we consider when we plan, the most important is the *human resources* God has entrusted to us. Most of our resources are renewable, but people are not. Once we've lost people, we may never get them back, especially if we have stifled their ardor and commitment through casual and careless misuse. Therefore when you plan, look first at the people God has given you. Ask yourself, "Do we have the gifts we need in our church to do what we want to do well?" That word "well" is a vital word. If we can't do something well, how can we claim we are doing it for God's glory? No matter how much you may want and need a particular ministry, you can't implement that ministry if you don't have the kind of people you need to lead it. Or you may have to face the fact that although you once had the kind of people you needed to develop a ministry, you no longer have personnel to maintain it. There-fore you may be forced to drop something you have been doing, even if has been successful.

When you consider your human resources, look at all you are doing in your ministries. How much can you ask of people in light of their limited time and physical energy, their family and career demands, and their level of spiritual maturity? Most churches of small and moderate size do not have enough available human resources to start more than one or two new ministries a year if they are also going to keep their other ministries healthy. You can move people from one ministry to another, but you must be careful that you don't end up with two weak ministries where you once had one strong one. Just as no sane person maims himself in the name of progress, so we should not maim our churches in the name of God. Don't start a new ministry unless you can keep your other ministries strong and effective. Do everything you can to avoid overextending people in God's name.

We also need to consider our *physical resources*. Do you have the facilities needed to implement your plan? If you don't have the buildings you need now, can you have them by the time the plan calls for them? Often a church can be creative, by renting schools, leasing a service club, using a hotel conference room, or asking people to park at a shopping center and take a shuttle bus to church. When they have needed more space, many churches have used portable buildings or even a tent. People will put up with many physical limitations if their spiritual needs are being met. Even though all this is true, good planners must take the need for physical facilities into account and do everything they can to create the best relating/learning/growing atmosphere possible.

Another resource to consider is *finances*. Although many people start here, good planners don't. How often do we hear it said that we can't do something because we don't have the money? Ultimately a church may be forced to make this decision, but they'll never know until they have looked at all the possibilities. Good planners consider every opportunity and develop every option before they allow money to become a deciding factor. They know money can be moved from one ministry to another or a new idea may be so attractive it will replace an old practice or that new ideas can generate new income. They also know God is generous and loves to be trusted to do what only He can do. For this reason good planners always consider budget expansion after identifying the opportunities available to them.

Money follows ministry. If a ministry is effective, the money will be there to fund it. But *money should never master ministry.* Money should never make the ultimate decision about ministry. In other words, first plan your ministry, then count your money. After that, make the final decision on what you will plan to do. Be like a thorough shopper—never spend your money until you have considered all the possibilities and determined how you can get the most for it.

Plan to Change Your Plan

Everything changes—so every planner must plan to change. Planners are far more ready for change than nonplanners. Change comes in unlimited and often unexpected forms, sometimes for the good and sometimes for the bad. A developer unexpectedly buys land next to a church and puts two hundred homes on it, so new families move in right next door. Or a new high school opens up just a few blocks away, and suddenly the church has several hundred high schoolers passing by daily. Or the neighborhood slowly changes, and a church realizes it must change with it or move. Maybe the city council enacts a new ordinance that makes it impossible for the church to build where it planned to move. The culture changes continuously, constantly keeping you off balance.

The point is that ministry has a life of its own, taking pastors and churches into new and ever-changing situations, creating both opportunities and roadblocks. For this reason we must be prepared to change our plans. However, churches that never plan don't recognize new opportunities, let alone prepare themselves to take advantage of them. The question to consider is, How do we decide when to change our plans? What objective standards do we use so we are not blown about without intention or aim? The following five paragraphs address these questions.

- Make changes carefully and purposefully. Any change that doesn't fit your purpose should not be made. Thus if a large donor comes to you with a pet project that alters your plan or dilutes any one of your core values, you should not make the change. No matter how good the idea, the opportunity, the person involved, or the amount of money offered, if the change in the plan takes you away from your purpose or violates one of your core values, you must not make it. Going against your purpose and core values will weaken your ministry. Then it will be only a matter of time until you become a cheap imitation of what you could have been.

- You also should not change your plan for any opportunity that calls for you to use resources you do not have or cannot get by the time you need them. If you lack funds, space, or people to accomplish a task, turn from that task and concentrate on what you can do. Grow your ministry, attract people, raise funds, build space, and then pursue the opportunity. If someone else has already taken advantage of that opportunity by the time you are ready to do it, this is in the hand of God, and He will be well pleased with your discipline and dedication to use your resources well. Do not make this decision lightly. Pray diligently, seeking God's direction concerning any opportunity you may be considering, remembering that people and their trust are your most precious resources. If there is genuine conviction from God on the part of all involved that you should go after an impossible dream, do it. Tell everyone what you are doing, so they all understand the step of faith you are taking and how much you need their prayers, support, and participation.

- If an opportunity is an unusually good one, but you cannot do it when you first see it, put it off until you can. Lay the foundation by adding it to your plan when you update your thinking. Every plan should be reviewed and updated annually. Let's say you are working with a three-year strategic plan. Once you accomplish the first-year's aims, evaluate where you have been and where you are going and then develop another set of goals for the next three years. In this way you always have a rolling three-year plan and are never more than two years away from a new major initiative. If you see you can move some steps from one year to another in order to make room for a new and challenging opportunity, do so. That way you can respond to unexpected developments in a wise and orderly fashion.

- What if you make a mistake in your planning? If you make your mistakes prayerfully, you can be sure they are all part of figuring out where God wants you to go and how to get there. Paul planned to go to Bithynia, but God planned for him to go to Macedonia.

Paul got to the right place by attempting to go to what turned out to be the wrong place (Acts 16:6–10). Because he prayed, he made a mistake only in intention rather than in action. Without a plan, however, Paul would never have needed to pray and find new direction from God. Seek God's purpose for you and your ministry, and you will find it. Surely you know God is more interested in having you in the right place than even you are. Pursue Him, and He will guide you.

- Never let a plan become a set of shackles that imprisons you in useless goals. The purpose of planning is to set you free, not put you in a stockade or turn your ministry into a sinking Titanic because of its leaders' shortsightedness. Ministering without a plan is like driving without a map. Plans provide a vision map for your ministry. They are useful only so long as they are guiding you to the right destination. When changes come that demand redirection to a new destination, develop a different map. If you are lost *with* a map, you have a way of finding out where you are so you can get to where you're going. But if you get lost *without* a map, it is difficult to find your way since you don't know where you are or how to get where you are going.

Plan to Achieve Your Plan

Besides the fact that I am not a planner by nature and my former conviction that it is unspiritual to plan, there was one other reason I did not plan strategically. No one had ever shown me how to do so. I didn't have the slightest idea how to go about doing strategic planning, and everything I picked up on the subject was daunting and discouraging. The writers made it seem so complex and confusing that I quit before I even started. I felt it would take me months to learn how to do the process, and I didn't have months to spend just learning how to do strategic planning.

Of course, natural strategic planners don't understand this, and they always set out to show someone like me how simple it is if I will just work at it. Then they swamp me with reams of technical terms, charts that cross my eyes, and exercises that take pages to describe and hours to complete. When they're finished, I'm ready to quit all over again. What I needed was a simple strategic planning process, and I found one in Bobb Biehl's book *Masterplanning*.[2] When you are ready to learn to do strategic planning, this is as good a book as there is.

Let me whet your appetite by showing you the core of Biehl's thinking, which uses a simple six-step process built around the acrostic *Doctor*.

- *D: Direction.* To begin the strategic planning process, you must determine the direction you want your ministry to go by defining its purpose, values, and key goals.

- *O: Organization.* In this step you determine how you will structure your ministry to accomplish your plan by projecting how many volunteers and staff members you need. You should also look ahead to see how many you will have to add to your team.

- *C: Cash.* Here is where you budget—after you have decided what you want to do and who will do it. Of course, when you see the size of your vision and your budget side by side, you may have to go back and make some choices as to what you can do, but avoid allowing money to control your plan's development. Find creative ways to carry out your plan with limited means. If you start with a focus on money, you will never break free and take new and risky steps.

- *T: Tracking.* Once your plan is in place, track your progress by holding everyone involved accountable on a regular basis for how well they accomplish their goals.

- *O: Overall Evaluation.* After you have been tracking for a while, you will need to do an evaluation to determine not only how well you are doing, but also how wisely you planned in the first place. Perhaps you will discover some new needs that should be met or old ideas that should be discarded.

- *R: Refinement.* At this stage you refine your plan to move in new directions based on your evaluation. These new directions need to conform to your purpose and core values. More than likely, you will have to revamp your organization, especially if you add or reduce personnel. When you evaluate and make changes, you need to go back and take another look at direction, organization, and cash. Once you do this, you can begin tracking again.

Start with this simplified version of strategic planning and move forward from there.

Plan for Others to Own the Plan

Many writers assume that the leader of the organization does all the strategic planning. This is not wise because you will miss an opportunity to create ownership of the purpose, values, and vision by those who have to implement it. Many churches have no sense of purpose. The people come to church for self-centered reasons, not for the bigger purpose of worshiping God, serving each other, and reaching those who do not know Christ. Unless these people learn to care for others and understand that the church exists to do more than meet their needs, they will never grasp God's purpose for their fellowship. If they are allowed to remain on the sidelines during the planning process, they will become spectators, judges, and critics rather than owners of the final product, responsible for its implementation.

You can't directly involve everyone in the planning process. You can, however, involve the entire congregation through representatives from all the interested groups: elders, deacons, Sunday school teachers, small-group leaders, staff members, men's and women's ministry leaders, youth sponsors, and any others who need a voice.

Before you involve anyone else, you should define the parameters of the plan, that is, frame the canvas on which the plan will be painted. These parameters must be the biblical standards that govern every church: the Great Commission, the principles of discipleship, the practices of leadership development, the theological truths that are essential for church health—anything critical to your church's purpose and core values. Train the people who will lead the planning process under your direction in these essential elements until you are confident they understand them, are committed to them, and can explain them to others.

Even before the planning process goes public, make every effort to help the entire church understand the aim of the plan and the underlying principles on which you are building. Remember, you are not painting on a small canvas. You're painting a mural, not a landscape, so it will take multiple artists working under your guidance to produce the final work. Remember, too, that if strategic planning is not your greatest strength, let one who is particularly good at it lead the process. Your job is to see that the church determines to obey God. Sometimes you can give greater input from the side, where you don't have to worry about managing the process, than from the front, where you are responsible for guiding the flow of thought.

You will have to spend a large block of time planning to plan, especially if you want to involve as many people as possible. You must know generally what you want the final plan to look like, although you can't predefine all that will be in it. Train those who will serve as leaders under your guidance, and plan how best to involve the many voices who need to be heard. The number of people who are listening when you present your final plan will depend entirely on the number of voices you listened to in developing it. If you do not allow voices to speak, you will never get hands working. Trust the people by honoring their gifts, and the Holy Spirit will give you a plan most will own.

PLAN

Once you have planned to plan, do your planning. Be sure to have a format designed for all to follow, so the results come back to you in a common and easy-to-handle form. This will save you an immense amount of time when you start to organize your thinking. Since you are as much a member of the church as anyone else, you should certainly see that your point of view is represented in the plan. Not everyone's desires will make it into the plan, of course, but God's certainly should. Wherever possible, incorporate an idea, but do not turn from God's call for His church in order to satisfy some member's misunderstood idea of what the body of Christ should be doing. Once the plan is completed, do everything you can through everyone you can involve to make it known throughout the church. Do not make the mistake of thinking that because you told them the vision once, they heard you and now come to church committed to it every week. They need to hear some facet of it at least once every three weeks to remember what their church is all about.

Plan to Implement Your Plan

The greatest problem with planning is not that plans get in the way of the sovereign God (what can get in the way of the sovereign God?), or that plans replace the Holy Spirit, or that we do what we want to do rather than God's will. No, the greatest problem with planning is that very few planners become implementers of what they planned. Unless you intend to implement your plan, don't plan.

Plan for Excellence

In your planning, develop a sense of excellence. Don't strive to impress others with what you are doing, because that is ego, not excellence. Excellence exalts God because we do things that glorify Him and are worthy of His name. For some reason many think God isn't interested in quality, but He is. Just think of the tabernacle He directed Moses to erect in the wilderness. The materials He told them to use were the best obtainable. This is not to suggest we become extravagant; but we should strive for excellence that is worthy of God within the means He provides. Excellence is not a matter of competition or superiority. Excellence means we do our best with the resources God gives us. All of us can do this.

Plan to Be Accountable

We plan to be accountable when we keep the judgment seat of Christ in mind at all times throughout the planning process. This is another way of bringing our self-centered desires for success in line with God's values—by remembering that He will hold us accountable for all we do. When we plan to use people, we send wood, hay, and stubble on ahead (1 Cor. 3:12–13), even if our plan brings more people into our churches. Our plans are failures if they do not attract others to Christ, strengthen people's relationship with Him in their families and friendships, and release them to be what God created them to be.

Pastors are notorious for requiring people to serve *them* in order to advance *their* cause and *their* career. Many churches demand that their attendees be involved in activities several nights a week. In such situations the church divides families. When pastors burn people out, we will face accountability for our actions at the judgment seat of Christ. Our plans must build others in maturity and ministry, not drain them of spiritual strength and health.

One way to test a plan is to ask yourself and others if those involved in implementing it will grow in Christ or be stunted in their development. Unless your plan enables those implementing it to grow spiritually, you have hindered God's aim. Good planning keeps in mind the fact that we are tending Christ's sheep and that He will hold us accountable for what we do with them.

CONCLUSION

I have come full circle in my thinking about planning. Once I saw it as a hindrance to pleasing God. Now I see planning, when done according to God's purpose and principles, as one of the most motivating ways to please God. I have seen a plan increase prayer because it gave the planners specifics to pray about. I have seen a plan increase faith because God answered prayers and showed His greatness to those who called on Him. I have seen a plan energize a team as they saw things they could do, new ways to move forward, and new opportunities to serve Christ. I have seen a plan unify a group once they saw what a difference they could make while working toward a common goal.

Plans can replace our dependence on God; there's no doubt about that. But plans don't *have* to replace His role in our lives. They didn't get in the way of Moses, Joshua, Nehemiah, Jesus, or Paul. Certainly God's plans don't get in His way. One of the exciting things about the planning process is that it can be the means of getting us in touch with the Lord's sovereign aims and purposes. What could be greater than seeing Him work His sovereign will through our finite thoughts and actions? Implement the planning process in submission to God, and you will see this happen.

CHAPTER THIRTEEN

LEADING CHANGES

SEPTEMBER 14, 1969, was a great day in our lives—the day we held our first service at South Hills Community Church in San Jose, California. For five months we had planned for this moment, and God blessed us with an amazing beginning. One hundred fifty people came to worship with us that Sunday.

NOT JUST ANOTHER CHURCH

When we started we knew one thing for sure: This would not be just another church. South Hills was going to be special, unique, different, a church that would make a mark. The ministry would belong to the saints. The pastoral staff would equip the saints to do the work of the ministry. The elders were to be real Acts 6 leaders—they wouldn't just sit in meetings and vote. Instead, they would be men of the Word and establish themselves as models who led in their families and led in our ministry. And that is exactly what they became.

There were things we would not do. We would not expect unbelievers to give. We would not have a choir. We would not be traditional in any way. And most importantly, we would not build a building. Period. How can anyone justify spending so much money on wood frame and stucco? We certainly couldn't and wouldn't. We determined to spend that money on missions and reaching the lost. Our money would be living money—invested in the lives of people serving Christ with energy and power, not dead money rotting away in real estate.[1]

SOUTH HILLS MEETS CHANGE

So we rented the facilities of the Cambrian Park Seventh-Day Adventist Church; they used it on Saturdays, and we used it on Sundays. It was a great arrangement until we grew into two services and began to look like we planned to be permanent renters—which we did. That's when the Seventh-Day Adventists introduced South Hills Community Church to change! And what an introduction it was. They told us we would have to vacate their facility when our lease was up in two years. Unfortunately there was no other facility we could rent, so we were forced to build.

We had sold the people of South Hills on our plan not to build, and no one protested that decision. Everyone marched in the same direction, according to the same cadence—South Hills will not build, South Hills will not build. Now we needed to do an about-face and march to a different beat—South Hills will build, South Hills will build. The problem was that we had trained everyone to march forward, but we had not taught anyone how to turn around and go in a new direction. The result? Three hundred people broke ranks and dug in to resist the change. They were not mean-spirited; they just didn't understand why we had to make this change after taking a strong stance on the issue of not building. It was difficult for them to accept the fact that we now had to build.

Sometimes naiveté is a wonderful friend. I had no idea change could be divisive and destructive. There were a number of things I did know:

- Our work was cut out for us.
- We would lose people.
- We would have to communicate better than we ever had before.
- God alone could get us through this change.
- Our faith would have to grow.

None of us had seen God do anything this big before. None of us had any idea how He would do it, but He did meet our needs and more. We discovered that *times of change are great times for the God of change to show Himself to His people.* Though change may be unwelcome for many, it is actually a mentor that teaches us to trust God in ways we have never done before.

UP THE EVEREST OF CHANGE

Change, especially when we don't know much about it, is like climbing a glacial mountain. What we've learned from those who have struggled on Mount Everest's slopes is that glacial mountains are constantly changing. We can't control change, though we can prepare for it. Change by its very nature means we are always facing new territory, places we've never been, sights we've never seen. Even when we climb up the same mountain trail of change that others have climbed before us—such as building projects or explosive growth—the mountain is not the same. Glaciers have shifted, storms have blown in, avalanches have covered the trail, ropes have been lost, and we struggle to find our way. Change can never be conquered, so we must learn to navigate change. Change means uncertainty; it is full of surprises, the unexpected rules supreme, and fear can dominate our response. Like mountain climbing, it is thrilling yet dangerous; but since it is utterly unavoidable, we must strive to survive its rigorous demands.

People in our churches fight change because they face it everywhere else—in their families, their careers, their communities, even their bodies, but they don't want it to happen in their churches! They want one place in their lives that doesn't change, and that place is the church. They seem determined to die and take their church with them, and some of them will succeed. But people make a bad choice when they select a church as their bastion of consistency, because God is the One who decides what the church is about and God is about change. What greater change could there be than to turn us from hell to heaven and deliver us from death to life? He takes us from self-centeredness to self-sacrifice, from decay to glory. All of life is growth in grace, a constantly growing change. God has called the church to be the most significant change agent in the world, so as our culture changes we must change, while, like God, we remain unchanging in our essence. Our theology never deviates, while the communication of that truth constantly develops to meet the new issues and opportunities created by the changes around us.

In bringing about change in a church, we are like climbers on Mount Everest: We are climbing a constantly shifting glacial mountain. Maps are helpful on this climb, but techniques for climbing are more important. So even though we need a map for the change we are making, it is more essential that we learn the techniques for leading change. Techniques first, then the map—that's what we need to navigate change. Techniques for leading our churches in change fall into four categories: preparation, communication, implementation, celebration.

PREPARE FOR CHANGE

Pray

I don't mention prayer simply to "baptize" the change process and somehow make it more spiritual. Prayer is not an add-on; prayer is the heart and essence of all we do.

Careful and wise planning is critical to achieving change, but prayer makes the difference between futile effort and fruitful impact. That is why prayer is part of every step along the way. For this reason establish a prayer plan that supports each change step; have specific intercession goals for every action you take. Have special times of prayer at key points in the plan and be sure to seek God's face to make certain you are still going in His direction, not your own.

Start with the End in View

Know where you want to go before you announce a change. Anyone who sets out to climb Mount Everest knows exactly where he wants to go—to the summit. This target defines every step he takes, each piece of equipment he obtains, and each member of the support team he will have to recruit. If he overlooks even one need, he could make a fatal mistake, especially if he is the leader of the expedition. Many other climbers could die because of his failure to prepare carefully. So it is when we navigate the glacial mountain of change: We must know where we're going, how we will get there, what kind of team we need, and who will lead us to reach the top. Unless we prepare with great care, we'll fail and take many with us. To help others find their way through change, we have to be as focused on our goal as Everest climbers.

Whenever you institute change, you must answer four vital questions:
- Where are you going?
- Why is going there better than staying where you are now?
- How are you going to get there, that is, what is your plan for implementing change?
- Who will take you there, that is, who are the fellow-leaders who support the plan and are joining you in climbing the mountain?

These questions need to be answered before you move ahead.

Determine If the Timing Is Right

Success in making change depends as much on timing as it does on the quality of the idea or the process used to accomplish it. A good idea introduced at the wrong time makes it a bad idea. Often a pastor tries to bring about a needed change—to build a building, relocate the church, add a staff member, or develop a contemporary service—but the church rejects the change, and him along with it. After he moves on to another church, a new pastor comes and does the very thing the former pastor wanted to do but couldn't. Why? Because the timing was better for the second man.

Sometimes one pastor's efforts help prepare for change by the next pastor. Sometimes a pastor's ideas fail because he didn't test the water to find out if people were ready for change, or he may not have included enough people in the preparation process. Other reasons may be that he didn't ask the right questions or didn't talk with others who climbed the mountain before him. Whatever it was, he slipped and fell on the sheer ice of bad timing.

The following steps can help you determine when the timing is right.

Step 1: Discuss your idea with each of a few trusted individuals before you present it to any groups.

Step 2: Listen to those whom you consult and adjust your thinking accordingly. Your initial group should include your church elders. If they are opposed to the change, you can't go any further until you win them over. Once they approve the idea, you have freedom to move forward to the next circle of influencers.

Step 3: Expand your test group as appropriate until you have included as many as needed. Be sure this group is made up of all interested parties. Even if you fear someone's opposition, don't leave that person out. People with an interest in a change who are not consulted beforehand will almost certainly oppose it, even if it is a good idea. That's because they may feel rejected, sensing that you didn't trust them. It is better to slow down and wait for the reluctant changers than to be forced to turn back as you approach the summit by a sudden storm of howling protest.

Taking these three steps will help you know who favors the change and why, who may resist the change and why, the primary obstacles you must overcome in making the change and what you will have to do to overcome them, and the primary sources of resistance and how you can win them over.

Decide to Make the Change

Once you know the timing is right, decide with your leaders to make the change and then plan the steps you need to take to move forward.

Evaluate Your Trust Account

As the pastor-leader of your flock, think of the trust you earn from your church as a bank account—a leadership trust account—into which you make deposits. In times of change your success depends entirely on how much trust you have established with your church. If your account is low, you will have a difficult time bringing about change. On the other hand, if the people trust you, they will follow you in any credible direction you establish. Be certain of this: Since change depends on trust, change depends on relationships. The best thing you can do toward bringing about change is to build relationships constantly—especially during times of nonchange. If you show up suddenly because you want to make a change, you will lose both trust and respect. People will not only suspect you; they will also know you are using them.

Make the Withdrawal

What do you do if you have worked and waited for a unified commit-ment to a change, but it's evident it isn't coming? This is when you will need to decide whether to make a major withdrawal from your trust ac-count. If the need is great, if the future of the church is at stake, you must make the withdrawal. However, be sure you understand what it will cost you in terms of anger, unfair judgment, false accusations, and behind-the-back attacks. Some changes are worth risking everything to accomplish—just be sure you are willing to pay that price before making a withdrawal from your trust account.

Our building project at South Hills Community Church demanded almost a total withdrawal from the trust account all of us as leaders had built after several years. Our motto for the building project was "Building Buildings to Build People," taken from our church purpose statement, "Building People to Disciple the Nations." Some questioned whether we were building buildings to build people or building buildings to build Bill Lawrence. I heard that sentiment and felt its bite. Why were we build-ing? Was it to help others grow in Christ or was it to feed my ego? I knew the objective realities—the Seventh-Day Adventists had given us a firm deadline to move, and we had no choice. There was no place to go; it was either build or shut down. Our elders and staff had no interest in feeding my ego. We made the decision on the basis of the facts, not emotions; yet I had to be sure we were building people before I could lead us into this change. So I sat down in my rented office one day and asked myself, Are we building people or is this just a slogan? What I discovered was amaz-ing and encouraging.

God had used us to build up a significant number of people since we started seven years before. Many families had been healed, many divorces prevented, many who grieved had been comforted, many had come to Christ, many had entered full-time ministry. I did not accomplish this. It was a total church effort, and we were building people. Once I saw these facts objectively, I was confident we were undertaking this project for the right reasons. There was no need for me to doubt myself, our direction, or God. He had to be in this, or He would not have raised up a ministry of developing all these people only to shut it down for lack of a place to meet. We had to move forward despite a handful of naysayers—and by that time there were only a handful. Before we completed the building, the church was totally unified around the project, and it has gone on to erect additional facilities. That was a time when it was well worth the risk to make a major withdrawal from our trust account.

Build the Change Leadership Team

Once you decide to go ahead with a change, build the team who will implement the process. If it's an all-church change, you need an all-church team, that is, elders, deacons, and representatives from every interest group in the church. If it's a ministry change (for example, a new approach to your youth ministry), you need full representation from that interest group, including parents, youth, staff, and volunteers. Recruit them on the basis of their willingness to go forward with the change once they are convinced from a careful study of the Scriptures and other evidence that this new way will meet the needs of the church more effectively.

Recruit a diverse team: administrators, action-takers, encouragers, communicators, writers, artists—any gift and talent you need to accomplish the change. Draw from the people in the church as much as possible; hire from the outside only when you must. Do not involve divisive people on the team, but if you can invite known opinion-makers to participate, it will help everyone realize you are not trying to control the process for your own ends. Whatever you do, pursue excellence in every step you take. Slipshod change will make the steep climb extremely dangerous.

Develop a Plan for Making the Change

You may have already developed much of the plan as you thought through where you want to go and how you want to get there. That's good, but don't deny your change-making team the opportunity to contribute to the process. If you do, you will deny them ownership in the change, and they won't support it as you want them to.

Communicate the essence of your plan as you recruit your team members, while helping them understand they will have genuine opportunities for input along the way. They need to know you have given this change significant thought, and they will want to follow your lead as much as they can. As you recruit them, ask for their responses to your thinking; give them plenty of opportunities to ask questions, express opinions, offer suggestions—and use as much of their thinking as you can from the very beginning.

Establish a Time Line from Start to Finish

Identify the completion date for your project, lay out the mileposts along the way that will tell you when you have finished each step, and assign each of these an end date. This will give everyone involved a sense of progress and opportunity to enjoy success throughout the process. Specify when you will arrive at the foot of the mountain, when you expect to get to base camp, when you plan to start for the top, and how long it will take you to arrive at the summit. There's nothing like a series of small gains along the way to keep you going on the treacherous climb up the mountain of change.

Use a Private-Pilot-Public-Permanent Process to Introduce Selected New Ministries

Suppose you want to establish evangelistic home Bible studies in your church, but you want to be sure the ministry will go well before you announce it to everyone. Begin with a *private* effort in which you engage a handful of carefully chosen people in an unpublicized effort. Let the elders know your plan, but keep your effort private in the beginning. Once you're sure you know what you're doing and have a few trained leaders to stand with you, announce a *pilot* project to the core leadership. You are still not ready to go public, but your key leaders are informed about your efforts. After you have completed the pilot effect, move to a *public* project. Now the whole church knows what's going on and is asked to pray, for example, for three different Bible studies, each being led by people you have trained. Then include the ministry as a *permanent* part of your activities with a special celebration and a *plan* to involve a significant number of people in this opportunity.

The advantage of this process is that you can stop it at anytime. And it allows you to experiment without running a major risk of failure. Nothing hinders your leadership more than starting something without finishing it, especially in the public arena. Every time you plan a change or plan to develop a new ministry, do everything you can, even before you begin, to be sure the idea will succeed.

COMMUNICATE THE CHANGE

Communicating the change to the larger group (the *public* aspect of the change) may be the most difficult and significant task in the transition process. Unless the people affected by the idea understand and accept the need for change and the way you plan to make it, they will never set out on the journey with you. What could be worse than to have spectators on Mount Everest when you need helping hands? If others don't see the need and they decide not to go with you, no one will make it to the summit. Or, if you do make it, participants will be angry and resentful over those who refused to be involved. No leader can afford to have his followers so divided.

Pray

Pray for clarity in communicating both the aim and the process of the change. Involve your team in prayer at this critical point so that all of you are relying on God when you make your plan public.

Communicate in Advance of Any Public Announcement

Before you make any public announcement about change, prepare your congregation for what is coming. Depending on the nature of the change, you may write an article for your church newsletter, develop a brochure, make a series of short announcements, or announce a special Sunday when all will come together to hear what God is leading the group to do. Whether it is an all-church change or a ministry change, those who have an interest in what is coming must be prepared for it. Never surprise your church with an unanticipated change.

Show the Need for the Change

Because change is so difficult, few people will agree to it without good reason to turn from the comfortable patterns of the present to the threatening risk of the unknown. Even when the need is obvious, people are reluctant to step into uncharted territory. For example, the Scriptures clearly show that believers are to pursue the Great Commission, but many Christians are unwilling to take the steps demanded to obey this command. There are those who would rather disobey God than change, and for this reason, when you have clear biblical sanction for the change, you must show them from the Scriptures that their refusal to implement it actually means disobedience. If you can't do that, you need to think long and hard about why you are calling them to change. Why make a change that won't glorify God, help His people become more of what He wants them to be, and bring others to Him?

Of course, you will not be able to show a direct biblical link with changes such as moving to two morning services or constructing a new building, but if you aren't taking such actions for biblically based reasons, why take them? Don't claim scriptural authority when it isn't there, but show clear links when you can. Be careful you don't use the Scriptures as a club to get sensitive people to do what you want, because you won't keep them with you very long. They will realize what you are doing, and you will lose credibility in their eyes.

In the case of South Hills Community Church, we had to build because if we didn't we couldn't continue to exist and develop people to disciple others. This is what gave us the confidence to challenge our people to sacrifice financially for the project after we had told them we would never do this. We could show them that if we didn't exist as a church, we couldn't reach others for Christ and disciple them.

Use every means at your disposal to communicate the need and the plan for change. *Preach* on the issue so people can see for themselves what God's Word has to say about the change. Use *testimonies* from others who believe in the change because they see its benefit. Present *videos* to support the steps you are taking. Display *posters, banners,* and other *visuals* to make your point. Write *articles* in your church newsletter, put *quotes* in the church bulletin, use appropriate *skits* in the services. Communicate what you are doing in every way possible and make your communication honest, accurate, and excellent.

Answer Key Questions When You Communicate

Remember the four critical questions you must answer if you are to have a positive response: Where are we going? Why is going there better than staying where we are now? How will we get there? Who will take us there?

These four issues must be stressed constantly if you are to get the unity you need. This is especially critical the first time you introduce your plan. Therefore, when you are presenting the change to the whole church, show not only the biblical reasons for the change, but also the practical ways you intend to accomplish it. Don't forget that their trust in you is at stake, so make as small a trust withdrawal as possible to accomplish your aim.

Introduce the Change Leadership Team

Introduce the change leadership team as part of your initial presentation and keep the spotlight on each member so that everyone knows who is involved. Explain each person's role, why he or she is on the team, and give selected members an opportunity to speak in support of the change. This team will add to your credibility as a change leader and will strengthen the people's trust in you.

Call for Commitment

At the conclusion of your initial presentation, ask the congregation to commit to the new direction. You may choose to make the commitment a public one or you may ask for a heart commitment to be communicated in writing at a later date. Or you may want to proceed as many churches do when they call for faith-promise commitments, by asking the people to fill in a response card during the service or at another time.

Some churches have held a series of home meetings to inform the members about the change, and then they sponsor a banquet as a climax to the communication efforts.

If the change is one that requires a congregational vote, you will have to call a special business meeting and you will know the outcome at that time. Research shows that typically 16 percent of the people in any group will resist a change on general principles—keep that in mind no matter what the vote tally says. This is a good reason not to make your required approval percentage so high that you're set up to fail. Of course not every church falls into statistical norms, but it will help to be aware of this.

IMPLEMENT THE CHANGE

Pray

Pray now for the plan as you pursue the steps to bring about the change. Have your change leadership team pray both individually and together throughout the entire implementation process. Keep their prayers fresh and focused—don't allow them to count on the plan to make the difference. Help them remember that only God can bring about the results you desire.

Do What You Said You Would Do

When you announced the change and the way you planned to get to the mountaintop, you called for people to commit themselves to go with you. This agreement became a covenant between you and your people, so they will hold you accountable. For this reason, deviate as little as possible from what you first said. It is extremely unwise to change direction in the middle of the process because followers will lose confidence in you. Like people lost on a climb who no longer trust their guide, they will take over the map and try to decide among themselves where to go and how to get there. This can be disastrous in the middle of a major change.

Seek to bring as much stability into the change process as you can. To keep the people's trust, keep your word throughout the period of change.

Change the Process for the Better as Appropriate

Although keeping your word is essential, it is possible to make improvements in the change process along the way. While it is true that the more thoroughly you prepare the more effective your change process will be, no one can think of everything, and some good ideas may surface as you progress. If someone does think of an improvement that can be introduced into the process without confusion, don't hesitate to introduce it. Just do so carefully, and explain fully why you are bringing something new into the plan.

If God does intervene and redirect your plan, follow Him. Explain the change carefully and show why it is the result of God's sovereign hand and not your sloppy thinking. However, if you are forced to deviate because you didn't foresee something you should have, don't blame God. Before you announce the adjustment, review all you are doing to be sure you are not missing anything else; then take responsibility and acknowledge what you did wrong. The wisest thing you can do is listen to God during the preparation stage and get it as right as you can. However, the Lord has His own reasons for waiting until we are underway to redirect us, and we must be ready to follow Him wherever He takes us.

Report Successes along the Way

Nothing encourages the heart more than success, no matter how small it may be. For this reason don't wait until the end to rejoice. Each time you complete a milepost, celebrate the achievement and turn the people's eyes ahead to the next step. Joy from the Lord strengthens us (Neh. 8:10), so the more we lead the people in rejoicing, the stronger they become in trusting God and pressing on toward the change. Tell everyone what God has done. Feature some member of the congregation who contributed to this achievement. Produce a video that shows what has been accomplished so far. Do everything you can to show you are making progress in a timely way toward your target. When you are doing the right thing, you will face spiritual opposition, and the people need to know how this is being overcome. If you can accomplish your plan without God's supernatural intervention, your vision isn't big enough nor is it from Him.

Review the Need and Anticipated Results at Least Monthly

People need constant reminders if they are to stay on target. Old habits and thought patterns take a long time to change, and new thinking is fragile, long after we think others have accepted it. Because of this, you help ensure the acceptance of change by reminding people what need you are meeting and how meeting it will glorify the Lord. Reminding followers about change is like telling our mates we love them—saying it once is not enough. As new people come, you need to draw them into the new direction you are taking. Of course, the more often the regular attendees hear what you are doing, the more they will understand and commit to the change.

CELEBRATE THE CHANGE

Pray

Pray with praise and thanksgiving to God for His faithfulness in enabling you to navigate a difficult trail and arrive at the change you set out to accomplish. He is the One who enabled you to accomplish the change, and He must be acknowledged as your Enabler. Lead the people in special times of worship and rejoicing as you celebrate His faithfulness.

Celebrate the Successful Completion of the Change

If the change is church-wide, hold an all-church celebration in a Sunday morning service. If it's a ministry change, hold a special time of celebration with those who lead that ministry. If the change in a specific ministry is a significant one, hold a special time in a morning church service to tell everyone what it means to that ministry and therefore to the whole church.

Many workers, both volunteer and staff, never receive adequate appreciation for their efforts. Recognize them publicly when they do something special; this will greatly encourage them. Plan a special time with the change leadership team to thank them for their faithfulness and to rejoice with them at what they have accomplished.

Acknowledge the Change in a Visual Way

Frequently Israel looked back to celebrate what God had done. God instituted seasons of remembrance through Israel's annual feasts. Also He directed them to take twelve stones from Jordan's riverbed to be set up as a sign of His faithfulness at their first camp in the Promised Land (Josh. 4:1–7). This is exactly what we did at South Hills Community Church when our building was completed. At the suggestion of one of our staff members, we took large rocks and incorporated them into our landscaping in front of the church. These rocks became a testimony to God's faithfulness when we had all but lost hope that we could ever complete the building project. This encouraged us to look back and say, "Remember when . . ." and to recall God's provisions in difficult times.

CONCLUSION

In June 1979, ten years after we started South Hills, we moved into our new building. Nine months before this, in mid-September 1978, our elders and staff gathered for a retreat in the Santa Cruz mountains. For six months our building program had been shut down because of an investigation by the State of California. Early in our planning we found no bank willing to lend us money to build, so we chose to self-finance our project through a company that had successfully assisted many churches in selling bonds to their members. Our leadership had investigated this company carefully and found nothing in its history to indicate any problem, so the state's intervention was a blow to us. As a part of the investigation, the state impounded all our money when we were only ten thousand dollars short of our goal. During that six-month period real estate and construction materials in California inflated at one of the highest rates in the state's history.

Just before the retreat the state gave our bond company a clean bill of health and released our funds so we could continue with our plans. We came to our time together with the expectation that we would quickly get moving, sell out the remaining bonds, and get the project started within weeks—all in time to vacate the Seventh-Day Adventist Church by the deadline they had given us. Instead the chairman of the board brought us some shocking news. He had met with the contractor and learned the cost of our building had escalated by one hundred thousand dollars, and he didn't see any way for us to raise the additional money. With that he began to weep, because he was so overwhelmed by this news.

As I listened I thought back to an experience I had two nights before. On that Thursday I woke up in the middle of the night, something I rarely do, and began to pray. As I was praying, I felt impressed to recommit myself to stay as pastor of South Hills Community Church for an indefinite period of time. That was an unusual response since I had no desire to leave. While the chairman was speaking, it occurred to me that God would not call me to recommit myself to a ministry He planned to shut down in a matter of months.

I told the men that story, and we got down on our knees to pray. When we got up we had no idea where we would get the additional funds, but we knew God would provide. So we planned a celebration day the last Sunday in October, and we went home to tell our people about the need God had created for us. These were the people who eighteen months earlier had questioned our need to build and whether the project was God's will. But they had undergone such a great change that when they were asked to give, many of them donated funds directly rather than lend money in the form of bonds. On the Wednesday before Celebration Sunday the earth-movers were on our site creating the pad for our building, and we had the one hundred thousand dollars with a little left over!

We learned much from that experience. For one thing, we discovered the money we thought we were saving by not building wasn't going into missions and reaching the lost, but was being used by the people to buy homes, furniture, cars, and vacations. These were all valid expenses until we presented a higher use for those funds.

We also learned God uses change to build faith in those who follow Him through the transition process. In fact, the greatest change that came out of our project was not on our building site, but in our souls. We truly were building buildings to build people; we just didn't know we were the people God was building.

I call you to lead your sheep into change by the hand of God. If you have the courage to do this, you will be the most changed person among them. You and they together will scale heights of faith you never thought possible as you climb up the Everest of change.

CHAPTER FOURTEEN

FINDING THE BEST—FOR YOU

THE KEY to building a great team is getting round pegs in round holes of approximately the same size."[1]

When it comes to hiring staff, no words could be more true. Your object is to find the round peg that most nearly fits your round hole. Of course, no round peg will exactly fit your round hole, so you are left with the reality of "approximately." This means no more searching for a modern appearance of the apostle Paul, no more Superman Syndrome.

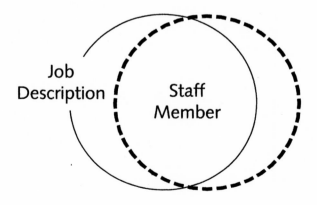

In the diagram on the preceding page,[2] the solid circle represents the position to be filled, and the broken circle represents the person who will fill it. If you can get an 80 percent overlap between the person and the position, you are doing well. People usually don't come "tailor-made" for job openings. That's why the correlation between the round hole and the round peg will always be approximate and never exact.

Begin with this fact when you hire staff members and you will take the first step toward making a good hire. Since you will virtually never find a perfect fit for any position you seek to fill, build your job description and evaluation standards around this fact. Don't let the person you bring on board change the job unless it should be changed. Sometimes you may adjust the position to get a person you really want. Or you may trade responsibilities with another staff member, thus moving two people to their greatest areas of strength. However, other times you may have to give up an outstanding candidate because a forced fit would mean failure for everyone involved. When a staff member fails, especially in the first two or three years, the fault is yours for making a bad hire. It is neither right nor wise to force someone into a position he or she doesn't fit just because you are attracted to his or her giftedness and temperament. No matter how attractive a person may be, someone who doesn't fit the position doesn't belong on the team. You will have to swallow hard and keep looking.

How do you go about finding the best person for a position? That's the question addressed in this chapter. We'll look first at the major categories in the process, and then at the specific steps we must take.

THE STANDARD-SETTERS

"Standard-setters" are those who define the roundness of the hole, that is, the people who set the standards and write the job description for the position to be filled. Typically, there are five possible standard setters: the senior pastor, the staff team, elders and/or deacons, volunteers who will serve under the new staff member, or a combination of the above.

Depending on the position to be filled, my choice is a combination of all five, with the senior pastor participating in some way in every hiring decision. If the addition is someone who reports directly to the senior pastor, he must lead the search. However, if the new person reports to another staff member (for example, a children's pastor reporting to the Christian education director), the latter should lead the search with appropriate help from elders and volunteers who have a direct interest in the children's ministry. Because every staff position is critical to the ongoing health of the ministry, when I was a pastor, I participated in every hiring in some way. Though a senior pastor shouldn't make every hiring decision, he should interview every full-time staff level candidate.

I conduct a short interview with the two or three final candidates for each full-time position for three reasons: (1) to support the staff member doing the hiring, (2) to give my input in the decision, and (3) to show interest in the individual being considered for the position.

I tell every interviewee that I don't make the hiring decision and that I won't be involved in managing that person. However, I express my interest in the person and my willingness to make myself available should he or she be hired. Even with part-time positions, I want to get to know the individual and to make him or her feel comfortable being on our team. Senior pastors should not be distant from their staff. Anyone who has the gifts and maturity to be on a pastoral staff should have access to the senior pastor and be comfortable with him.

THE STANDARDS

Standards for possible candidates should include the following elements:

The job description—including the position title, the reporting structure, the desired duties, and other elements listed below.

The spiritual requirements—including spiritual maturity, personal disciplines, and character development.

The physical requirements—including health, discipline, and preferred age (be sure to check any legal stipulations that might govern these areas).

The theological concerns—including doctrinal agreement with the church, especially any doctrinal issues unique to your church (for example, charismatic issues, eternal security, the role of women, church government).

Educational requirements—such as a college degree, seminary graduation, continuing education, and informal training.

Pilgrimage experiences—such as formative relationships and experiences that have made the candidate who he or she is, times of brokenness, ministry experiences God has used in particular ways to form his or her identity.

Marital/family elements—such as marriage and children, commitment of one's mate to the ministry, divorce, attitudes of anger or resentment over past family history that come out in bitter, harsh words.

Work history—positions held, length of time in those positions, skills developed and demonstrated, tasks carried out.

Expectations of the candidate—including such things as daily and weekly work hours, the spouse's role, philosophy of ministry issues (for example, the place of the Great Commission, the role of women, worship perspectives, the place of elders in the church).

Application forms for the position should be kept as short as possible. While it is essential for you to get as much information as you can about each potential candidate, some churches demand untold hours from people they will never hire. This is not fair. Make sure you need all the information you ask for in the forms you develop.

All the candidate needs to see of this information early on in the process is the job description. The rest will be disclosed as necessary and appropriate as he or she progresses through the interview process. Yet the search committee must have all this information and should use it to develop questions to help them evaluate each candidate in light of their needs.

THE SEEKERS

Who will be on the search committee? Since their aim is to find the finest round peg of approximately the same size as your round hole, you need to find the best people you can for this committee.

Not all the standard-setters need be on the search committee. Frequently the position will be of such significance that all of the staff will discuss the nature of the job and the kind of person who should fill it.

Then the appropriate staff member should take this information to the ministry leaders involved, for example, the Christian education committee or the youth parents' council. From there, the proposed standards go to the elders. Each of these bodies will have input into the position description and final standards.

The search committee should consist of godly and mature men and women selected from the staff, the board, the ministry to be led, and the general church membership. I don't believe the task of establishing the position standards should be delegated to the search committee. However, a number of those on the committee should have participated in establishing the standards so they can clearly represent them to potential candidates.

THE PROCESS

Finding Where the Best Fish Feed

The biggest problem a leader faces in hiring a new staff person is finding the most qualified candidates for the position. The quality of our final choice depends on the quality of our candidate pool. So how do we find the best people possible?

The answer is found in one word: networks. There is a network for every position we seek to fill, for example, a Christian educators' network, a disciplers' network, a worship pastors' network. These and many other kinds of networks exist because people of similar skills and interests associate together. In fact, there are networks within networks, so the Christian educators' network may include specialties such as preschool and elementary school directors. Also the best fish tend to congregate in the same holes. This means there is a quality network within every network, a set of relationships in which you will find those who are best for you. So how do you find the networks in which the best fish feed? Places to "fish" include the following:

- friends
- professional associations
- conference centers where professional gatherings are held
- influential pastors and churches
- seminary professors

- publication placement services (for example, the Employment Opportunities portion of the Marketplace section in *Christianity Today*)
- denominational placement services, including leaders such as district superintendents or bishops
- seminary placement services
- the Internet.

Many pastors question the value of placement services. They feel the names they get from such sources represent people who are anxious for valid or invalid reasons to make a change, "damaged goods" who can't make it where they are and have to leave. While it may be true that some, perhaps many, of those who use seminary and denominational placement services want to make a change for a variety of reasons, including the fact that things are not going well for them in their current setting, that doesn't necessarily make them bad options. Some very good people have some very difficult struggles at one time or another. What's more, the directors of effective placement services find joy in bringing about a good "marriage," not in getting names off their list or "scalps on their belts." Because this is the case, a good placement service gives you not only the names of people who want to consider making a change, but also the names of people who don't even know they're being recommended. You can always ask the director of the placement service for specific background information on the person being recommended.

Making Sure There's a Fit

Remember, you have to define what the word "best" means for you. If you are hiring a music pastor and your church favors traditional church music, you don't want to hire a person whose interest lies only in contemporary music, no matter how good he or she might be. You may hire the most skilled, educated, and experienced person you can find, but if that person isn't the right "fit," the best will become the worst staff addition you could make. *By "fit" I mean the appropriateness of a candidate for your ministry, both professionally and personally.* A person fits well professionally when he or she has all the requirements needed to fulfill your job description— the gifts, education, experience, and character required for the task. A person fits well personally when he or she "belongs," that is, when the "chemistry" is right.

At least four factors need to be considered before you have a good fit.

The biblical convictions of your church. Every church has biblical convictions in relation to doctrine, purpose, and values.

Doctrinal compatibility is critical. You may have members who create theological havoc, but you don't need staff who, whether subtly or overtly, undermine the unity of your church by raising doctrinal questions. You can help avoid this by assuring yourself of theological compatibility through a well-developed doctrinal statement and carefully thought-through questions to surface any critical differences. There will, of course, be differences. What you must decide is when a difference rules out a candidate.

Your church purpose and values grow out of your biblical convictions and are a way of determining your critical practices. (See chapter 12 on planning.) Many do not realize how agreement on this is essential or how disagreement in this area can tear a church apart. Some concerns may include worship and music, the way you teach your children, how you conduct youth ministry, the role of women in the church, how you minister to the poor, and other issues.

If you hire someone with a strong difference of conviction in the area of purpose or values, you will introduce divisive controversy into your church. If, for example, you see your church as one that equips its members to reach the lost in their neighborhoods and not in the church, and the new staff member desires a seeker-centered thrust, you will find yourself at odds. He will want to move in a direction different from you, and this will mean constant tension. Soon some may accuse you of not caring for the lost or preferring irrelevant worship. Controversy in these areas is a fire storm to avoid.

The governmental practices of your church. If you are convinced the Bible teaches that elders should lead the church, and the possible candidate believes in a congregational form of church government, he may soon have a core of people who want to go his way. Government is an expression of authority, and it will be difficult for you to have someone on your team who resists the governing structure of your church. You can serve with people who differ with you, but you need some assurance it will work out before you bring such a person on board.

The sociological structure of your church. Is your church an urban church? Then you need to be sure a suburban person will fit in. Is your church a blue-collar church? Then be sure a white-collar person will be comfortable in your setting. Yours may be an ethnic church or a church made up of older people or a church consisting mainly of those who are forty and under. People can cut across these sociological barriers, but not easily. Before you hire, do your best to avoid unnecessary conflict by getting the best sociological fit you can find.

The cultural preferences of your church. There is a close relationship between sociology and culture. People of the same race, the same income, or the same age tend to be similar in their thinking and preferences, but this is not always the case. Therefore we must recognize the critical role cultural preferences play in our ministries. For example, some people in their twenties prefer a contemporary expression of praise, while there are others who are drawn to liturgical worship. Few things divide the church more today than issues of culture. Previously healthy churches have been torn apart by style of worship, focus of ministry, and other concerns that are not as sharply defined by Scripture as we may think. Do everything you can to prevent such divisions by knowing your ministry and the candidate exceedingly well. Painful as it may be to say no to someone you want to hire, it is far less painful than removing that person after a long and difficult struggle.

Paper Weights

How will you evaluate the many resumés you will receive? You may receive scores of resumés for a well-publicized opportunity. With that much paper, you must decide beforehand how you will weigh each piece of information you receive. First, you should ask, Is the resumé written in a professional, well-organized manner? Then you should seek to determine how you feel about each applicant's fitness for your opening. This will be determined by how well each resumé describes a person who meets the standards you established earlier in your process.

- Do the applicant's gifts fit the needs listed on the job description?

- Is his or her experience diverse and adequate enough to warrant a further look? Does the cover letter introducing the resumé show the level of communication ability needed to be effective in your church?
- What character traits show through the resumé?
- Is there any unusual creativity that makes the resumé stand out?
- Are there things about the resumé that make it look more gimmicky than professional?
- What is unique about this resumé that you like?
- Do you see any statements about the person and his or her goals and life dreams that make you want to know him better?
- What gets your attention that causes you to say, "I want to talk to this person further?"

Playing Telephone Tag

When you interview a potential candidate over the telephone, and you don't yet have a resumé from that person, follow these steps:
- Introduce yourself by giving your name and the church's name.
- Explain why you are calling.
- Tell how you got the interviewee's name.
- Give a short and precise summary of the position you are seeking to fill.
- Inquire as to any interest the interviewee may have and offer to continue the conversation if desired.
- Expand on the major aspects of the job by explaining the level of the position (associate, assistant, director) and the key opportunities and outcomes it represents. (For example, "This position provides an opportunity for the one who fills it to change adult education in our church and to create a biblical training program found nowhere else in our community.")
- Ask if the person has any questions of you and answer the questions raised.
- Ask selected questions of the interviewee, such as the person's current tasks, length of service in present ministry, and openness to further conversation.
- Tell the person where you are in the hiring process.

- Ask for a home address where you can write the individual. (This is usually better than writing to the church where the person is serving.)
- Explain how and when you will follow up the phone call.
- Send a short follow-up letter expressing appreciation for his or her time and confirming any plans for further contact.

If you are responding to a resumé, you can be more direct in your conversation.

Ask more specifically about his interest level. "What attracted you to our position? What do you think qualifies you for this position? What is there about your current position that makes you willing to leave?"

Ask more specifically about the potential candidate's experience and qualifications. "Tell me about your current job description. What are you doing now that is similar to the tasks in our opening? What is not similar? What makes you ready to make a change?" Raise questions about previous positions to gain insight into the person's long-term experience and how it might fit with your position.

If you are calling on the basis of a reference from a friend, you should tell the interviewee this, even if you can't reveal the name of the person who suggested the contact.

Whatever you do in the hiring process, keep your word to everyone you contact. Churches are notoriously poor in keeping promises they make to possible candidates, so your integrity in this regard will make you stand out and will help you build a positive relationship with the person you hire. It may even help you get the attention of an otherwise uninterested potential candidate.

Keep your first call short—no more than fifteen or twenty minutes unless there is an unusual spark, and you think the person may be a likely candidate. Whatever you do, don't make any promises, implied or stated, during a phone call other than those agreed on beforehand by the search committee. Be sure all of you say the same thing to every candidate you contact in the initial stages. Be sure you all agree on what the spokesperson for the committee will say when talking to potential candidates.

Telephone only your top fifteen or so candidates. To do this, divide up the names among your search committee and have the callers use an agreed-on form for taking notes. When you no longer have interest in someone, let that person know, so he doesn't think he is still a candidate when he isn't. Though it is difficult to do, it is gracious to notify by telephone someone you have eliminated, rather than by an impersonal letter. Do this as soon as you have decided a person is no longer a possibility for your position. Be gracious, kind, and truthful, and you will earn additional respect as a first-class church.

When you decide on six or eight potential candidates to pursue, appoint members from your search committee to make weekly contact with the potential appointees. Once every week each member should telephone the candidate, tell him or her what the current status is, and answer any questions or concerns that are raised. As each one is eliminated, make a gracious call of appreciation, answer any final questions, and bring the process to a gentle close.

Face to Face

Once you select your three top candidates, conduct a face-to-face interview with each one. You will benefit most if you go to each interviewee's current city and conduct your interview in a neutral setting, such as a hotel conference room. You also will gain great insight by visiting each one's home.

During this time ask specific yet open-ended questions. Never ask questions that can be answered simply by yes or no. Always ask questions that will make the interviewee think and not be able to give rehearsed answers. When the interviewee responds, "That's a difficult question," or "I'll have to think about that one," you know you have asked a question that will give you insight into the person. Use short case studies as scenarios to evaluate the candidate's experience. Don't let anyone simply tell you what he or she has done by saying things like, "I pastored a church that built a new building for cash," or "I grew a youth group from twenty to sixty in eighteen months." Instead, ask interviewees to describe what they did, what attracted them to the task, how they went about it, what the situation looked like before and after they were involved, what they intended to do, and what they actually did.

As important as it is to know what your possible candidates have done in the past, it is more important to know how they did it. This will tell you much of what you need to know about their professional and personal fit with your church.

Also ask the candidates to define ministry-related terms they use, such as "discipleship," "evangelism," "worship." These are key words we all think we understand, but you may discover that what they mean by a certain word differs significantly from what you mean. If you don't ask staff candidates to define and illustrate key terms, and you hire that person, problems may develop. You might even accuse each other of misleading or misrepresenting what you really thought, when all you did was use common terms in different ways with no malice intended.

When you have interviewed your top three candidates, you are ready to select your first choice and to invite that person to come to your church for the final candidating steps. Do not invite a person unless you are almost certain you want to hire him or her. Also invite the person's spouse and children. This final step should last up to five days and should consist of as much contact as possible among the staff, elders and/or deacons, those serving in the ministry involved, and other key leaders in the church. Reserve a hotel room for the candidate and give the person plenty of time alone to process the decision. Also get the family into as many homes as is reasonable. Strive to be understanding of their children—no one's children do their best in a strange and demanding situation. Be wary if the family is too perfect. A child's temper tantrum or crying because of fatigue gives you a great opportunity to see your candidate's response to everyday realities. Don't set it up so this happens, but be patient and observant when it does.

Most of the questions at this point in the process should be repeat questions asked by those who have not had an opportunity for previous interaction. Some of the questions may pursue more details than before. If the process up to now has gone well, there may not be too many new questions. Ask open-ended questions that require the candidate to think and speak carefully and deeply about the answers. Also be sure to answer the candidate's questions, introduce him or her to the church in appropriate ways, have the person minister, and then follow the process you have established for issuing a call to a new staff member. Be sure to include everything needed for the person to make a decision: job description, salary, benefits, and any agreed-on steps.

KICK-OFF

Shaking Hands: The Transition from Out-of-Towner to Newcomer

Seek to make the transition for your new staff member into your ministry as smooth as possible. Here are a few pointers to keep in mind.

You can't say hello until you've said good-bye. If there were bad feelings about the former staff member, such as unresolved struggles, past wounds, or leftover issues, don't make your new staff member clean up an old "mess." He didn't make it and he shouldn't have to correct it. Either have those who created the situation correct it or appoint someone else to get it done before the new person comes. If you make the new appointee correct something he didn't do, people will be angry and feel alienated over things that person had no part in. Also be sure the new person does the same thing in the ministry he or she is leaving. If that person is leaving a difficult situation in which he or she was attacked and treated unfairly, be sure those issues are resolved and that the new employee comes with no residual anger.

Old houses make for old worries. Do everything you can to help your new staff person make a smooth move into the new situation. If that individual is moving from another city, contact a real-estate professional to help in the housing transition. Be sure to cover the moving costs so the staff member can afford to move. Don't force the person into unwanted debt because the budget you provided was too small for the move. Also, if real estate is more expensive in your area than in his or her former area, consider a joint equity arrangement in which you advance a significant portion of the down payment for the new home. Then later, if the staff person leaves, he or she and the church can share proportionately in any equity profit or loss made during the time the employee served with you. Another step you could consider is to forgive 10 percent each year of the advance you made. So if the staff worker stays ten years, the advance will be totally forgiven. This gives both of you an additional incentive for longevity, which means financial reward for the individual and stability for you.

New town, new friends. Encourage people in the church to befriend the new staff member's family. Children and youth sometimes find it difficult to get established in new settings. They have to give up old friends and make new ones, which can be an overwhelming task. Encourage them by helping the family find stability as quickly as possible.

Getting lost is not fun. Being lost is frustrating, especially when you are under the pressure of getting started on a new job. You can be lost on the streets of a town you don't know or lost in a stack of files hunting for something you can't find. Give your new staff member paid time to learn the area and also to get his office set up before the pressure of delivering on the job sets in. The sooner the new worker is organized, the sooner he or she will deliver.

Up and Down the Hall: The Transition from Stranger to Friend

If you have gone about the hiring process effectively, your new staff member is already a new friend rather than a stranger. Your object in this introductory time is to seal the friendship by making the family feel as welcome as possible in their new church, ministry, and community. The following steps can go a long way toward helping your new worker feel "at home" in the new job.

- Assign someone to help set up the worker's office. Provide furniture, file cabinets, and supplies. Try to anticipate these and related needs as soon as possible so time is not wasted searching for the tools required to be effective from the beginning.
- Assist him or her in hiring support staff. The new staff member may not have to do this, but if he or she does, help get the interview process started as quickly as possible. Your new person may need to wait awhile before true needs are best determined, but be prepared to get this done just as soon and as well as you can.
- Review the job description. One of the first things you should do is review and solidify the job description and establish both immediate and annual goals. Most of this should have been done during the hiring process, but you still need to review what has already been decided to be sure you are in agreement. Include some tangible goals

the person can accomplish in the first three months on the job. Getting something done this soon will give him or her the feeling of being a contributor and a member of the team.

- Encourage the worker to spend time with lay leaders. During the hiring process your new staff member should meet key lay leaders with whom he or she will be working, but it is necessary for the new person to get back in touch with them again as quickly as possible. Work to clear schedules and set up meetings as desired. The sooner he or she begins building relationships with lay leaders in his or her area of ministry, the sooner the staff person will gain trust and be able to make the difference you hired him or her to make.

- Acquaint the new person with the history of your church. Few things hurt more than an unwitting mistake made early in a new ministry. So be sure your new employee knows the history and distinctives of your church. This can help him or her avoid making any offensive comment or suggesting an unworkable change. The more you can do to help here, the more that one can help you for years to come.

- Review the operating procedures of your church. If you have an operating policy handbook, see that the staff member gets one before arriving on the job. Explain what the spending limits are, how budgeting is done, whom to consult before committing to spend money or add people, how retirement and health policies work—all the administrative procedures anyone must understand to work efficiently in a well-managed organization.

- Have a "welcombration." A welcombration is a party, a welcome, and a celebration at the same time. Bring as many people from the church together as appropriate, and make the staff member and family feel special and wanted. As part of your welcombration, you could have a pounding—an old-fashioned way to welcome someone by having every family in the church give the new family a pound of food or supplies, anything from sugar to nails.

These things will demonstrate how delighted you are to have the person on board.

CONCLUSION

Few decisions are as critical as your hiring decisions. Keep the following four facts in mind when you hire.

First, hire to your limitations; don't clone yourself. Don't be afraid to hire people who are better than you are at what they do. If they aren't better than you, why are you hiring them? Must you surround yourself with inferior people because you are too afraid of gifted, excellent people? Hire to complete yourself, to expand the impact of your church, and to maintain the excellence already established in your ministry.

Second, do not believe the myth that staff members always save you time. To the contrary, new staff persons will cost you time, especially when you first hire them. Too many pastors think the staff's purpose is to advance their career, and they end up frustrated and angry when a newcomer doesn't want to be used in this way. Don't hire staff to serve you and make you successful.

Third, remember that it takes time for new staff to get settled in and become productive. This is why a thorough orientation process is important. The more time you invest at the beginning of a new staff member's tenure, the more time you will save later. Be prepared to give each new hire the time needed to get off to a good start and to become effective as soon as possible.

Fourth, realize that even the best of new staff members will have their own set of problems. All of us have disappointing character struggles, irritating personality patterns, behavioral blindspots, unexpected gift flaws, inefficient work habits—any number of marks that cost time and energy and detract from the goal of getting ministry done. Some will rebel against you; others will decide they can do your job better than you; a few will deceive you and turn out to be unqualified for the job you gave them. Some will talk about you behind your back and undermine you in the eyes of others so they can build themselves up. Unless you are prepared to face such realities, you will fail as a leader of the staff God gives you.

However, nothing is more rewarding than working together with a dedicated band of self-starters who are committed to excellence in serving the Lord. Even in the best situations some head-knocking may occur along the way as you learn to come together. I have never known anything more satisfying than to work with a team of ministry leaders who are as different from me as they can possibly be, yet who are committed with me to a common purpose and common values and who strive to accomplish that purpose through dependence on the Lord. My hope for you is that you will find those round pegs to fit in your round holes of approximately the same size so you will see that you, they, and the Holy Spirit can do more together than any of you ever imagined possible.

RESOURCES

Hiring the Best by Martin Yate(Boston: Bob Adam, 1990), is the best book I've seen on hiring. Yate offers a thorough "tour" of the hiring process, both generally and specifically. He covers information like eight reasons why we hire poorly and three criteria for outstanding hires, six steps to defining your real needs, seventeen personality traits of successful employees, what to look for in a resumé, how to go from phone interviews to a short list of potential candidates, the art and science of interviewing, specific questions to ask whether hiring a secretary or a chief executive officer, legal issues to consider when interviewing, and four ready-to-use outlines to use as starting points when hiring. *Hiring the Best* is written for business hires, so you will have to transfer the concepts to the church, but this can be done easily. Read this book carefully before you make your next staff addition.

The Leadership Handbook of Management and Administration, edited by James D. Berkeley (Grand Rapids: Baker, 1997), is the most comprehensive work on church management and administration I've found. Buy it for a reference book, a kind of lexicon of management and administration. Keep it handy and consult it whenever you have a question in these areas of ministry. The chapter on hiring is an excellent one written for the local church.

CHAPTER FIFTEEN

SCULPTORS OF THE SOUL

THE BLOCK OF MARBLE that became Michelangelo's larger-than-life sculpture of David lay almost untouched in the cathedral storehouse in Florence, Italy, for decades. Two other sculptors had attempted to make something of it before it was offered to Michelangelo. One started working with it, but soon quit because his talents lay in more delicate work. The great Leonardo da Vinci turned down an opportunity to transform it, preferring to pursue another project more suited to his taste. When offered the opportunity, Michelangelo agreed to do what others couldn't or wouldn't do. He built a shed around the block of marble, which he kept locked at all times. For three years he labored to transform it from its natural state to an eternal work of art. At first Michelangelo examined the marble minutely to see what poses it would accommodate. He made sketches and models of various possible creations and then tested his ultimate image in a small-scale wax version of his final result. Finally he picked up his mallet and chisel and began to work.[1]

When Michelangelo looked at that block of marble, he didn't see what it couldn't be; he saw what it could be. He didn't reject it because it was flawed. He saw a way to work around the flaws, even to incorporate them into his design. What he did was so great, even evident flaws could not scar its beauty. There are drill marks in David's thick curled hair, some of the original quarry marks are on the very top of the head, and one can see traces of the cuttings made by an earlier sculptor who, forty years before, failed to do what Michelangelo did: create one of the greatest master-pieces of all time. Michelangelo, the sculptor of David, is a picture of a pastor who is able to see potential that many others have missed.

THE EYE OF AN ARTIST

When I first started pastoring, all I saw in people were their flaws. I saw the reasons they could not be elders or teachers or be equipped to serve others. I was a critic rather than an artist. This was all I saw because I was looking at people with the eye of a critic rather than through the eye of the Artist. I saw what they were in themselves, not what they could be in Christ. It wasn't their flaws that kept them from becoming all Christ created them to be; it was my critical judgment that blinded me and kept me from seeing how Christ could transform them. I missed seeing all He was doing through those very people I regarded as unqualified to be used by Him. My heart was as hard as a block of marble, and I didn't even know it. I had to change, but I didn't understand how much, although I realized I needed to see people in a new way. I needed to see people as Michelangelo saw that block of marble he transformed into his David.

Equipping Disciple-Makers

A great deal of confusion exists today as to what pastors are to be. Are they chaplains, CEOs, preachers, managers, or counselors? Paul gave us the an-swer long ago: They are to be equippers (Eph. 4:7–16). We are to be equippers, who pray for the sick and comfort the sorrowing. We are to be equippers, who lead others and call them to godly vision. We are to be equippers, who proclaim God's Word wisely and well. We are to be equippers, who plan thor-oughly and administer carefully. We are to be equippers, who listen intently and advise biblically.

We are not chaplains, CEOs, preachers, managers, or counselors. We are equippers, disciple-makers, just as Jesus was an equipping disciple-Maker. In fact, we are to have exactly the same goal for our min-istries Jesus had for His: to present every man complete in Christ (Col.

1:28–29). This is what we're about. We are to be sculptors of souls, completers of others for Christ.

COMPLETE IN CHRIST

The men and women we serve are on a search for glory, seeking a lasting significance and security that will give them identity and meaning in life. They look everywhere for this glory. They look for it in achievements and success, in heroes and entertainers, in sexual pursuits and chemical dependencies, in adventures and excitements, but they never find it. So they live barren, empty lives, and they continue to seek for glory.

Our great privilege is to tell them that their only hope of glory is already in them, or can be if they put their trust in Christ. This is the glorious mystery Paul spoke of in Colossians 1:27, the sacred secret God has now revealed to us who were once separated from Christ, strangers to the promise, having neither hope nor God in this world (Eph. 2:12).

When they see Christ in us, they see hope at work in our lives. This is what attracts them to us. They see in us Christ's glory, security, stability, and strength. They see a confidence they can't account for, a vulnerability that seasons and matures us. Many of them can see where once there were the sharp marks of selfish ambition, arrogance, and pride. Or they can discern the scars of fear and insecurity left behind by sin's once powerful grip on us. They can see the difference Christ has made as the Sculptor of our souls.

THE SCULPTURE OF A PASTOR'S SOUL

Earlier in our lives, our sculpture may have been a striking one that caught attention and drew others to us, but it may not have been warm or inviting. Now we are different. We have discovered our true glory, not in preaching, acquiring fame, or having any form of so-called success, but through knowing Him and His presence in us. We now realize no riches, whether material or professional, match the riches of Christ in us, and the hope He brings. We have been softened by experience and the reality of our limitations. We have been tested; we have been judged; we have succeeded; we have failed; we have been humbled. There's a new strength in our souls, a new depth in our spirits. Formerly, people were attracted by the clarity and brilliance of our lives; now they are attracted to the warmth of our hearts. There is something inviting about us that wasn't there before. Now they stop to study what Christ is doing in us, to enter in and explore what this new glory is. They are curious about what it might be and what it might offer them.

The old chisel marks and sometimes conflicting cuts are still there, but that's all right with them. The marks show we are real and give them hope for themselves. We are not perfect men as we once might have presented ourselves to be. Instead, we are growing, which is exactly what they long to be doing. They have discovered that their riches turn out to be poverty. Could it be, they wonder, that the new riches they see in their pastor's life will turn out to be true wealth? The answer is yes if, when they step inside our lives, they discover Christ in us, and realize He is their hope of glory also.

This is why Paul wrote that we are to proclaim *Christ*. *He* is our life message, and everywhere we go *He* tells others about true riches and true glory through us. We don't even know this is going on as we still wrestle with old prides and fears. But there is one thing we now know: We want every person to hear this truth, both those who need to be warned and those who need to be taught (Col. 1:28). Some need their hearts set right while others need their heads informed. Whether it be warning, correction, and exhortation on the one hand or instruction on the other, we want everyone to know the true wealth of Christ's glory. We have the down payment for that glory already deposited in our lives, and anyone who will can open a new account by putting faith in Christ. Our aim in equipping disciple-makers is to present everyone we serve as mature adults in Christ.

This is what an equipping, disciple-making pastor is all about. He sees the potential riches of real glory in everyone he serves. It may not be there yet, but it could be, and he will do all he can, whether it be to warn or to teach, to develop it in them. He sees these riches in the unlikely and the unlovely, the hopeless and the helpless, the poor and the unwanted, the attractive and the winsome, the clever and the successful. He grieves with Christ when the modern rich and young turn away as the rich young ruler did. The equipping pastor yearns for them to grow in Christ so when it comes time for them to enter the Lord's presence he can present them to Him complete and mature, fully grown up in Christ.

But how does a pastor do this? How do these changes come in those he serves? How does this glory become evident in them? Only through the wisdom he seeks to impart to others (1:28). What did Paul mean by wisdom? Was it knowledge? Insight? Understanding? It was all this and more. Paul told us that wisdom is Christ Himself (1 Cor. 1:30), and it is demonstrated through the foolish things of this world, especially the Cross. Wisdom is Christ crucified, foolishness to the world, but true wisdom to those who understand how God thinks.

People come to us full of the world's wisdom, which means they are full of foolishness and folly. They come striving to control life with the expectations of success and power they expect God to meet, but He refuses to meet these expectations and constantly calls them to take up the Cross. Every time the Cross comes up, ego comes out. The pain of even thinking about the Cross is so great it forces the ego to assert itself and resist the death it must die.

For us to do as Paul described—to admonish and teach every man with all wisdom (Col. 1:27)—we must know Him, for He alone is wisdom. When we know Him, we also know God's power and God's wisdom in Christ (1 Cor. 1:24). Thus as disciple-makers we seek to help every person we meet to turn to Christ so they may know Him as we know Him.

But how do we do this? How do we warn and teach people so they become mature in Christ? The answer doesn't lie in materials, methods, and techniques, even though these things are helpful. The answer lies in our labor and His enablement.

No pastor is adequate for this task, yet this is the task every pastor must pursue. How can pastors do something for which we are utterly inadequate? By drawing on the very riches of the hope of glory we now possess, by drawing on Christ in us. We can no longer cover our inadequacies; we can no longer run from our fears; we can no longer deny our deficiencies. Instead, we find our adequacy in Christ.

This is what makes us real. We are inadequate and we know it, but He is adequate and He shows it through us. This is what softens the sharp angles of our lives, what brings depth and warmth to the marble of our souls so we become inviting to others who once stood at a distance rather than enter into relationship with us. Our hearts have been turned from stone to flesh (Ezek. 11:19).

So with Paul we labor—hard, back-breaking, heart-breaking labor—agonizing over the souls of men and women, boys and girls. There is pain in this labor; we face resistance and rejection in this labor. People don't want to give up their glory, nor do *we* want to give up our glory. It's not easy to warn pride-filled, self-seeking, angry people of their foolishness, especially if we're just like them. It is not easy to teach unteachable people who don't want to take up the Cross and follow Jesus. Like the apostles before Jesus' resurrection, the Cross makes no sense to many people today. They have no idea what resurrection can mean in their lives and they won't until, with Peter, they are finally forced to face their baseless self-confidence.

So we labor until we become physically exhausted, emotionally spent, and spiritually dry. And then we labor some more. How? By His energizing, enabling power, the power that works with amazing might within us. Then the resistant become responsive, the broken whole, the empty filled with a glory never seen before.

Christ in us, the equipping disciple-Maker, takes our minds and mouths, our words and works, and makes them His. As we turn from the futility of the self-focused mind to the mind of Christ, He transforms our deficit thinking into abundance thinking, our emptiness into His fullness. Then He takes our inadequacy and fills it with His adequacy. When we depend on Him to feed the five thousand, He takes what we do not have and multiplies it so greatly we have leftovers when we thought we'd have a shortfall. When we must walk on water, He gives the courage to step out on the waves and then overcomes the storm. Through us, He transforms men and women and makes us sculptors of the soul.

FROM HEARTS OF MARBLE
TO SCULPTURES OF DAVID

The people whom we shepherd come to us with quarry marks and cuttings made in their lives by other sculptors long before we begin our ministry to them. They have flaws from their past. Shame, guilt, anger, bitterness, pride, fear—scars of the soul caused by decades of sin and selfishness. Like Michelangelo, we mustn't allow these flaws to stop us from taking our Cross-like mallet and beginning to cut away at the marble of their hearts. Of course, we consult with the master Artist, spending long blocks of time in prayer for them, seeking to discern from His Word how to meet their needs. We chip away at the fault marks of their souls, tapping gently first, then firmly, until the pride, the anger, the hatred, the fear—whatever it is—falls away, and a little bit more of *David* appears. Ours is not a three-year project, of course; ours is a lifetime project, or as much time as the master Artist chooses to use our hands to create His work of art in them. Gradually we see the marble of their hearts transformed into the beauty of a masterpiece, and we rejoice that the day is coming when they will be complete in Christ. It will be a great day when He decides where they should be placed on view for eternity.

What a privilege to know we've participated with Christ in creating an eternal work of art in the hearts of men and women. He has chosen to place them in our hands, and we have chosen to give Him our hands. So it is we labor, even agonize, over these works of art, while He mightily empowers us to transform flawed souls into completed men and women.

This is pastoring: serving as sculptors of the soul. No honor could be greater, no responsibility higher, no accountability more serious. Let us join with Paul and bow our knees before our Father in prayer for His enablement as we undertake this task.

> For this reason, I bow my knees before the Father, from whom every family in heaven and on earth derives its name, that He would grant you, according to the riches of His glory, to be strengthened with power through His Spirit in the inner man; so that Christ may dwell in your hearts through faith; and that you, being rooted and grounded in love, may be able to comprehend with all the saints what is the breadth and length and height and depth, and to know the love of Christ which surpasses knowledge, that you may be filled up to all the fulness of God. Now to Him who is able to do exceeding abundantly beyond all that we ask or think, according to the power which works within us, to Him be the glory in the church and in Christ Jesus to all generations forever and ever. Amen. (Eph. 3:14–21, NASB)

ENDNOTES

CHAPTER 1—TO KNOW HIM

1. C. S. Lewis, *Mere Christianity* (New York: Macmillan, 1981), 103 (italics his).

CHAPTER 2—THE DREADED LEADER'S DISEASE

1. John D. Grassmick, "Mark," in *The Bible Knowledge Commentary, New Testament,* ed. John F. Walvoord and Roy B. Zuck (Wheaton, Ill.: Victor, 1983), 132.
2. Ibid., 130.
3. William L. Lane, *The Gospel According to Mark*, New International Commentary on the New Testament (Grand Rapids: Eerdmans, 1974), 228.
4. Ibid., 228–29.
5. Ibid., 232.
6. He also did this for another Gentile, the Roman centurion, in healing the soldier's paralyzed servant (Matt. 8:5–13).
7. Our Lord's purpose at this time was to help His disciples understand what their hardness of hearts was doing to their faith. Although the miracle did point up the contrast between Israel's religious leaders and the gentile Syrian-Phoenician woman, this was not Mark's major point. Our Lord focused His teaching primarily on His disciples throughout the rest of His ministry, and this was the case here as well.

8. Grassmick, "Mark," 136.

9. Ibid., 137.

10. Ibid., 138.

11. Surely they knew this as early as the first Galilee storm (Mark 4:35–41) when they awakened Jesus in the stern of the boat, and He stilled the storm. They were amazed because they knew only God could do this. Their problem was in the quality of their faith.

CHAPTER 3
DELIVERANCE FROM THE
DREADED LEADER'S DISEASE

1. Henry T. Blackaby and Henry Brandt, with Kerry L. Skinner, *The Power of the Call* (Nashville: Broadman & Holman, 1997), 19.

2. Ibid., 18.

3. David Rhoads and Donald Michie, *Mark as Story* (Philadelphia: Fortress, 1982), 91–92.

4. "The dispute over greatness indicates the degree to which the disciples had failed to understand Jesus' solemn affirmation concerning his abandonment to the will of men (Ch. 9:31f.). It also shows how impregnated they were with the temper of their own culture where questions of precedence and rank were constantly arising" (Lane, *The Gospel According to Mark, 339).*

5. Grassmick, "Mark," 146.

6. Eugene H. Peterson, *Under the Unpredictable Plant* (Grand Rapids: Eerdmans, 1992), 4–5 (italics his).

7. Ibid., 382.

8. Grassmick, "Mark," 152.

9. A. B. Bruce, *The Training of the Twelve* (1883; reprint, Grand Rapids: Kregel, 1971), 273.

10. Ibid., 179.

11. When He wanted to strengthen His point Jesus often used the "Amen" formula, an emphatic way of speaking (unique to Him) (Lane, *The Gospel According to Mark*, 144).

12. Ibid., 513.

13. Ibid., 15.
14. Ibid.
15. Ibid., 16.
16. Of course, scholars debate where Mark ended his Gospel, whether at 16:8 or 16:20. Grassmick suggests that Mark finished writing at 16:8 and an inspired anonymous Christian writer composed the remainder of the chapter under the Holy Spirit's inspiration ("Mark," 194). Assuming that all of chapter 16 is inspired, I find it significant that the concept of hardness of heart comes up one more time in 16:14. This is certainly a key concept in the Gospel, and is, I believe, the major barrier in our Lord's efforts to develop His men as leaders.

CHAPTER 4—DISCIPLE-MAKING CHURCHES

1. Robert D. Culver, "What Is the Church's Commission? Some Exegetical Issues in Matthew 28:16–20," *Bibliotheca Sacra* 125 (July–September, 1968): 245.
2. LeRoy Eims, *The Lost Art of Disciple Making* (Grand Rapids: Zondervan, 1978), 75.

CHAPTER 5—WHAT'S A PASTOR FOR, ANYWAY?

1. Harold W. Hoehner, "Ephesians," in *The Bible Knowledge Commentary, New Testament*, 634.
2. Ibid.
3. Lothar Coenen, "Bishop, Presbyter, Elder," in *New International Dictionary of New Testament Theology*, ed. Colin Brown (Grand Rapids: Zondervan, 1986), 1:349.
4. Fritz Rienecker, *A Linguistic Key to the Greek New Testament*, ed. Cleon L. Rogers, Jr. (Grand Rapids: Zondervan, 1982), 614.
5. For an extensive discussion of Paul's teaching ministry see Roy B. Zuck, *Teaching as Paul Taught* (Grand Rapids: Baker, 1998).
6. Erich Beyreuther, "Shepherd," in *New International Dictionary of New Testament Theology*, 3:565.

CHAPTER 6—THE ORDER OF THE TOWEL

1. A study of the conversation between Jesus and Pilate in John 18–19 shows this to be true even though Pilate had the power to condemn Jesus to death.

2. Leon Morris, *Expository Reflections on the Gospel of John* (Grand Rapids: Baker, 1991), 478–79.

3. Rienecker, *A Linguistic Key to the Greek New Testament*, 250.

4. Morris, *Expository Reflections on the Gospel of John*, 471.

5. C. K. Barrett, *The Gospel According to St. John*, 2d ed. (Philadelphia: Westminster, 1978), 437.

6. Ray C. Stedman, *Exploring the Gospel of John: God's Loving Word* (Grand Rapids: Discovery House, 1993), 363. Stedman also discusses the related passages of Matthew 18:18–20; Galatians 6:1; and James 5:16.

CHAPTER 7—SERVING GOD, LEADING OTHERS

1. H. Bietenhard, "Beginning," in *New International Dictionary of New Testament Theology*, 1:165.

2. H. Bietenhard, "Lord," in *New International Dictionary of New Testament Theology*, 2:518.

3. Ibid., 2:519.

4. Walter Bauer, William F. Arndt, and F. Wilbur Gingrich, *A Greek-English Lexicon of the New Testament and Other Early Christian Literature*, 2d. ed., rev. F. Wilbur Gingrich and Frederick W. Danker (Chicago: University of Chicago Press, 1979), 421.

5. Rienecker, *A Linguistic Key to the Greek New Testament*, 60.

6. Ibid., 118.

7. Henry Alford, *The Greek New Testament*, rev. ed. (Chicago: Moody, 1968), 1:205.

CHAPTER 8—THE PASTOR'S AUTHORITY

1. Coenen, "Bishop, Presbyter, Elder," 1:191.
2. Henri Nouwen, *In the Name of Jesus* (New York: Crossroad, 1993), 58–60.
3. Ibid., 63.
4. This concept was developed by Gene A. Getz, senior pastor, Fellowship Bible Church North, Plano, Texas.

CHAPTER 10—FEED THE WIDOWS AND STARVE THE CHURCH

1. I am not saying the apostles formed a local church board in the modern sense, because they didn't. But they were the functioning leaders of the church and in that sense they were similar to contemporary church boards. Certainly they are a legitimate model of what church leaders should be in any age.
2. Stanley D. Toussaint, "Acts," in *The Bible Knowledge Commentary, New Testament*, 367.
3. Bauer, Arndt, and Gingrich, *A Greek-English Lexicon of the New Testament and Other Early Christian Literature*, 413.
4. Stephen Covey, *The Seven Habits of Highly Effective People* (New York: Simon & Schuster, 1989), 146–82; and *First Things First* (New York: Simon & Schuster, 1994), 32–43 ("The Urgency Addiction"), 77–102 ("Quadrant II Organizing"), and 322–41 ("Appendix B: A Review of Time Management Literature").
5. Covey, *First Things First*, 37.
6. Although these definitions are largely my own, the concepts of purpose and core values are taken from James C. Collins and Jerry I. Porras, *Built to Last* (New York: Harper Business, 1994), 73.

CHAPTER 11—VISION OR VACUUM

1. John Haggai, *Lead On* (Waco, Tex.: Word, 1986), 12.
2. Source unknown.

CHAPTER 12—PLANNING FOR NONPLANNERS

1. For a much deeper and richer development of our Lord's plan, read Bruce, *The Training of the Twelve,* and Robert Coleman, *The Master Plan of Evangelism* (Grand Rapids: Revell, 1993). See also Roy B. Zuck, *Teaching as Jesus Taught* (Grand Rapids; Baker, 1996), 115–27.
2. Bobb Biehl, *Master Planning* (Nashville: Broadman & Holman, 1997), 10.

CHAPTER 13—LEADING CHANGE

1. Looking back on these convictions, some of them seem silly and irrelevant today, but they reflected our hunger to make a mark for Christ. Many churches we had seen were in bondage to things like an undue emphasis on giving, traditions that limited them, and heavy debt that kept them from making an impact. We wanted to be alive for Christ, and in the thirty years since then South Hills Community Church has seldom known a dead moment. That is due to the grace of God, because in many ways we didn't know what we were doing.

CHAPTER 14—FINDING THE BEST—FOR YOU

1. Biehl, *Master Planning,* 85.
2. I first saw this concept developed by Ralph Mattson, president of Doma Group, Minneapolis, Minnesota.

CHAPTER 15—SCULPTORS OF THE SOUL

1. Charles H. Morgan, *The Life of Michelangelo* (New York: Reynal, 1960), 59–64.

BIBLIOGRAPHY

Anderson, Leith. *A Church for the 21st Century.* Minneapolis: Bethany House Publishers, 1992.

Adams, Jay E. *Shepherding God's Flock.* Grand Rapids: Baker Book House, 1979.

Beall, James Lee, with Marjorie Barber. *Your Pastor, Your Shepherd.* Plainfield, N.J.: Logos International, 1977.

Baker, Benjamin S. *Shepherding the Sheep: Pastoral Care in the Black Tradition.* Nashville: Broadman Press, 1983.

Baxter, Richard. *The Reformed Pastor.* Edinburgh: Banner of Truth Trust, 1997.

Brachter, Edward B. *The Walk-on-Water Syndrome.* Waco, Tex.: Word Books, 1984.

Callahan, Kennon L. *Twelve Keys to an Effective Church.* San Francisco: Harper & Row, Publishers, 1983.

Criswell, W. A. *Criswell's Guidebook for Pastors.* Nashville: Broadman Press, 1980.

Finzel, Hans. *Empowered Leaders.* Swindoll Leadership Library. Nashville: Word Publishing, 1999.

Hayes, Ed. *The Church: The Body of Christ in the World Today.* Swindoll Leadership Library. Nashville: Word Publishing, 1999.

Hughes, R. Kent, and Barbara Hughes. *Liberating Ministry from the Success Syndrome.* Wheaton, Ill.: Tyndale House Publishers, 1988.

Lutzer, Erwin W. *Pastor to Pastor.* Chicago: Moody Press, 1987.

Luecke, David S., and Samuel Sothard. *Pastoral Administration.* Waco, Tex.: Word Books, 1986.

McKenna, David L. *Power to Follow, Grace to Lead.* Dallas: Word Publishing, 1989.

Macchia, Stephen A. *Becoming a Healthy Church.* Grand Rapids: Baker Books, 1999.

Malphurs, Aubrey. *A New Model for Church and Ministry Leaders.* Grand Rapids: Baker Books, 1999.

Peterson, Eugene H. *The Contemplative Pastor.* Grand Rapids: Wm. B. Eerdmans Publishing Co., 1989.

Stedman, Ray C. *Body Life.* Glendale, Calif.: Regal Books, 1972.

———. *Authentic Christianity.* Waco, Tex.: Word Book Publishers, 1975.

Stott, John R. W. *Between Two Worlds.* Grand Rapids: Wm. B. Eerdmans Publishing Co., 1982.

———. *The Preacher's Portrait: Some New Testament Word Studies.* Grand Rapids: Wm. B. Eerdmans Publishing Co., 1961.

Stowell, Joseph M. *Shepherding the Church into the Twenty-First Century.* Wheaton, Ill.: Victor Books, 1994.

Tidwell, Charles A. *Church Administration: Effective Leadership for Ministry.* Nashville: Broadman Press, 1985.

Warren, Rick. *The Purpose Driven Church.* Grand Rapids: Zondervan Publishing House, 1995.

Westing, Harold J. *Multiple Church Staff Handbook.* Grand Rapids: Kregel Publications, 1985.

Scripture Index

SUBJECT INDEX

The
Swindoll Leadership Library

ANGELS, SATAN AND DEMONS
Dr. Robert Lightner

The supernatural world gets a lot of attention these days in books, movies, and television series, but what does the Bible say about these other-worldly beings? Dr. Robert Lightner answers these questions with an in-depth look at the world of the "invisible" as expressed in Scripture.

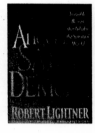

THE CHURCH
Dr. Ed Hayes

In this indispensable guide, Dr. Ed Hayes explores the labyrinths of the church, delving into her history, doctrines, rituals, and resources to find out what it means to be the Body of Christ on earth. Both passionate and precise, this essential volume offers solid insights on worship, persecution, missions, and morality: a bold call to unity and renewal.

COLOR OUTSIDE THE LINES
Dr. Howard G. Hendricks

Just as the apostle Paul prodded early Christians "not to be conformed" to the world, Dr. Howard Hendricks vividly—and unexpectedly—extends that biblical theme and charges us to learn the art of living creatively, reflecting the image of the Creator rather than the culture.

EFFECTIVE PASTORING
Dr. Bill Lawrence

In *Effective Pastoring*, Dr. Bill Lawrence examines what it means to be a pastor in the 21st century. Lawrence discusses often overlooked issues, writing transparently about the struggles of the pastor, the purpose and practice of servant leadership, and the roles and relationships crucial to pastoring. In doing so, he offers a revealing look beneath the "how to" to the "how to be" for pastors.

EMPOWERED LEADERS
Dr. Hans Finzel

What is leadership really about? The rewards, excitement, and exhilaration? Or the responsibilities, frustrations, and exhausting nights? Dr. Hans Finzel takes readers on a journey into the lives of the Bible's great leaders, unearthing powerful principles for effective leadership in any situation.

END TIMES
Dr. John F. Walvoord

Long regarded as one of the top prophecy experts, Dr. John F. Walvoord now explores world events in light of biblical prophecy. By examining all of the prophetic passages in the Bible, Walvoord clearly explains the mystery behind confusing verses and conflicting viewpoints. This is the definitive work on prophecy for Bible students.

THE FORGOTTEN BLESSING
Dr. Henry Holloman

For many Christians, the gift of God's grace is central to their faith. But another gift—sanctification—is often overlooked. *The Forgotten Blessing* clarifies this essential doctrine, showing us what it means to be set apart, and how the process of sanctification can forever change our relationship with God.

GOD
Dr. J. Carl Laney

With tenacity and clarity, Dr. J. Carl Laney makes it plain: it's not enough to know *about* God. We can know *God* better. This book presents a practical path to life-changing encounters with the goodness, greatness, and glory of our Creator.

THE HOLY SPIRIT
Dr. Robert Gromacki

In *The Holy Spirit,* Dr. Robert Gromacki examines the personality, deity, symbols, and gifts of the Holy Spirit, while recapping the ministry of the Spirit throughout the Old Testament, the Gospel Era, the life of Christ, the Book of Acts, and the lives of believers.

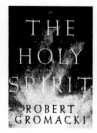

HUMANITY AND SIN
Dr. Robert A. Pyne

Sin may seem like an outdated concept these days, but its consequences remain as destructive as ever. Dr. Robert A. Pyne takes a close look at humankind through the pages of Scripture and the lens of modern culture. As never before, readers will understand sin's overarching effect on creation and our world today.

IMMANUEL
Dr. John A. Witmer

Dr. John A. Witmer presents the almighty Son of God as a living, breathing, incarnate man. He shows us a full picture of the Christ in four distinct phases: the Son of God before He became man, the divine suffering man on Earth, the glorified and ascended Christ, and the reigning King today.

A LIFE OF PRAYER
Dr. Paul Cedar

Dr. Paul Cedar explores prayer through three primary concepts, showing us how to consider, cultivate, and continue a lifestyle of prayer. This volume helps readers recognize the unlimited potential and the awesome purpose of prayer.

MINISTERING TO TODAY'S ADULTS
Dr. Kenn Gangel

After 40 years of research and experience, Dr. Kenn Gangel knows what it takes to reach adults. In an easy-to-grasp, easy-to-apply style, Gangel offers proven systematic strategies for building dynamic adult ministries.

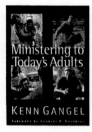

MORAL DILEMMAS
J. Kerby Anderson

Should biblically informed Christians be for or against capital punishment? How should we as Christians view abortion, euthanasia, genetic engineering, divorce, and technology? In this comprehensive, cutting-edge book, J. Kerby Anderson challenges us to thoughtfully analyze the dividing issues facing our age, while equipping believers to maneuver through the ethical and moral land mines of our times.

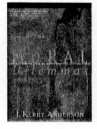

THE NEW TESTAMENT EXPLORER
Mark Bailey and Tom Constable

The New Testament Explorer provides a concise, on-target map for traveling through the New Testament. Mark Bailey and Tom Constable guide the reader paragraph by paragraph through the New Testament, providing an up-close-and-to-the-point examination of the leaders behind the page and the theological implications of the truths revealed. A great tool for teachers and pastors alike, this exploration tool comes equipped with outlines for further study, narrative discussion, and applicable truths for teaching and for living.

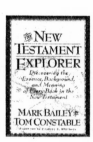

SPIRIT-FILLED TEACHING
Dr. Roy B. Zuck

Whether you teach a small Sunday school class or a standing-room-only crowd at a major university, the process of teaching can be demanding and draining. This lively book brings a new understanding of the Holy Spirit's essential role in teaching.

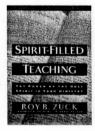

TALE OF THE TARDY OXCART AND 1501 OTHER STORIES
Dr. Charles R. Swindoll

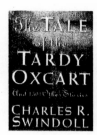

In this rich volume, you'll have access to resourcing Dr. Charles Swindoll's favorite anecdotes on prayer or quotations for grief. In *The Tale of the Tardy Oxcart,* thousands of illustrations are arranged by subjects alphabetically for quick-and-easy access. A perfect resource for all pastors and speakers.

WOMEN AND THE CHURCH
Dr. Lucy Mabery-Foster

Women and the Church provides an overview of the historical, biblical, and cultural perspectives on the unique roles and gifts women bring to the church, while exploring what it takes to minister to women today. Important insight for any leader seeking to understand how to more effectively minister to women and build women's ministries in the local church.

Printed in the United States
19311LVS00003BA/118-126

9 780849 913532